Recommendations

Practical and proven principles of prayer! Simple and yet profound lessons are demonstrated by a husband, father, and pastor as he brings prayer principles to life by the true stories in this powerful little volume.
— Samuel R. Schutz, M.Div., Ph.D.

"He prayed."—perhaps this is what Gideon Thompson will choose as an epitaph. It would not only fit on his gravestone; it would be fitting. While Dr. Thompson could claim many other more public accomplishments —inspiring preacher, strategic church planter, visionary leader—I believe that he'd want to be remembered first and foremost as a faithful pray-er. His public ministry has been the fruit of his private prayer. With the publication of this book, he welcomes us into his prayer closet so that his private prayer does not remain a secret. At times, personally vulnerable, at other times prophetically challenging, Dr. Thompson provides Biblical, practical instruction in *Lord, Teach Us to Pray: Learning How to Release the Power Potential of Prayer* that will benefit both new believer and experienced prayer warrior.
— David A. Currie, M.Div., Ph.D.
Dean of the Doctor of Ministry Program & Ockenga Institute
Associate Professor of Pastoral Theology,
Gordon Conwell Theological Seminary

"Out a rich history of study and practice, Bishop Thompson has produced an invaluable handbook on prayer. His combination of Biblical insights and personal experiences will provider readers with practical tools for increasing intimacy with God and improving ministry effectiveness. This is a must read for anyone wanting to benefit from the power potential of prayer and better understand the impact prayer, when rightly understood and practiced, has on one's total relationships. I highly commend this book to all; especially persons who are leaders of others."
— Rev. Ronald J. Fowler, Pastor Laureate, Arlington Church of God (Akron, OH);
Distinguish Minister at Large, National Association of the Church of God; Former Special Assistant to the President, Kent State University; Founder/Director of L.E.T.'S Network, a mentoring/coaching ministry to Lead Pastors.

It is an honor and a privilege to recommend this wonderful book by my pastor and mentor, Bishop Gideon Thompson! Through heart-warming personal stories (many of which I remember hearing from his pulpit) and careful scriptural exegesis, he exposes the modern problem of prayerlessness and then carefully explains the "what", "why", "who", and "how" of prayer. Bishop Thompson writes comprehensively and persuasively. Even though I've heard his teaching on several occasions, I found my heart "strangely warmed" by it and gained a new determination to upgrade my own prayer life.

Don't read this book in an effort to advance in God's Kingdom by duplicating someone else's ministry (something I have been tempted to do in the past). Instead, let the truth in these pages, born out of Bishop Thompson's decades of experience, guide you into a more intimate walk with the Lord and into the unique calling that he has for you. I've had the privilege of sitting under Bishop Thompson's ministry as he was learning these lessons - often at a great personal cost that I've been able to observe at first hand. May God bless you as you take the truth of these pages to heart and put it into practice in your own life!

—Rocklyn E. Clarke Sr.
Senior Pastor, Life Church Boston
Former Administrative Pastor @ Jubilee Christian Church
Former Board Chair - Emmanuel Gospel Center
Volunteer Staff with InterVarsity Christian Fellowship Black Scholars
and Professionals

"At this very time in my life, I am so grateful for this book, and for it's author, who has already impacted my life in so many ways. A business school professor told me recently that 'entrepreneurs do to learn, while managers learn to do'. Bishop Thompson makes the same point with regard to effective prayer and I am ready to set off to do that which I have only given lip service to for most of my life as a follower of Jesus, this time on my (new) knees and with great expectations. Pray for me."

James L. Bush,
president, Bush & Company

Profound, prolific, and powerful. A contribution of great importance. A must read for every pastor and church leader regarding the establishment of a culture of prayer, an essential discipline for every Christian believer. "Remember to focus on where you are headed and not where you have been."

Rev. Dr. Rudolph Moseley Jr.
Founding and Senior Pastor of Bread of Life International Worship Center, Providence, RI
Executive Director of TIMES 2 STEM Academy, Providence, RI

More than 20 years ago, I met Bishop Thompson in Boston as he was living out the practice of prayer. Hundreds gathered in his church every morning to pray for the city and nation. I witnessed God exponentially grow that ministry while changing tens of thousands of lives. What I learned from him then greatly affected my own life and deep commitment to prayer.

"LORD TEACH US HOW TO PRAY?" powerfully captures the extraordinary insights that I have heard Bishop Thompson teach and practice for decades.

As I read this new work, my life was profoundly touched afresh! This book is not just a great read, but it opens up an even greater experience for the reader

Rev. Hurmon Hamilton
Senior Pastor New Beginnings Community Church
(NBCC), Mountain View, CA
Former Senior Pastor Roxbury Presbyterian Church,
Boston, MA
President GBIO in the Greater Boston Area

It is obvious that "Lord Teach Us To Pray" is not simply an attempt to write a book on the subject of prayer, but the culmination of a life dedicated to the things of God with prayer, communication with God and commitment to his Word as the foundation. Bishop Thompson makes his case for the importance of prayer by integrating the scholarly basis for and a practical application to prayer that is thorough in every way. In some ways this book is a how-to manual for the successful Christian life. It is informative and transformative, and imparts to the reader the motivation to have a vibrant prayer life, a faith filled walk and the impact in the world that we all have been called to have. A must read for the believer that desires a deeper more effective relationship with God.

Joel. A. Brooks Jr.
Senior Pastor, Stones Church
Kalamazoo and Grand Rapids, Michigan

The message is the messenger. Anyone who knows Bishop Gideon Thompson knows that he personifies prayer. *Lord Teach Us To Pray* is not a compilation of mere thoughts on prayers—it is an overflow of who the author is. When you squeeze a fruit its juice comes out. When you squeeze Bishop Thompson, prayer comes out. You will read this book. You will get books for others to read. You will use this amazing resource as a teaching tool. Your small groups will love this. *Lord Teach Us To Pray* is a life changer.

Sam Chand, Leadership Consultant and
author of Leadership Pain (www.samchand.com)

Prayer is like an ocean of endless possibilities and solutions. Some people are afraid to jump in because they are weighed down with doubt. Some people prepare to jump in wearing a lifejacket - just in case prayer doesn't work. Then, there are people like Bishop Gideon Thompson who jump into the ocean of prayer with wild abandonment. This book bids you to come and join him.

Terri McFaddin-Solomon
Psalmist, Evangelist, Bible teacher to entertainers,
Writer, Wife, Mother, and Grandmother

LORD
TEACH
US TO
PRAY

LORD TEACH US TO PRAY

DR. GIDEON ANDREW THOMPSON

XULON PRESS

Xulon Press
2301 Lucien Way #415
Maitland, FL 32751
407.339.4217
www.xulonpress.com

Unless otherwise indicated, Scripture quotations taken from the Holy Bible, New International Version (NIV). Copyright © 1973, 1978, 1984, 2011 by Biblica, Inc.™. Used by permission. All rights reserved.

Printed in the United States of America.

ISBN-13: 9781545642801

When I shut up the heavens so that there is no rain, or command locusts to devour the land or send a plague among my people, if My people who are called by My name, will humble themselves and **pray** and seek My face and turn from their wicked ways, then will I hear from heaven and will forgive their sin and will heal their land.

—2 Chronicles 7:13-14

I searched for a man among them who should build up the wall and **stand in the gap** before Me for the land, that I should not destroy it; but I found no one.

—Ezekiel 22:30 NASB

Very early in the morning, while it was still dark, Jesus got up, left the house and went off to a solitary place, where he **prayed**.

—Mark 1:35

Pray in the Spirit on all occasions with all kinds of **prayers** and requests. With this in mind, be alert and always keep on **praying** for all the saints.

—Ephesians 6:18

I Found the Answer
Johnny Lange

I was weak and weary, I had gone astray,
Walking in the darkness, I couldn't find my way.
Then a light came shining, to lead me from despair,
All my sins are forgiven, I was free from care.

Chorus:
I found the answer, I learned to pray,
With faith to guide me, I found the way.
The sun is shining for me each day,
I found the answer, I learned to pray.

I was sad and lonely, all my hopes were gone,
My days were long and dreary, I couldn't carry on.
Then I found the courage to keep my head up high,
Once again I'm happy, and here's the reason why.

Keep your Bible with you, read it every day,
Always count your blessings and always stop to pray.
Learn to keep believing and faith will see you through,
Seek to know contentment, and it will come to you.

ACKNOWLEDGMENTS

FIRST, LET ME ACKNOWLEDGE THE ONE GOD USED TO PREACH THE HELL out of me, the late Rev. Horace W. Sheppard. Not only was he used of God to win me to Christ but to also ground me in the love of truth. His illustrative accounts of prayer exploits impregnated me with a hunger to be one who "prays through." Within his church were significant prayer warriors who taught me by their examples to seek the Lord with all my heart. Pastor Sheppard's powerful preaching created in me a passionate hunger to communicate truth in the pulpit like my spiritual father.

Second, let me acknowledge Mae Gadpaille, a dear woman old enough to be my grandmother whom God used to keep me rising early in the mornings for prayer long after I regretted ever starting Early Morning Prayer Meetings at our church. For five years, between 1986 and 1991, I met prayer warriors from 5:00-6:00 AM, Monday through Friday, and from 7:00-9:00 AM on Saturdays to pray, and 99% of the time, Mother Gadpaille was there—winter, spring, summer, and fall. If she arrived before me, she would lovingly scold me with the words, "My mother taught me it is better to be an hour early than to be a minute late." Knowing she would be on time at our place of prayer forced me into a faithful diligence that birthed a prayer-warrior anointing in my life and ministry.

Third, I wish to acknowledge my appreciation for Rev. Ernest G. Billingsley. We became acquainted at the Church of God Youth Convention in 1965, and little did I realize that fewer than three years later I would relocate to Chicago from Philadelphia with my new wife and our firstborn to enter the bachelor's degree program at the Moody Bible Institute (September 1968–June 1971). This dear brother, old enough to be my father, pastored a Church of God congregation on the north side of Chicago, and during my matriculation at Moody and then at Garrett Theological Seminary we became great friends. God used him greatly to encourage me toward excellence both spiritually and educationally. He never purchased a Scriptural reference book without also buying one for me. He was the consummate instructor: one who delighted in posing a theological question that would catapult us into a lengthy discussion surrounding biblical truth. His practical wisdom and literary erudition were amazing; I was fortunate to have him as a fatherly mentor. When I received an invitation to fly to Boston to preach for a church I knew was looking for a pastor, Pastor Billingsley actually took me aside and told me what to expect and exactly how to respond to various questions and statements. And he was also the only mentor during that post-college graduation/seminary season of my life who consistently urged me to pray. Before I departed for Boston to become the senior pastor of the small Church of God congregation in Boston, Billingsley's last words to me were, "Brother Thompson, whatever else you do, don't forget to pray."

I wish also to acknowledge my appreciation for two prayer partners whose long-term consistent prayerful influence regularly facilitate my prayer growth and development. The first is Rev. Roland E. Cooper, a man of deep abiding prayer and piety. We have witnessed over the years, through the faithful intercessory covering of each other and our families, all of our offspring becoming passionate for Christ and His kingdom, and our individual lives achieving a Joshua 1:8 and Ephesians 3:20 level of benefit and prosperity. At this writing, for the past 30-plus years, the agreement between us has resulted in the multiplication of discipleship and the establishment of a unity that has brought about a dominion in our spheres of influence that make us rejoice.

And finally, I wish to acknowledge my deepest appreciation to the wife of my youth, Yvonne, who has been my best friend, companion, and confidant for the past 49-plus years. Her love for Christ, our family, our church, and me have been a source of strength that served to anchor us in growing paths of ministry. You are one in a million; one who through all of the unfortunate rough aspects of pastoral ministry coupled with the expected adversities of life remained focused and steadfast. Thank you for never discouraging me from pursuing God's presence and purpose. Thank you for your faithful agreement with God's will that positioned you to walk with me through countless fasting and prayer vigils. Thank you for your constant word of encouragement over the years, "Do all that is in your heart, man of God." I love you.

CONTENTS

SECTION FIVE: The WHO of Prayer

SECTION SIX: The HOW of Prayer

FOREWORD

I N 1978, RICHARD J. FOSTER WROTE A BOOK ENTITLED, CELEBRATION OF *Discipline: The Path to Spiritual Growth*. Dr. Foster examines what is universally considered the twelve disciplines of the spiritual life. I am not sure to what degree most believers faithfully practice all twelve of these, but I am absolutely convinced that the *inward* disciplines of *prayer*, *fasting*, *meditation* and *study*, are the absolute essentials to the core of a godly life.

I only know Dr. Foster through his books but I have known personally Bishop Dr. Gideon A. Thompson for more than three decades. He and his wife Yvonne are some of our dearest friends in life. Gideon is an outstanding man of God, a loving husband, a proud father of eight children and many grandchildren and great grandchildren. He, more than any of my close friends who are ministers, my acquaintances who are also ministers, young and old, women and men has epitomized what it means to be a person of prayer. I do not mean to imply that many of my acquaintance don't pray, in fact, one of my most admired friends and mentor, Dr. Jack Hayford's book, *Prayer Is Invading The Impossible* has impacted my life greatly. My walk with Bishop Gideon has been "up close and personal" and my times of fellowship with him in ministry of various kinds have given me a window into "the house that prayer built."

The Gospel of Mark gives an account of a father's frustration with Jesus' disciples inability to heal his demonized son and after Jesus efficiently dispatches the evil spirit and sets the child free, and the disciples' puzzlement as to their inability to do something they had already done. In their *what did we do wrong session* they inquired the reason for such a failure. "And when He had come into the house, His disciples asked Him privately, why could we not cast it out? So He said to them, this kind can come out by nothing but prayer and fasting." (Mark 9:28–29 NKJV) Although some translators take issue with the words "***prayer and fasting***," and therefore do not include it in some of the popular translations; I would venture to say it ought to be included, since it has been proven through the centuries of the church.

Jesus gave the twelve and the seventy the authority to cast out demons, however the terms prayer and fasting were never linked to that initial authorization. It is also clear that prayer was not a part of their personal or corporate discipline from their request to Him in Luke 11:1 "...Lord, teach us to pray." Furthermore, it seems obvious that fasting and prayer was not a part of their lifestyle, since Jesus had to respond to the questions concerning the absence of the practice of fasting and prayers in the lives of His disciples (Mark 5:33 - 34).

Fasting is one of the missing disciplines, and while the church is beginning to awaken to its effectiveness, it has been a very vital part of Bishop's life of prayer. Numerous seasons of forty-day fasts color in the picture of his and Jubilee's prayer life. Since fasting has been a central part of my life in ministry, I have been encouraged by his personal commitment to this means of "intensifying prayer" as Dr. Derek Prince so powerfully taught. A church that has been trained, taught and led in these two things will excel in many arenas of ministry. I believe it's the primary reason that Jubilee Christian Church rests under an "open heaven."

If New England is a desert and waste place, then Jubilee Christian Church in Boston, Massachusetts is the oasis. Their vibrant and passionate worship couched in the most incredible music, their constant pursuit of excellence in every endeavor, their phenomenal growth and outreach to the greater Boston community all testify to the power of prayer. JCC defies the often famous quotes that it is the "preacher's graveyard," "the frozen chosen," or "nothing spiritual grows there." Jubilee has grown from a handful to a multi-site congregation of more than seven thousand, but their open secret is not church growth principles but church growth principles informed and sustained by prayer! These two terms, church growth and prayer are not in contradistinction to each other, in fact they are immutably inseparable. Multiple services on their campuses reminds me of the famous saying by the late Yogi Berra, former manager for the New York Yankees who said, "Nobody goes there anymore, it's too crowded."

Bishop Thompson has often been asked the question, "How did you build this ministry?" When he answers, "Prayer," there always seems to follow the perplexing phrase, "Yes but." It is as though each inquirer is looking for another answer — but prayer is all Bishop Gideon and Jubilee have. I have often heard the idiom, cited but I believe is incorrect: "Those who can, do; those who can't, teach." This book is about doing and teaching, an experience birthed out of trial and failure; it is in fact--a template and a model for building, "A House of Prayer." I commend it to anyone wanting to do just that, and I urge it upon persons who desperately need to come to this conviction. In Bishop Gideon A. Thompson, we have a skilled and faithful guide and mentor.

Bishop Joseph L. Garlington, Sr.
Presiding Bishop
Reconciliation! A Network of Churches and Ministries
Founding Pastor
Covenant Church of Pittsburgh

WHY SHOULD YOU READ THIS AUTHOR'S BOOK?

N THE SPRING OF 1964, AS A 17-YEAR-OLD HIGH SCHOOL GRADUATE, I heard Pastor Horace W. Sheppard preach the good news of God's love for the lost demonstrated by the sacrificial death of Christ on the Cross, and responding to an altar appeal, I repented of my sins. Afterwards, I was encouraged to faithfully come to church and read the Bible. Being around serious believers pulled me away from the profligate lifestyle of pleasure into one conducive to spiritual growth. I started attending the Youth Fellowship gatherings and joined the Youth Choir. When pastor recommended the spiritual discipline of fasting, I added fasting one day a week to my spiritual schedule.

But while I received a great sense of satisfaction with my personal Bible study and corporate worship and church services, I was not satisfied with my prayer life. Though I was praying and had even gone on several extended fasts for the purpose of drawing closer to God, I nevertheless sensed my prayer life was inadequate.

Years later, after learning how to pray effectively in faith, it dawned on me: *I don't remember ever hearing a sermon on prayer.* We were encouraged to pray; we had midweek prayer and Bible study meetings, and I can remember pastor quoting the words of Paul to "pray without ceasing," or the words of Jesus that "men ought always to pray and not faint," but I do not recall ever hearing any minister teach specifically on how to pray effectively. Since then, I've discovered most of us are knowledgeable of *what* is needed to succeed, but ignorant about *how* to make the "what" a reality. It is fun, and even easy, to tell people *what* to do, but painstaking and difficult to teach them *how* to do it. That requires another level of expertise that most teachers do not possess. I've thought to myself, "Maybe my teachers did not teach me how to pray effectively because they didn't know, or maybe those who did know didn't know how important it is to teach others *how* to do what they did well."

I taught my first prayer seminar in 1986, 22 years after my conversion. This caused me to think in retrospect that I probably would have missed many mistakes and overcome some significant hindrances much sooner had I only been taught the *how* of effective praying. I probably would have progressed toward spiritual maturity more rapidly and with fewer setbacks had someone taken the time to enlighten me about the principles of effectual, fervent prayer.

<u>That being said, why should you read my book on prayer?</u>

1. Because in prayer, I'm a doer; someone with experiential knowledge.

Several years ago, I heard a pastor friend, Ernest W. Frye, make the statement, "I don't take swimming lessons from drowning men." I don't know if the statement originated with him, but for me, the meaning was obvious: some things cannot be learned from inexperienced teachers. The person who instructs you needs to be doing what he or she proposes to teach you. On the student's end, this means you should look to learn from doers, not just from good talkers. There is a process called *impartation*. Ostensibly, it means that an experienced teacher is able to *impart* a hunger and an understanding to students that are open just by being around them. The truth of impartation makes sense of the old expression, "More is caught than is taught." Also, that teacher can illustrate from his own experience his answers to questions about *how* he continued and *what* he specifically did to be consistent during difficult or dry seasons in prayer.

In prayer, I am a doer. I'm writing this book on prayer out of my experience with *praying through*[1] in faith to results. I've discovered there is an authority, even an anointing, that accompanies the teaching or training by someone whose knowledge and insight comes from experience. As a prayer warrior, it is my privilege to spend one to three hours of most of my mornings in the presence of the Father. I'm not claiming perfection, but God answers my prayers, and I walk in a victory every true believer has a right to expect. I'm not just someone with knowledge but also someone with the experience and expertise of prayer proficiency.

2. Because I've taught effective prayer principles and seen others prosper.

Without a doubt, prayer is one of the most important disciplines in your spiritual walk, and you rarely rub shoulders with a knowledgeable resource that can help. This is a resource written by a teacher with experiential knowledge. The expression "experience is the best teacher" is true more so in positive areas, than in negative. Let me explain.

You can certainly learn from a negative experience and hopefully not repeat it, but if you learned how to listen and follow instructions, you can learn from the advice or counsel of someone you respect and avoid having to experience the loss of an eye or a finger in the process. You should not have to be burned before you learn that fire is hot. Someone once said, "Blessed is the man who learns from his *father's* burns and not his own." That makes sense doesn't it? This is why honoring your parents and submitting to their authority is so important. The fact that the fifth of the Ten Commandments[2] is the first commandment with a promise is significant in the matter of long life. Many young people have actually lost their lives or were seriously injured because they did not listen to the wise warnings of their parent(s).

In positive areas, especially in areas where you are expected to answer questions about what you did when the way was harder than expected and the goals were delayed, you need a teacher who can speak from the wisdom of experience. Truthfully, there are areas in life where the qualification to speak is only by reason of your experience. No doubt, in some areas, you really do not *know* something until you have done it. Personally, I would not agree to be the passenger on a plane piloted by someone who has never flown a plane safely from takeoff to landing. I wouldn't care how many books he'd read on flying or classroom courses he'd passed on being a pilot. His lack of experience would give me pause. The classroom work or books read only qualify him as an apprentice pilot who is now ready to get some experience flying a plane. I'd rather wait until he got that real experience before I put my life in his hands.

So it is in this area of prayer. My teaching you in this book can only bring you to apprenticeship, the beginning steps of becoming a proficient prayer warrior. To become a journeyman prayer warrior will take some doing on your part. However, this beginning instruction is extremely necessary, so keep reading.

3. Because I've outlined the spiritual principles underlying prayer proficiency.

We will cover the fundamentals of prayer effectiveness and share how to strengthen your hearing the word of faith (Romans 10:6-17). Faith comes from a *heard word*. We'll share more about that later. Knowledge of the truth of Scripture will lay the foundation for you hearing the truth by spiritual revelation that sets you free (John 8:32) from the bondage of ignorance and deception. The truth in this book will first, free you from the bondage of prayerlessness and therefore increase your intimacy with the Father, and second, strengthen your ability to hear the Holy Spirit.

Please be aware that the principles I will share in this book are applicable to those seeking success in every area of life: spiritually, physically, relationally, and financially. Life is connected, meaning you can expect the strength in one or more areas to influence the other areas; and the opposite is also true—you can expect the weakness in one or more areas to influence the other areas.

This drives home the truth we've all heard, "balance is the key to life." True! It would be unrealistic for you to expect that becoming a prayer warrior will automatically solve your physical, relational, or financial problems. Learning the principles leading to prayer proficiency will not bring you to physical health if you refuse to discipline your poor eating habits, or to marital bliss if you refuse to treat your spouse with loving respect as a joint-heir, or financial prosperity if you refuse to live within your means. Make sense?

4. Because my pastoral success in Boston can't be explained apart from prayer.

In all probability, the Boston area is one of the most liberal if not the most liberal parts of our country. And the spiritual life reaching beyond the four walls of the average inner city church was almost non-existent. Though some growth in local church numbers was evident in the 1970's, the reality of seeing a large auditorium packed with worshipers hungry for God in multiple services was only a dream. One might say that the liberal state of affairs in Massachusetts negatively affected the strength of faith, and therefore, local inner city churches felt the impact of that faith-robbing dilemma.

A historical example of the liberal strength of Massachusetts is when the Republican President Richard Milhous Nixon ran for reelection that he won every state in the union but one — Massachusetts. After the proof of the president's involvement in the Watergate scandal, and Nixon resigned to avoid impeachment and trial, residents from my state put a bumper-sticker on their cars that read, "Don't blame me, I'm from Massachusetts."

Finally, though I've been a pastor in New England for more than 40 years and have seen my ministry grow from a handful of faithful followers to thousands meeting on Sundays in five services in two locations, the truth that is foundational for success in ministry will work in every area of life. Principle-centered living is a walk of faith, anchored in believing the truth of God's Word and applying that truth to your everyday life. It influences how you think, what you will or will not say, how you act and react, the kind of lifestyle choices you will make, and, in essence, the kind of person you are. Let us pray:

> Father, thank You for the work of Christ on the cross for our sins; thank You that we are saved by Your grace through our faith in His shed blood and resurrected life. Thank You for the privilege of believing Your Word and praying in faith. Open our eyes, we pray; give us wisdom to understand Your truth that will free us from error and deception so that Your goodness and mercy can follow us all the days of our lives. In Jesus's name we pray. Amen.

Now let's look in detail at this matter of becoming a prayer warrior, one who knows who and whose you are, what you have and can do, where you are seated in Christ, and how you can accomplish the great work of the kingdom. My prayer is that the Lord of the harvest leads you into fruitful paths of prayer proficiency to the glory of God.

—Gideon Andrew Thompson

SECTION ONE

PRAYERLESSNESS: THE PROBLEM CONSIDERED

"Prayer is one of the most powerful yet underutilized resources available to the Body of Christ." GAT

CHAPTER ONE

PREAMBLE

DR. ANTHONY C. CAMPBELL, A DEAR FRIEND AND FORMER PASTOR OF the Eliot Congregational Church in Roxbury, died of a massive stroke in October 2002. For a few years, after retiring from the pastorate, he'd become a professor at my alma mater, Boston University School of Theology. Though only 63 when he died, he left behind a legacy of being a brilliant orator, an effective teacher, a loving pastor, and friend. On several occasions, we met for lunch as colleagues for fellowship.

After the funeral a fellow seminarian engaged me in conversation. He knew me as one of the few seminary students who was older, married with children, a homeowner, and the pastor of a small church in Boston. Having heard about the growth of my church, he asked, "Thompson, what are you doing?"

"What do you mean?" I replied.

"I mean, how have you gone from pastoring a handful of people to preaching every Sunday to thousands? What's your secret? I want to know!"

"You really want to know?" I responded, as I stared at him thinking, *how do I begin to share something so simple yet so profound?*

"Yeah man, I *really* want to know. I've been a pastor since we graduated, but I'm not experiencing your level of success.

Seriously! Share with me brother. I really *need* to know what you're doing."

In my mind, I began to prepare myself to have a heart-to-heart talk with him, one that clearly would require some time, maybe going to lunch somewhere, so I started by saying, "I'm praying!"

But before I could say more, he interrupted, "Yeah, but what are you DOING?!!" His emphasis unfortunately exposed his belief that prayer is not something you can DO that will make a difference in the church. Clearly, he was unfamiliar with the power of prayer. In spite of the fact that I tried again and again to explain I was not just praying the kinds of liturgical, sermonic prayers we are accustomed to praying in church, but was spending the kind of time in prayer where my intimate relationship with the Father increased, he never got it. He never understood. It eventually dawned on me, as I stood frustrated with my failure to get through to him, that he represented the thinking of many pastors of the many denominational churches in America. Even the average Bible-believing, born-again pastor who really loves the Lord spends very little time in prayer. Regrettably, those with an experiential knowledge of the power of prayer are few. Most see prayer as something we do ceremonially, and not as the necessary, valuable resource and discipline we need to develop for effective intimacy with God, multi-generational ministry, productive personal relations, and successful business and financial dealings. Thus, in many orthodox Christian circles, *prayer is the most powerful yet underutilized resources available to the Body of Christ.*

When I was a fairly new seminary graduate, and the pastor of a small, inner-city church, I gradually came to realize and determine to discipline my life to pray. Unfortunately, the importance of prayer was nowhere to be seen in my seminary; no professors taught it, nor reflected its power in their lessons. But by the grace of God, the more I prayed as a pastor, I saw how utterly dependent I was on the resource of prayer, and what's more, I know the same is true of believers in secular disciplines. In your daily life you may get by or even experience some level of success, but learning how to pray effectively will take you to a needed place of balance and focus in order to triumph not only in business but in life.

I propose to teach you what I've learned by experience in over 50 years of being committed to the lordship of Christ, over 40 years as a full-time senior pastor of a growing local church in New England, and over 15 years of being a bishop who gives pastoral care to senior pastors in states as far north as Massachusetts, as far south as Florida, and as far west as California. In addition, my wife and I are best friends, have been married for 51 years, have eight grown, married children, all of whom are passionate for the gospel of Christ and actively involved in the work of the church. As of 2018, we have 34 grandchildren who are being raised in Christian homes by godly parents.

As a mature believer, I determine to walkout the words of Paul, *"By the grace God has given me, I laid a foundation as an expert builder, and someone else is building on it. But each one should be careful how he builds. For no one can lay any foundation other than the one already laid, which is Jesus Christ."* (1 Corinthians 3:10-11) Teaching you how to build intimacy with God the Father through prayer is laying the foundation in Christ you can build upon. The multiplication goal is that as a mature believer who obeys the Word and prays in faith, the Lord will use you to change your world. In essence, this is the prosperous success Jesus summarized in the Sermon on the Mount, *"Therefore everyone who hears these words of mine and puts them into practice is like a wise man who built his house on the rock. The rain came down, the streams rose, and the winds blew and beat against that house; yet it did not fall, because it had its foundation on the rock."* (Matthew 7:24-25; cf. also James 1:22)

When you put the truth of the Word into practice by your obedience, it will effectively bring into balance every area of your life, including your prayer life that will enable your witness, by precept and example, to affect the lives of others. Literally, you will set in motion the miracle of impartation—others will hunger and thirst for intimacy with God they witness in you. The devotional lifestyle of worship, the study of the Word, and the faith to intercede for others you know, to—**Stand in the Gap**—on their behalf will result in you seeing the power of the prayer of faith saving and transforming lives. (Ezekiel 22:30) And the greater joy will be when you witness God using those you've influenced, praying to influence others. Regardless of your job, business, calling, or giftedness (spiritual or secular), prayer effectiveness that increases your intimacy with the Father will greatly benefit you and the people in your life. Do not allow yourself just to go to church without becoming proficient in the most important spiritual discipline in the entire world—*prayer.* Let me encourage you to run with perseverance this spiritual, rewarding race.

Finally, the people you influence may remember some of what you say, but they will never forget what you do and who you are. My purpose in writing this book is to influence you to see the incomparable benefit of developing a prayer life that will absolutely transform you from being just a hearer of the Word to becoming an obedient, effective doer.

Pray this prayer:

Father, strengthen me to grow in grace and in the knowledge of Christ. Help me to become an obedient doer of the Word; one You can use to touch the people in my life. As I read this book, I pray that You will enable me to rebuild my life on the solid rock of obedience as I determine to be a prayer warrior, in Jesus name. Amen.

CHAPTER TWO

AN INTERESTING COMPARISON

WHAT IS PRAYER? WHY SHOULD DEVELOPING A CONSISTENT PRAYER life be something you should prioritize? How important is the Bible, faith, and agreement in achieving answers to prayer? What part does theology, or morality, or lifestyle, or purpose play in this matter of prayer and relationship with God? Where do I begin? Can the development of a consistent worship and prayer life affect what happens and how you view and react to what happens in your spiritual, physical, relational, social, and financial life? What steps should be taken to achieve results?

Strangely enough, in many Christian circles, even where the theological perspective is orthodox, questions like these are not adequately answered because most Christians, even pastors and adjunct spiritual leaders in the church, have no consistent prayer life. This book is birthed out of my experience as an effective prayer warrior. In that regard, allow me to use the words of Jesus, "Very truly I tell you, we speak of what we know, and we testify to what we have seen" (John 3:11). In light of these words of Jesus, allow me to say, "I speak of what I know and testify to what I've seen and experienced. Experience is key!"

Consider this Comparison

George Barna, in a January 12, 2004 online article entitled "Only Half of Protestant Pastors Have a Biblical Worldview" stated, "The most important point is that you can't give people what you don't have."[3] The article is about a survey based on interviews with 601 Senior Pastors nationwide, representing a random cross-section of Protestant churches. Barna reported that only half (51%) of the country's Protestant pastors have a biblical worldview. The following excerpt from the article speaks to how fundamental is the matter of knowing and believing when it comes to communicating and imparting truth:

> The low percentage of Christians who have a biblical worldview is a direct reflection of the fact that half of our primary religious teachers and leaders do not have one. In some denominations, the vast majority of clergy do not have a biblical worldview, and it shows up clearly in the data related to the theological views and moral choices of people who attend those churches. Our research among people who have a biblical worldview shows that it is a long-term process that requires a lot of purposeful activity: teaching, prayer, conversation, accountability, and so forth. Based on our correlations of worldview and moral behavior, we can confidently argue that if the 51% of pastors who have a biblical worldview were to strategically and relentlessly assist their congregants in adopting such a way of interpreting and responding to life, the impact on our churches, families and society at-large would be enormous.[4]

Here's my contention given Barna's assessment: suppose a local church became a house of prayer, where prayer agreement is taught by the pastor and practiced by the members, where a prayer cover is provided by the members for each other, their families, and their community. Or suppose in the secular sphere a business owner consistently spends the first 15-30 or more minutes of his day in worship, intercessory prayer, and Bible study and pulls leaders in his business into that spiritual discipline; or suppose a worker on any particular job determines to prioritize prayer and devotional reading as part of his daily schedule—what do you think would be the impact? I believe if we recognize, study, analyze, and apply the spiritual discipline of prayer and obeying the Spirit's leading to mirror the character of truth in our daily actions and reactions, in the words of Barna, "the impact on our churches, families, and society at-large would be enormous." Again, I am speaking as a senior pastor of 40-plus years of experience, as one who committed his life to Christ in the 1960's, as a baby-boomer who grew up in church and is painfully familiar with church polity and procedures. All my ministry experience has been in major cities: born and raised in Philadelphia, PA, schooled in Chicago, IL and Boston, MA, and a pastor in Boston since 1972. I believe the truth-principles of church health and growth will work anywhere, whether in the church, in the family, or in the workplace. Uncompromised truth will work anywhere. I also believe the truth-principles taught in this book, if practiced sedulously, will result in strength and success in business and family; meaning this matter of becoming a praying believer will elevate you above whatever success you now experience. Becoming a believer who prays, hears Christ, walks in faithful obedience to what he hears, and seeks by precept and example to influence and impact his world for Christ will achieve a success, in the words of the great apostle Paul, immeasurably more than all you ask or imagine (Ephesians 3:20).

Speaking of uncompromised truth: while it is appropriate for compromise to influence methods and strategies, compromise has no place in foundational biblical principles of spiritual health and development. Church, business, relational, or personal health and growth are connected to principles of truth. As the old adage says, "Methods are many, principles are few; methods always change, principles never do." Your growth problem can be both theological and methodological. It can be theological in that what you believe is right or wrong, moral or immoral, and it will affect what you will or will not do. It is methodological because it is important to keep step with the times and communicate in a way your message can be heard by as many segments of society as possible. In your struggle to succeed and achieve your goals, make sure you care enough to examine what others like you have done to achieve success. Be open to learn from some of the methods they used, why those methods were helpful, and how they were structured. Reading this book about learning how to pray effectively can be a beginning for you in your spiritual, physical, relational, and even financial quest for success.

THE WHAT OF PRAYER
(PART I)

Considering definitions, answers, and procedures

CHAPTER THREE

WHAT IS PRAYER?

Introduction

PRAYER IS ONE OF THE CHRISTIAN DISCIPLINES THAT CAN MAKE THE difference between success and failure in your life. Prayer is a work that builds intimacy with God. Though you are saved by grace through faith and not by works (Ephesians 2:8-9), yet being God's workmanship that is created to do good work is part of who you are and of what you are called to do (Ephesians 2:10). While work does not save you, it does make you grow stronger. You either "grow in the grace and knowledge of our Lord and Savior Jesus Christ" (2 Peter 3:18), or you don't. And whether you do or don't in large measure depend on the work you do. That's reality. Though works don't save you, when you are truly saved by grace, the work of being a godly person is an expectation God and people have. You will not live the fulfilled life God intends for you without godly works.

Since it is true you reap what you sow (Galatians 6:7), if you do not sow, you cannot reap. There are seeds of love, mercy, generosity, kindness, etc. that when sown will produce fruit you reap. Make no mistake—you are called to sow and bear fruit (John 15:5). If you neglect doing (sowing) this work of the kingdom, you will suffer on the reaping end. There is work God expects you to do as a true believer and prayer is a necessary part of that work.

One way to define disappointment is not getting what you expect. Don't let it be true that Christ who paid the price for your destiny with potential and purpose is disappointed because His expectations of you are not being met. It's time to learn and practice the fundamentals of prayer proficiency. There are four basic definitions for prayer:

1. Prayer is Talking to God

The first definition sees prayer as simply talking to God, a monologue where you make your requests known to the Father, or even where you cry out to God through your pain or anguish of heart. When most believers pray, this basic definition is the understanding they have. If asked, "What is prayer?" they'd answer, "Prayer is talking to God, my Heavenly Father."

2. Prayer is Communion with God

The second definition sees prayer as communion with God, where you speak to God and He speaks to you. Some feel this listening aspect of prayer is unnecessary since we have the written Word, the Old and New Testaments. While it is true one of the major ways God speaks to you is through Scripture, you shouldn't allow anyone to theologize God Almighty into silence. There is absolutely no scriptural evidence to support the belief that God no longer speaks. Granted, present humanity has surrounded itself with the noises of fast-paced modern living, and has failed to quiet itself enough to hear God, yet the Scriptures testify that God spoke to the prophets, priests, kings, and apostles of old, and contemporary evidence testifies that God still speaks today. He is both transcendent and immanent, as the prophet Isaiah makes plain: "I live in a high and holy place, but also with him who is contrite and lowly in spirit..." (Isaiah 57:15b). If you quiet and humble your heart, prayerfully seek His face, and determine to do His will, you will hear Him direct your path. He is immanent, preparing to be found by those who seek Him with their whole heart (Jeremiah 29:13). He'll commune with you, speak words that encourage, enlighten, guide, direct, and inspire you to be your best for Him. You need to have this kind of relationship with the Father: one where you unburden your heart through petition and intercession, and where He speaks directive words you desperately need to hear. Open wide your heart, dear friend, to receive this level of intimate relationship with your Heavenly Father. He promised to show Himself strong on behalf of those whose hearts are fully committed to Him (2 Chronicles 16:9). Simply stated, God is looking to use you commensurate to your total surrender. This level of spiritual surrender grows out of a deep and abiding love for God where you desire to know Him better (Philippians 3:10). Jesus summed this up in the Sermon on the Mount, "Blessed are those who hunger and thirst for righteousness, for they will be filled" (Matthew 5:6). Unfortunately, this level of spiritual hunger and thirst is rare today, but let me encourage you to surrender to God in prayer, and position yourself to experience the spiritual fullness of spiritual encounters with your Heavenly Father.

Any genuine believer has access to God's grace by faith (Romans 5:2). The word "genuine" is used because there are those who call themselves "believers," but they've only given intellectual assent to the truth of the gospel without having made a heart commitment to walk by faith in its truth. Many act as though a commitment to Christ is nothing more than joining church, shaking the preacher's hand, and jumping through a few "religious hoops" without experiencing any change in lifestyle whatsoever. But the truth of eternal salvation by grace through faith in Christ is real and requires repentance and faith (Acts 20:21). Actually, Jesus warns, "Unless you repent, you too will all perish" (see Luke 13:1-5; cf. 2 Corinthians 7:10). Though Jesus did not come to condemn you but to save you (John 3:17), you should hear His warning of the pending doom of those who refuse to repent.

Therefore, live a life of change. Be an empty, yielded vessel, one that God can fill with His power and use in ways beyond what you could ask or imagine. "The creation waits in eager expectation for the sons of God to be revealed" (Romans 8:19). Will you say, "Yes," to become one God will use to fulfill that which creation needs? Will you determine to be an example others can follow?

Will you pray to be empowered to call those you know "from the dominion of darkness…into the kingdom of the Son he loves"? (Colossians 1:13) At your eternal "yes," God will break through the silence you've experienced and speak words of faith and direction that will lift you into a new realm of understanding and truth. Begin this salvation-journey of revelation knowledge by believing with all your heart that your Heavenly Father desires to make Himself known to you. You'll discover in prayer the incredible, confirming joy of relational intimacy with Him.

When God speaks, the miracle is that through a simple word or phrase, He downloads a paragraph of understanding and insight about where you are in your journey. It can be revelation about what you should do at the time, or how you should act or react in the circumstance. His spoken word brings you exactly where you need to be. Oh the supreme benefit of His wise and powerful words of counsel and comfort!

3. Prayer is Warfare

The third definition of prayer is warfare. Understand that practicing this type of prayer, the battling against the enemy, is a level of praying needed in certain circumstances to achieve prayer effectiveness. In preparation for warfare prayer, you need to put on the full armor of God because there are unseen adversaries that seek to thwart or hinder your prayer life. Paul made us aware of this struggle surrounding those who pray in Ephesians 6:10-18,

> *[10] Finally, be strong in the Lord and in his mighty power. [11] Put on the full armor of God, so that you can take your stand against the devil's schemes. [12] For our struggle is not against flesh and blood, but against the rulers, against the authorities, against the powers of this dark world and against the spiritual forces of evil in the heavenly realms. [13] Therefore put on the full armor of God, so that when the day of evil comes, you may be able to stand your ground, and after you have done everything,*

> to stand. *¹⁴ Stand firm then, with the belt of truth buckled around your waist, with the breastplate of righteousness in place, ¹⁵ and with your feet fitted with the readiness that comes from the gospel of peace. ¹⁶ In addition to all this, take up the shield of faith, with which you can extinguish all the flaming arrows of the evil one. ¹⁷ Take the helmet of salvation and the sword of the Spirit, which is the word of God. ¹⁸ And pray in the Spirit on all occasions with all kinds of prayers and requests.*

Let's look for a moment at the elements of the armor of God.

1. <u>Belt of truth</u> – The King James Version (KJV) says, "loins girt about with truth." Because reproduction comes through your loins, you understand that you're called to reproduce truth in the lives of others; this includes bringing others to a commitment to the lordship of Christ who is "the way, the **truth**, and the life" (John 14:6, emphasis mine). It also includes being filled with the Spirit (Acts 1:8; Ephesians 5:18-19); being aware that the Holy Spirit who lives in you (John 14:17) is called the "Spirit of truth" (John 16:13); thus you have "truth in the [your] inward parts" (Psalm 51:6 KJV).

2. <u>Breastplate of righteousness</u> – Understand righteousness is both vertical and horizontal. It is vertical in that righteousness is received by faith as a gift (Romans 5:17) when you are declared right with God, "justified through faith" (Romans 5:1). Righteousness is also horizontal. We are exhorted by Christ to "...seek first his kingdom and his righteousness..." (Matthew 6:33) Seeking His righteousness includes seeking to establish God's kingdom of truth, justice, equity, fairness, honesty, integrity, etc. in the world of people. Your spheres of influence may be small or large dependent upon your access or gifts, but donning the breastplate of righteousness means you understand the importance of God's grace *to* you and *through* you, and you commit to being the "light" God calls you to be (Matthew 5:14). Your understanding of the importance of righteousness is connected to being the "righteousness of God

17

in Him (Christ)" (2 Corinthians 5:21 KJV [parenthesis mine]; cf. also John 16:7-10 where the earthly presence of Christ is seen as the picture of righteousness, and because the ministry of His earthly presence was ending, He promised to send the Holy Spirit to be in you [John 14:17] for you to be the picture of righteousness in your own spheres of influence). Finally, Paul wrote, "Christ Jesus... has become for us wisdom from God—that is, our **righteousness**, holiness, and redemption" (1 Corinthians 1:30, emphasis mine).

It's amazing how differently the world looks when viewed through the eyes of righteousness. In the Frank Capra movie, "It's a Wonderful Life,"[5] George Bailey, the main character, is constantly doing the right thing. Out of his selfless honesty and integrity, he constantly helps people, and his world, Bedford Falls, gradually, through struggle, becomes a better place. He doesn't recognize the hand of God using him until a crisis, the loss of $8,000, threatens to ruin him and he contemplates committing suicide. His eyes are eventually opened when the Lord, through George's guardian angel, Clarence, shows him what the world would look like if he'd never been born. Mr. Potter, a selfish, self-centered, old man full of greed, in George's absence, literally turns Bedford Falls into a dive where every form of immorality reigns. George is horrified by the hole, the absence of his life, would leave in the lives of everyone he knows: his mother, his brother, his uncle Billy, his cab driver friend, Ernie Bishop, his childhood friend, Violet Bick, the druggist, Mr. Gower, the pub owner, Mr. Martini, and countless others who bought homes, built productive lives, didn't go crazy during the financial crash... on and on. The life of a righteous person, George, touched everyone he knew. Faced with the revelation that his life has meaning and purpose even in the midst of trials and difficulties, he prays, "Please God, I don't care what happens to me; take me back to my wife and kids. Please God, I want to live."

If you could only see your life through the eyes of righteousness, you would run from greed, dishonesty, and immorality like it was a plague. George Bailey being born is like you being born again. Follow the path of righteousness and life, the "Wonderful Life" God intends for you will be *abundant* as Jesus promised (John 10:10 KJV).

3. <u>Feet fitted with the readiness that comes from the gospel of peace</u> – Understand that by virtue of your commitment to the gospel of Jesus Christ (Romans 1:16-17), you wear the shoes of the gospel of peace. And whatever else you might do as an adult to earn a living (business owner, professional, white-collar or blue-collar worker, etc.), as a mature believer, you are chosen, called, and commissioned to make disciples of all nations (Matthew 28:19-20; John 15:15-16). The shoes are called "the gospel of peace" because wherever you go (walk, run, or travel) you have the God-given responsibility and privilege to help the lost come to peace in Christ (Romans 5:1). Notice the text says, "feet fitted with the readiness that comes from the *gospel* of peace." The kerygma of the gospel is "Christ died for our sins according to the Scriptures, that he was buried, that he was raised on the third day according to the Scriptures" (see 1 Corinthians 15:1-4; Romans 5:1). Your feet need to be transformed to accommodate walking a path where you communicate by life and by lip the good news of eternal peace through faith in Christ. It is not that the shoes of the gospel need to be sized for you, but that your feet need to be "fitted," your walk needs to be sized, transformed to meet the task of being one who walks out its truth.

4. <u>Shield of faith</u> – Understand faith is called a shield because it protects you from the flaming arrows of the evil one. There are several names for your enemy, a few are: the accuser of our brothers and sisters (Revelation 12:10), the adversary (1 Peter 5:8 KJV), the father of lies (John 8:44), the ruler of the darkness of this world (Ephesians 6:12 KJV), the tempter (Matthew 4:3; 1 Thessalonians 3:5), and Satan (Acts 26:18; Romans 16:20). Faith is both defensive, part of your armor as a shield, and faith is also an offensive weapon where you speak in faith a confession of God's truth and experience blessing. Here, faith is pictured as a defending shield. What you believe aids in defending you from the lies of your adversary. Even the accusations the accuser may mount against you will not work because your steadfast faith is anchored in the truth of God's Word you believe. Your faith comes from believing with all your heart what the Word says; faith comes from hearing the message, and the message is heard through the word of Christ. (Romans 10:17) And

remember you are not alone, for the Lord promised, "Never will I leave you; never will I forsake you" (Hebrews 13:5). So be confident, prayer warrior, He is present in this faith-fight you endure.

5. <u>Helmet of salvation</u> – Understand a helmet protects your head so a blow to your head will not render you unconscious. Well, the experience of knowing the truth in your mind and heart sets you free (John 8:31-32) from being knocked unconscious and out of the Christian race by doctrinal error or personal falsehood. An integral part of the protection of your name and ministry is—knowing who you are and whose you are. Also, remember Christ is your head when you've made Him Lord:

> *²² God...appointed him to be head over every-thing for the church, ²³ which is his body, the fullness of him who fills everything in every way.* (Ephesians 1:22-23)

6. <u>Sword of the Spirit, which is the word of God</u> – Understand that while most of the "armor of God" you clothe yourself with is predominately defensive, this sword is predominately an offensive weapon. It can be used defensively as Jesus did when tempted by the devil after the 40 days of fasting (Matthew 4:1-11), but with respect to the sword being used in offense, remember the sword is not in your hand but in your mouth (Revelation 19:11-16, esp. v. 15). As the apocalyptic picture of Christ has the sword coming "out of his mouth," so you and I are expected to speak powerful words of faith that separate truth from deception, light from darkness, the worldliness of this age from the eternality of God's kingdom. Paul exhorted Timothy to,

> *² Preach the Word; be prepared in season and out of season; correct, rebuke and encourage—with great patience and careful instruction. ³ For the time will come when men will not put up with sound doctrine. Instead, to suit their own desires, they will gather around them a great number of teachers to say what their itching ears want to hear. ⁴ They will turn their*

ears away from the truth and turn aside to myths.
⁵ But you, keep your head in all situations, endure
hardship, do the work of an evangelist, discharge
all the duties of your ministry. (2 Timothy 4:2-5)

7. <u>Pray in the Spirit on all occasions with all kinds of prayers</u> –
Most Bible expositors do not include "prayer" as part of the "armor
of God" that believers are exhorted to "put on" (Ephesians 6:11),
and while I would not forcefully disagree, I would encourage you
to understand Paul's admonition to *put on the full armor of God* as
that which is inseparably connected to an effective warfare prayer
life. Actually, the figurative list of "the armor of God" is not *full*
apart from warfare prayer. They coexist—the armor and prayer—
strengthening each other. And while I would not require numbering
"prayer" as the seventh armor as I've done here, I've listed it as such
to say, "You cannot have one without the other."

The Seven Sons of Sceva

The account of the seven sons of Sceva, a Jewish chief priest,
is told in Acts 19:13-16. It warns of the danger in trying to do
Christian work apart from truly being Christian. Evidently, these
sons witnessed Paul's preaching and heard him cast out demons
in the name of the Lord Jesus, and they decided to use the words
and formula they witnessed in Paul but without taking into account
Paul's consecrated commitment to the lordship of Christ, his being
filled with the Spirit, and his understanding of his faith position
based on the Word of Christ. The result was tragic: the demonized
man "overpowered them all...(and) gave them such a beating that
they ran out of the house naked and bleeding" (v. 16).

The lesson from this is clear: you cannot fake faith and a godly
commitment to the lordship of Christ. You must be Christian
through and through, unswervingly committed to Christ and obedient to scriptural truth all the way down. The phrase "all the way
down" reminds me of an anecdote with the phrase "turtles all the
way down." There are numerous versions of the "turtles all the

way down" story. The version I heard from a banquet speaker goes like this,

> Professor William James while giving a lecture including the cosmology of the universe was interrupted by the statement of an old lady who told him the Earth was not round but a flat clump of ground resting on the back of a huge turtle. "But, my dear lady," Professor James asked, as politely as possible, "What holds up the turtle?" "Ah," she said, "That's easy. The turtle is standing on the back of another larger turtle." "Oh, I see," said Professor James, still being polite, "But would you be so kind as to tell me what holds up the second turtle?" "It's no use, Professor James," exclaimed the old lady, realizing he was trying to lead her into a logical trap. "It's turtles-turtles-turtles, all the way down!"

The phrase is usually used to describe a system that appears to have dependencies that never end. Well, allow me to use it to describe this spiritual truth—the never-ending spiritual dependency we have to stay inseparably connected to Jesus. In this matter of spiritual warfare, "It's **Jesus, Jesus, Jesus,** all the way down!" And it needs to be branded firm in the minds and hearts of every believer seeking to do kingdom work, whether it's saving the lost, healing the sick, delivering the bound, or simply teaching the truth. Genuine faith in Christ must be your center and His work your focus. In the Gospel According to St. John, Jesus said, "I am the vine; you are the branches. If you remain in me and I in you, you will bear much fruit; *apart from me you can do nothing*" (John 15:5, emphasis mine).

Jesus used the word "nothing." My rhetorical question to you is, "What part of 'nothing' don't you understand?" This faith fight is no joke; you can lose your life if you are not properly prepared and equipped. It's the rationale behind Paul exhorting the Ephesians to put on the full armor of God prior to warfare prayer to the Father. In prayer, you will engage the enemy. You must be prepared! The enemy's agenda is to "steal and kill and destroy" (John 10:10); to stop or hinder your contribution to the progress of God's kingdom of righteousness in whatever way he can. You must always be prepared with the sword of the Spirit, the Word of God (Ephesians 6:17), to take your faith stand upon the unshakeable foundation of the truth of God's promises.

Seriously, when you pray, prepare to engage the enemy — using the power of the Holy Spirit (Acts 1:8), the authority of the faith-filled Words of Christ (Romans 10:17), and in the name of the Lord Jesus Christ (Philippians 2:10-11).[6]

There is an old hymn of the church that says,

> The fight is on, O Christian soldier!
> And face-to-face in stern array,
> With armor gleaming and colors screaming,
> The right and wrong engaged today.
> The fight is on, but be not weary.
> Be strong and in His mighty hold fast.
> If God be for us, His banner o'er us,
> We'll in him sing the victors' song at last![7]

Seeing prayer as warfare will take you beyond the prayer recitations you hear read or recited by some as part of a liturgical church service format. This is by no means a criticism of those prayers, but simply serves to differentiate between written prayers recited as part of the liturgy of a worship service versus the travailing intercessory prayers made by a prayer warrior in his or her secret closet.

In the Name of Jesus

As a prayer warrior, you must learn to use the authority of the name of Jesus in prayer. Jesus taught His disciples about the kind of praying they should do when He would no longer be with them,

> [23] *"In that day you will no longer ask me any-thing. Very truly I tell you, my Father will give you*

whatever you ask in my name. *²⁴ Until now you have not asked for anything in my name. Ask and you will receive, and your joy will be complete"* (John 16:23-24).

Your prayer format, according to this text, is to pray to the Father *in the name of Jesus.*

In warfare prayer, you exercise authority over the enemy in the name of Jesus. The name of Jesus has authority in the three realms: *heaven–* in the realm of God and angels; *earth–* in the realm of mankind and animals; and *under the earth–* in the realm of the devil and demonic forces (Philippians 2:9-11). It should be used when praying for the lost, and especially when you suspect the presence of demonic activity. Jesus taught His disciples to use His name to drive out demons and when they lay hands on the sick (Mark 16:17-18), and you have authority in the name of Jesus to bind the forces of demonic opposition (Luke 10:17; Acts 16:18). Praying in faith means your prayer has a biblical foundation to it, i.e. you are in the will of God according to the Word of God as you are prayerfully ministering to someone. His will is made clear in His Word, just as your will is made plain by your words. Helping the helpless is what Jesus coming to earth is all about (Luke 4:18-19), and He's calling you to pray and fortify yourself with a confident faith based upon the promise(s) of His Word:

> *¹⁴ This is the **confidence** we have in approaching God: that if we **ask** anything **according to His will**, He hears us.* *¹⁵ And if we know that He hears us— whatever we ask—we know that we have what we asked of Him.* (1 John 5:14-15, emphases mine).

Jesus says in Matthew 18:18, "I tell you the truth, whatever you **bind** on earth will be bound in heaven, and whatever you loose on earth will be loosed in heaven" (emphasis mine). The same Greek word translated "bind" in 18:18 is translated "ties up" in Matthew 12:29: "...how can anyone enter a strong man's house and carry off his possessions unless he first ties up the strong man? Then he can plunder his house." This is where prayer is more than a request to the Father, but a faith command to the enemy. This is warfare! The binding of the enemy is a spiritual matter. It is where you, and hopefully a prayer partner, stand firm in faith against the oppression of the enemy as you rebuke him in the name of Jesus. It means you take a determined spiritual stand against the enemy's malevolent presence by the authority of the name of Jesus Christ. This tenacious stand in Christ is needed to secure deliverance for the bound. Important to remember here is that you cannot drive demons out of someone who does not want to obey Christ and be saved. But when you have one whose heart is fighting for freedom in Christ, who is seeking to "take hold[8] of...eternal life" (1 Timothy 6:12) and agreeing internally as you bind demonic forces, deliverance is possible because you **have the agreement necessary for victory.**

4. Prayer is Prophetic Intercession

The fourth and last definition of prayer is prophetic intercession. This is where you are praying the will of God for your life and including those runners who are with you in pursuit of that vision of God's will. It is where you have an understanding of what God is saying to you about the direction of your life, but you need a clearer view of how the vision God has given unfolds to reveal your place in His plan. In prayer, you actually come to the revelation of God's grace for you to be who He has created you to be and to do what He has called and gifted you to do. I've lived long enough to witness the lifelong journeys of some believers who never achieved their destiny simply because they did not hear God clearly enough to pray in line with His will for their lives. A classic Scripture demonstrating this fourth definition is in the Old Testament book of the prophet Habakkuk,

> *[1]I will stand at my watch and station myself on the ramparts; I will look to see what He will say to me and what answer I am to give to this complaint. [2] Then the LORD replied: "Write down the revelation and make it plain on tablets so that a herald may*

run with it. ³ For the revelation awaits an appointed time; it speaks of the end and will not prove false. Though it linger, wait for it; it will certainly come and will not delay." (2:1-3)

Out of the urgency of a serious complaint, Habakkuk positioned himself to hear from God. An excellent definition of vision is "seeing what God is saying." Habakkuk's prayer became a "watch," like a soldier standing guard. He is on the "ramparts" (the roof) of a tower allowing him visibility in every direction. The meaning here is clear: you must position yourself to hear God speak, to see God's vision by removing all distractions and hindrances. Like Habakkuk, you must determine to see what God is saying. Habakkuk's determination to experience an encounter with God, to have the vision, to understand the revelation of His part in God's plan, to speak to the "complaint," is the urgency of the prophet's prayer. That urgency must become yours as you pray, "I'm looking with believing expectation for You, Father, to direct my steps."

Understanding that a prayer-watch is part of being a faith-filled prayer warrior on assignment is key. Your watch in your sphere(s) of influence is where you exercise authority and an oversight-responsibility in the lives of others. With a pastor, the sphere of influence would be his church; with a business owner, the sphere of influence is his or her employees; with a parent, the sphere of influence is the children in the family. With Habakkuk, his dilemma was not just his but it was the complaint his people were making. What dilemmas are in the lives of the people for whom you pray? Do you know God wants to show you how to help them?

Remind yourself that vision is seeing what God is saying. A vision is a revelation of God's purposes being fulfilled in your life and in the lives of those you influence. When you see it, you will also see how others are included in what God is showing you. Strategize by writing down what you see, talk about what you see, and by all means earnestly pray about what you see.

Be aware that visions and dreams are not for you alone. In the realm of the spirit where prayers are spoken and faith is released, what's achieved is for many. This was true of the prophet Habakkuk:

as he sought the Lord with all of his heart in prayer, the Lord said, "Write the revelation down" (2:2). Making the revelation plain by writing it out is an important component to understanding the revelation's meaning for your individual life and how it connects and impacts others within your spheres of influence. Habakkuk was told to write the revelation down so those who were with him could read it and run with him in agreement. This agreement piece needs to be explored in more detail later, but let me simply say, you won't get very far by yourself, and you will never fully achieve the will of God or reach the fullness of your potential without reaching beyond yourself to include the gifts in others. Habakkuk saw this, and you must see it too. Yes, the prophet climbed to the ramparts of a tower to pray and seek God's face for some answers, and when he descended into the dilemmas that confronted him, he had the answers in the *revelation* God gave him, and part of the revelation was the necessary inclusion of others also called and gifted of God to read, agree, and run with him.

Finally, Habakkuk was told the revelation was for an appointed time that speaks of the end and will not prove false, and though it lingers, he must wait for it, it will surely come to pass and will not delay (2:3). These words of encouragement are especially needed between the time you pray and the time you actually receive—especially when that in-between time is delayed, like Abram leaving Ur of the Chaldeans to go into a land God promised to show him (cf. Genesis 11:31-12:1). The writer of Hebrews, recounting that historic event, wrote,

> *8 By faith Abraham, when called to go to a place he would later receive as his inheritance, obeyed and went, even though he did not know where he was going [nor how long it would take him to get there]. 9 By faith he made his home in the promised land like a stranger in a foreign country; he lived in tents, as did Isaac and Jacob, who were heirs with him of the same promise. 10 For he was looking forward to the city with foundations, whose architect and builder is God.* (11:8-10)

27

Praying prophetically means praying out of your communion understanding with God. God's revelation speaks of the end that will not prove false; it's a revelation that will surely come into being even though it may be delayed. All this must be understood so you don't get discouraged in prayer because your expectation of a swift answer to your prayer did not happen. You begin prophetic praying after you discern the prophetic revelation of a particular season in your life or the will of God for your life. And when you pray prophetically, though it sounds similar to the second definition of prayer, it is more than simply communing with God around a problem or issue. It is taking God's revelation of your future direction and vision and praying it through. The requirement of you *seeing what He is saying,* understanding fully the revelation of the vision, can be the difference between achieving or failing to achieve your God-given purpose.

Praying in the Spirit and Praying with Your Spirit

There is a difference between praying *in the Spirit* and praying *with your spirit.* Praying *in the Spirit* is prayer that is guided by the Holy Spirit according to the will of God. Praying in the Spirit is where you want to be in your prayer life. There may be times when you pray in the Spirit that the fervency of your prayer can seem to take on a life of its own, so to speak (James 5:16b KJV). Your prayer can become so intense that, as you become so yielded to the guidance of the Spirit that you pray in line with the Holy Spirit and the will of God for you, or for the need, person, or circumstance on your heart that the words of your prayer seemingly flow without you thinking about them. It is as though your spirit links with God's Spirit, and you passionately pray the will of God.

Your praying can be in the language of your understanding,[9] and it may include the language the Spirit enables as you pray *with your spirit*. Praying *with your spirit*, according to the apostle Paul, is associated with praying in other tongues:

> [14] *If I pray in a tongue, my spirit prays, but my mind is unfruitful.* [15] *So what shall I do? I will pray with my*

spirit, but I will also pray with my understanding; I will sing with my spirit, but I will also sing with my understanding. (1 Corinthians 14:14-15)

Earlier, in the same chapter, Paul teaches, "Anyone who speaks in a tongue does not speak to people but to God. Indeed, no one understands them; they utter mysteries by the Spirit" (v. 2). Paul also says in verse 4, "Anyone who speaks in a tongue edifies themselves" (cf. Jude 20 KJV, "But ye, beloved, building up [edifying] yourselves on your most holy faith, praying in the Holy Ghost"). So to "speak" in a tongue can be prayer that strengthens you. Faith-filled praying with your spirit in tongues, in your secret closet or war room, for needs of which you are aware they are the will of God, build you up spiritually and are where the Spirit is moving in your spirit in prayer.

My own experience with deep intercession is where I've gone back and forth between the two as the Spirit directs (cf. Paul's example in 1 Corinthians 14:13-15). In some instances, the back and forth can be the same prayer in the Spirit where the meaning of the praying in tongues is given in the back and forth with your praying in the language you understand.

Now, as a believer, praying in the Spirit, whether in the language of your understanding or of your spirit, is when you pray recognizing your need of the Spirit's help. It is going in faith before the throne of grace (Hebrews 4:16) while you are aware that demonic principalities will do all within their limited authority to stop or hinder your praying. But, when believers, clad in the armor of God and seated in Christ, pray, and demonic forces are powerless to stop or hinder them, that's the only praying worth taking the time to do—it is warfare, praying in the Spirit (see the section above under *Prayer is Warfare*).[10]

The Holy Spirit Helps Us

In some cases, we don't know what we ought to pray. In his letter to the Romans, the apostle Paul deals with this truth:

19 The creation waits in eager expectation for the sons of God to be revealed. 20 For the creation was subjected to frustration, not by its own choice, but by the will of the one who subjected it, in hope 21 that the creation itself will be liberated from its bondage to decay and brought into the glorious freedom of the children of God.

22 We know that the whole creation has been groaning as in the pains of childbirth right up to the present time. 23 Not only so, but we ourselves, who have the firstfruits of the Spirit, groan inwardly as we wait eagerly for our adoption as sons, the redemption of our bodies. 24 For in this hope we were saved. But hope that is seen is no hope at all. Who hopes for what he already has? 25 But if we hope for what we do not yet have, we wait for it patiently.

26 In the same way, the Spirit helps us in our weakness. We do not know what we ought to pray for, but the Spirit himself intercedes for us with groans that words cannot express. 27 And he who searches our hearts knows the mind of the Spirit, because the Spirit intercedes for the saints in accordance with God's will. (Romans 8:19-27)

In verse 19, Paul personifies "creation" as having an "eager expectation for the sons of God to be revealed." The overwhelming desire of the apostle, in a discerning moment, gives voice to creation concerning the destructive ways of sinful man; ways that can only be corrected by the righteous change that mature believers bring.

He continues in verses 20-21, "creation was subjected to frustration" apart from "its own choice, but by the will of the one who subjected it, in hope that the creation itself will be liberated from its bondage to decay and brought into the glorious freedom of the children of God." After the apostle gives creation human characteristics, he lifts the need for mature believers to see themselves as the tools God uses to fix what is broken in the world of humankind and in the world of creation._ Ostensibly, Paul links the salvation of humankind with the salvation of the earth in the matter of "creation itself will be liberated from its bondage to decay and brought into the glorious freedom of the children of God." So God's plan for you and me being mature "children of God" includes empowering us through prayer and faith to disciple the world to be kingdom-of-God- and righteousness-conscious (Amos 5:24; Matthew 6:33) in order that the social, political, and financial decisions leaders make are influenced by God's kingdom of justice, righteousness, morality, and truth. The need for God's agenda to become a reality is why the apostle Paul writes prophetically, "the whole creation has been groaning as in the pains of childbirth" (v. 22, emphasis mine), and that mature believers "who have the firstfruits of the Spirit, groan inwardly as we wait eagerly for our adoption to sonship, the redemption of our bodies" (v. 23, emphasis mine). Paul characterizing the groaning of creation and the inward groan of those who have the firstfruits of the Spirit connects the redemptive plan of God to save the planet and to save people together. Key to all of this is our being the mature believers God can use to bring redemption truth to the world of men and nature.

In verses 24-25, the apostle Paul masterfully connects the "hope" of our future in eternity with our present call to walk and work in faith, and to wait with patience for the fulfillment of our salvation in Christ. This is the perfect understanding you need to have in preparation for effective praying that's strengthened by the ministry of the Holy Spirit. Those who have the firstfruits of the Spirit are not called to sit idle until Christ returns. In fact, we are exhorted by Christ to "occupy," to do the work of the kingdom, until He returns (Luke 19:13 KJV), and that work of the kingdom can only be achieved by those who experience transformation through the power of prayer. Our weakness (v. 26) is that we do not fully know the will and plan of God in the life of an individual or in the season of a circumstance. Therefore, we desperately need the insightful help of the Holy Spirit who intercedes on our behalf, according to the will of God, with groans that words cannot express (note that this is not you praying in tongues in the Spirit, but the Spirit's own intercession for you). You who have the firstfruits of the Spirit and groan inwardly are not groaning for the sweet by and by but for change in the nasty now and now. You groan in prayerful intercession for the righteous transformation our world desperately needs.

Praying for April Joy

April is the fifth of our eight children. We named her April Joy because she was born on April 1, commonly known as April Fools' Day. She is indeed a joy and was an almost straight-A student in high school, graduated as the president of her senior class, and was one of the speakers at her graduation ceremony. She probably would have been accepted wherever she applied to college, but she only applied to the college from which her older sister, Theresa (number two in the birth order), graduated—Spelman, an excellent all girls black college in Atlanta, Georgia. After completing her freshman year at Spelman, she returned home announcing to her mother and me that Spelman was not for her even though she got all A's in every subject but two that year. She found the social life at Spelman difficult for her as a Christian young woman and missing her family almost unbearable. She decided to stay home and continue her college education at the University of Massachusetts. But UMass did not work for her either; it was too big, too impersonal, and just not the fit she needed, and without my knowledge, April's failure to matriculate meaningfully in college led to her experiencing depression, a first for her.

During my early-morning prayer time, one of the regular items on my prayer list is praying for my family by name and by need. I began praying for my wife Yvonne, went on to pray for my oldest, Andy, then the second-born, Theresa, the third, Matthew, the fourth, Philip and with all of them, I prayed as I usually pray for them: to be protected, healthy, open to the guidance of the Spirit, etc. I prayed for their needs to be met, their relationships to be secure, and their destinies to be achieved. If they were married, I also prayed for their spouses and their children by name and by need. During all of this prayer time for my first four children, I prayed in faith in English using the Scriptures appropriately to undergird my stand in faith for each petition.

But suddenly, as I finished praying for number four, Philip, and began praying for April, without warning my language changed and I was ushered into an intense intercession for April that lasted for several minutes. I remember thinking while I was praying with my spirit with such intensity, "Lord, what's up with April?" I understood none of the words flowing out of my mouth that seemed to come from some deep reservoir in my spirit, and when it was over, I followed the admonition of Paul,

> *[13] For this reason anyone who speaks in a tongue should pray that he may interpret what he says. [14] For if I pray in a tongue, my spirit prays, but my mind is unfruitful.* (1 Corinthians 14:13-14)

So I prayed for the meaning of this intense season of prayer for April.

In my mind, I saw a college campus I recognized because I'd actually visited that campus for an event. It was the small Christian college campus of Eastern Nazarene College (ENC) in Quincy, Massachusetts, a short drive from our house. Later that day, I sat with April, told her of my experience in prayer and the college I saw in my mind. The next day, April visited the campus, talked with the Registrar who lovingly welcomed her and gave her a tour of the campus. That evening, April shared with me her visit to ENC and literally wept for joy at finding a place that finally fit. She graduated from ENC and that experience taught me the importance of the prayer ministry that the Holy Spirit has within us according to the teaching of Paul in Romans 8. As a prayer warrior, you need to be open to the moving of the Holy Spirit as He guides you in prayer toward the will of God being accomplished in you and through you.

CHAPTER FOUR

WHAT PRAYER BASICS DO YOU NEED TO KNOW?

Your Position as a Prayer Warrior

AS A BELIEVER, KNOWING THE TRUTH OF YOUR POSITION IN CHRIST will strengthen you to persevere in faith as you exercise authority in prayer. Jesus taught the disciples to pray, "Thy kingdom come, Thy will be done on earth as it is in heaven" (Matthew 6:10 KJV). The prayer agenda of the mature believers in a local church is to establish the kingdom of God in the hearts and lives of those they influence. Intercessory prayer and the loving sharing of truth are two of the main tools in your spiritual briefcase. Only remember, you are called of God to teach by precept (words of instruction with principles and illustrations) and example (the truth being seen through your lifestyle and choices).

The Pillar of Holiness

Maintaining separation from the darkness of the world will strengthen your witness to others. Not being an example of godly conduct will hinder your witness. You cannot expect others to exercise confidence in you when you are entangled in the same web of deception in which they find themselves. A lukewarm Christian is a believer whose lifestyle does not reflect a serious, genuine commitment to Christ. And believers who are defeated by the dark deception of sin and rebellion and who have no effective prayer life have very little to offer those who are groping in darkness. If ever there was a time for you to grow up and be the Church—the balanced believer you need to be, the example people in your life need to see, and the mature praying Christian God is calling for you to be—it is now. As the apostle Paul wrote, "Now is the time!" (2 Corinthians 6:2) Begin by taking personal inventory of your walk (Hebrews 12:1): decide to lay aside the weights, repent of the sins, and fully commit your life afresh to the lordship of Christ. Then don't stop until you are filled with the Spirit (Acts 1:8) and are praying with dominion authority. The apostle John spoke against the love of this world, and the love of the wicked things or practices in this world: "...the lust of the flesh, the lust of the eyes, and the pride of life—comes not from the Father but from the world" (1 John 2:16; see also v. 15). And in verse 17, John issues a solemn warning to those who would play the fool in a kind of schizophrenic way of living where you act like a Christian in church and live like a heathen elsewhere. Notice John's warning: "The world and its desires pass away, but whoever does the will of God lives forever" (1 John 2:17). This verse within the context of all three verses (15-17) enables you to see the line drawn between those who live the lifestyle of a true believer, versus those who act out a commitment to godly character but are not true believers. While it is true only God can judge what is in a person's heart, you are responsible for warning those who play the fool that it's possible they are not true believers (cf. Matthew 7:21-23).

Though it is true that works do not save you, and that you are only saved by grace through faith (Ephesians 2:8-9), yet your works can indicate either the presence or absence of saving faith. The author of Hebrews and the Lord Jesus agree that holy living and purity of heart are not unrealistic expectations for true believers: "Make every effort to live in peace with everyone and to be holy; **without holiness** no one will see the Lord" (Hebrews 12:14, emphasis mine); "Blessed are the pure in heart, for they will see God" (Matthew 5:8). Beloved, in addition to God's expectation of you living a holy lifestyle, you will also need a firm grasp upon the truth of your spiritual position in Christ. No prayer warrior can be effective without the confident faith gained from the truth of his or her position in Christ.

Your Position "In Christ"

Some years ago, I was one of several prayer warriors called to a meeting in New Hampshire. The purpose was to discuss and plan strategy for ministering to the Seven Cultural Mountains in our society: 1) Arts & Entertainment, 2) Business, 3) Education, 4) Family, 5) Government, 6) Media, and 7) Religion.[11] As you can imagine, a significant part of the meeting was set-aside for prayer. Approximately 20-25 of us sat in a circle agreeing in prayer as various ones around the circle led us. After several sessions of prayer and intercession, a resource person who was not from New England, but was invited to assist in the discussion, took it upon himself to warn the group concerning what he considered a dangerous type of praying. Using the examples of people he knew who, according to him, had come under demonic attack because they'd prayed against the demonic influences of principalities, he cautioned us not to pray against a principality (a demonic ruler over a region).

Unfortunately, since his warning or caution was public it needed to be corrected publicly. I would have preferred, as one of the leaders, talking with him alone, but my pastor-mentors taught me: a correction must go as far as it is known. Contending, I said, "Then what is the meaning of Paul in Ephesians 6 where we are told we wrestle against principalities, powers, and the rulers of the darkness of this world; against spiritual wickedness in the heavenly realms? How do I wrestle against these demonic forces if I'm afraid that by confronting and contending with them in the name of Jesus, they can afflict me with a terminal illness?"

He then made a distinction between a demonic principality in the heavenly realms and a demon we cast out in the earth realm saying, "A demonic principality is *above* us and we need to be careful not to disrespect that principality; it could be dangerous."

In the process of trying to fortify his argument with Scripture, he referred to the passage in Jude, "But even the archangel Michael, when he was disputing with the devil about the body of Moses, did not himself dare to condemn him for slander but said, 'The Lord rebuke you!'" (Jude 9)

But my contention continued that to rebuke the enemy in the name of Jesus was what the Scriptures teach—that we "overcome all the power of the enemy; nothing will harm you" (Luke 10:17-19 emphasis mine; cf. also Philippians 2:10-11). I then took issue with the statement that "a demonic principality is *above* us," saying emphatically, "My brother, they may be above you, but they are not above me."

Understanding the truth of your positional power *in Christ* is one of the most important truths you must grasp in your faith fight against demonic forces. The apostle Paul writes in Ephesians of three benefits you experience because you are in Christ. The benefits are in the New Testament Greek aorist tense, meaning benefits received in the past continue to have effect in the present. Here is the text with the words in the **aorist tense** highlighted.

> *⁴ But because of his great love for us, God, who is rich in mercy, ⁵ **made us alive** with Christ even when we were dead in transgressions—it is by grace you have been saved. ⁶ And God **raised us up** with Christ and **seated us** with him in the heavenly realms in Christ Jesus*. (Ephesians. 2:4-6, emphasis mine)

The above passage basically says that because you are in Christ Jesus, you've been **made alive**, you've been **raised up,** and you've been **seated** with Christ in the heavenly realms. This is your spiritual *position* by virtue of you being *in Christ*. You are no longer dead in trespasses and sins because you have been **made alive**, born again, spiritually resurrected (John 5:24); you've also been **raised up**, delivered, empowered, treated with favor (Colossians 3:1-3); and, you've been seated **with** Christ on a throne to worship and exercise rule and authority (cf. Revelation 11:16-17).

Where is this place where you are **seated** "with him in the heavenly realms in Christ Jesus"? I'm glad you asked because this will make you shout for joy. The first chapter of Ephesians explains the location of the place, "in the heavenly realms."

> [19] *...That power is the same as the mighty strength* [20] *he exerted when he raised Christ from the dead and **seated** him at his right hand **in the heavenly realms**,* [21] *far above all rule and authority, power and dominion, and every name that is invoked, not only in the present age but also in the one to come.*
> (Ephesians 1:19b-21, emphasis mine)

When you know you are *in Christ,* you not only know you have been *made alive, raised up,* and *seated* in the *heavenly realms in Christ Jesus,* but you also know that the **heavenly realms** is "at his [the Father's] right hand...far above all rule and authority, power and dominion, and every name that is invoked, not only in the present age but also in the one to come." There is no demon, principality, rule or authority above the throne of Almighty God. When you know you are in Christ, your actual spiritual position is at the Father's right hand. Hallelujah!

Are there casualties of spiritual warfare? Yes; but not because believers wrestle against a principality in the name of Jesus, but because believers do not gird themselves with the truth of the armor of God (Ephesians 6:13f) and the knowledge of their spiritual position "in Christ."

What Are Your Procedural Weapons as a Prayer Warrior?

Let's consider some foundational prayer basics as you proceed toward becoming an effective prayer warrior: knowing and fully understanding the truth of the *blood of Jesus,* the *name of Jesus,* and the *Word of God* as spiritual conveyers of power and authority will bring focus and confidence to your prayer life. All three are primary in their importance, so do not deduce from the order in this presentation that one is more important than another.

The Blood

To begin, your faith in the *blood of Jesus* strengthens your assurance and your confidence in God's plan of redemption. Paul wrote in reference to the death of Jesus, "In Him we have redemption through his blood, the forgiveness of sins, in accordance with the riches of God's grace" (Ephesians 1:7). The word "redemption" means,

> ...deliverance from some evil by payment of a price... prisoners of war might be released on payment of a price which was called a "ransom" (Gk. *lytron*). The word-group based on *lytron* was formed specifically to convey this idea of release on payment of ransom. In this circle of ideas Christ's death may be regarded as "a ransom for many" (Mark 10:45).[12]

You must not take lightly the shedding of Christ's blood on the cross; His shed blood[13] was the price of your redemption. Since God's justice required punishment for sin, God, out of love and mercy, took our punishment upon Himself in Christ.

There are various ways to see this biblically. In the Old Testament, the prophet Ezekiel writes, "Behold, all souls are mine; the soul of the father as well as the soul of the son is mine. The soul who sins will die" (Ezekiel 18:4 NASB). And in the New Testament, the apostle Paul writes, "For the wages of sin is death, but the gift of God is eternal life in Christ Jesus our Lord" (Romans 6:23). In both passages, the same truth is taught—death is the punishment for sin. While it could be argued that the "death" refers to physical death, the truth of progressive revelation[14] teaches the second passage adds to the understanding of "death" in the first passage, meaning "spiritual death," or separation from God. Several passages in the New Testament teach the dichotomy of being alive physically but dead spiritually (cf. John 5:24-25; Ephesians 2:1-2; 1 Timothy 5:6). You are saved because you have placed your faith in the shed blood of Jesus Christ of Nazareth. No one is saved by their good works or damned by their wicked works. Simply stated—those with believing faith are saved and those without believing faith are lost (cf. 1 John 5:11-13).

In addition to the redemption aspect of the blood, with respect to prayer, you have access to God's presence by the blood of Jesus:

> *19 Therefore, brothers and sisters, since we have confidence to enter the Most Holy Place by the blood of Jesus... 22 let us draw near to God with a sincere heart and with the full assurance that faith brings.* (Hebrews 10:19, 22)

As a true prayer warrior, you must never be guilty of acting presumptuously, thinking because you are obedient, faithful in prayer and fasting, and experiencing a move of God in your ministry life, that you have access to the presence of God by your own works or efforts. Do not get this truth twisted. There are two ditches of failure: one on each side of the road to prayer access and power.

The first ditch is the sin of wrongdoing where, let's say, in an unguarded moment you failed to discipline your flesh and you do not confess it and repent (1 John 1:9). That failure, if not dealt with, can hinder your continued walk in the light of fellowship with the Father and thus hinder your prayer life (1 John 1:6).

The other ditch is the sin of arrogant self-confidence where you feel pride for how well *you* are doing in the things of God. You must guard against both ditches, and in prayer know emphatically that you only have access to God by your faith in the shed blood of your Savior, the Lord Jesus Christ (cf. Romans 5:2).

The Name

The second of the three benefits you need to know is the power of the *name of Jesus*. While both the blood and the name exert power when used in faith, they each supply different benefits: the *blood* is the redemption price for our salvation and therefore gains us access into the presence of God, and the *name* has the authority to break the chains that bind you and defeat demonic principalities and powers. Your knowledge and use of both will elevate you to the level of faith you need for effective praying. The importance of faith will be dealt with in greater detail in the section below entitled "The Necessity of Faith," but it's imperative that I touch on it here. This knowledge is more than intellectual ascent where there is no change in behavior. Jesus said that we would know the truth and the truth would set us free (John 8:32). When the truth behind the name of Jesus and the blood is known and understood experientially, change is the byproduct. Knowledge, when acted out in experience, results in faith coming to life in your heart. Speaking the name of Jesus over the life of someone who's bound and seeing him or her delivered will increase your faith in the authority of the name.

Reading in the Scriptures that the name of Jesus is above every name is one thing; experiencing the authority of that name in ministry to the sick or bound and seeing them healed and set free is another level of faith every praying believer needs to experience.

The apostle Paul, in Philippians 2:6-11, outlines the foundation for the authoritative power of the name of Jesus.

> *⁶ Who, being in very nature God, did not consider equality with God something to be used to his advantage; ⁷ rather he made himself nothing by taking the very nature of a servant, being made in human likeness. ⁸ And being found in appearance as a man, he humbled himself and became obedient to death—even death on a cross! [A horrific form of capital punishment.] ⁹ Therefore God* **exalted him to the highest place** *and* **gave him the name that is above every name**, *¹⁰ that at the name of Jesus every knee should bow, in heaven and on earth and under the earth, ¹¹ and every tongue confess that Jesus Christ is Lord, to the glory of God the Father.* (Emphasis and parenthesis mine)

A member of the Godhead, One equal with God, *emptied* Himself, made Himself *nothing*, and took *the very nature of a servant*. In theological circles, this passage is known as the *kenosis* passage—*kenosis* being the Greek verb used here which means, "to empty."[15] The interpretation is an explanation for the "how" of the incarnation—God becoming man. Understand, the Son of God always was, always is, and always will be God the Son; Christ could no more not be God than you or I could not be human. The miracle of the kenosis, the emptying (the incarnation), is Christ submitted Himself to do only the Father's will (John 4:34; 5:19, 30; 6:38) and to function only in the power of the Holy Spirit (Acts 10:38) as the perfect example for you and me to emulate (John 20:21). The following words to the disciples only make sense if the above is true: "Very truly I tell you, whoever believes in me will do the works I have been doing, and they will do even greater things than these, because I am going to the Father" (John 14:12).

Because of Christ's perfect sacrifice of obedience to die on the cross to reconcile the world to God (2 Corinthians 5:19), the Father exalted with power the name of Jesus above every name, in heaven (with God and angels), on the earth (with humankind), and under the earth (with the devil and all demons); thus, when the name of Jesus is used by a faith-filled believer in prayer, heaven stands at attention. And when people or demons are commanded by the authority of that name in the will of God, they must bow in obedience (Philippians 2:10). It has been said that the name of Jesus makes demons tremble (cf. Luke 4:34; James 2:19).

Before we go further, let me remind you of the necessity of being a genuine, mature believer when confronting the demonic. Be warned by the account I shared in some detail earlier about the sons of Sceva, who, according to Acts 19:13-16, tried to exorcise demons with counterfeit faith. Just be aware of the necessity to be real.

There are a few more passages you need to know that teach the truth behind the power of the name of Jesus. This truth is powerfully illustrated by the words of the 72 returning to Jesus after ministering in His name,

> *[17] The seventy-two returned with joy and said, "Lord, even the demons submit to us in Your name. [18] He replied, "I saw Satan fall like lightning from heaven. [19] I have given you authority to trample on snakes*

and scorpions and to overcome all the power of the enemy; nothing will harm you. [20] However, do not rejoice that the spirits submit to you, but rejoice that your names are written in heaven." (Luke 10:17-20, emphasis mine)

And the commissioning words of Jesus at the end of the Gospel according to Mark,

> *[17] And these signs will accompany those who believe: **In My name** they will drive out demons; they will speak in new tongues; [18] they will pick up snakes with their hands; and when they drink deadly poison, it will not hurt them at all; they will place their hands on sick people, and they will get well.* (Mark 16:17-18, emphasis mine)

And finally, the ministry of Paul resulting in deliverance in Philippi,

> *[16] Once when we were going to the place of prayer, we were met by a female slave who had a spirit by which she predicted the future. She earned a great deal of money for her owners by fortune-telling. [17] She followed Paul and the rest of us, shouting, "These men are servants of the Most High God, who are telling you the way to be saved." [18] She kept this up for many days. Finally Paul became so troubled that he turned around and said to the spirit, "**In the name of Jesus Christ** I command you to come out of her!" At that moment the spirit left her.* (Acts 16:16-18, emphasis mine)

Deliverance: A Personal Example

Within my own pastoral ministry, I saw the power in using the *name of Jesus* in deliverance demonstrated when a young college student—a believer and a faithful member of my church—asked for help after a Sunday morning service. He described what sounded like catatonic seizures. Each episode gripped and paralyzed him for several minutes each day at the same time. Discerning that the seizures were demonic, I made an appointment with him to come to my home. My wife planned to be with our children out of the house during the appointment, and I began by teaching him about deliverance from the Scriptures for approximately 20-30 minutes. Then we pushed my dining room table against the wall to make space for whatever would happen, and as he sat in a chair, I stood commanding the evil spirit to manifest in the name of Jesus. After approximately five minutes, he literally fell off the chair onto the floor and writhed like a snake. Instinctively, I stood over him and commanded the evil spirit to come out of him in the name of Jesus. Within seconds, he convulsed a few times and then lay still. I helped him up to sit again in the chair and laid my hands on him and prayed. From all appearances, he was delivered. Every Sunday following, when I talked with him in church, his testimony was one of victory. Praise God.

But after several months of victory, he approached me after Sunday service complaining of being bound again by the same seizure occurrences. Again, we scheduled an appointment at my home when my wife and children were out, and I began by questioning him about what happened. His words were telling; they revealed a very low level of faith. He said, "I was in the school library when I felt a slight touch on my thigh."

I then interrupted him saying, "And let me tell you what you said to yourself. You said, 'Ah man, I thought I was free, but I guess I'm not.'"

Looking at me with surprise, he said, "That's exactly what I said!"

"And when you said that to yourself," I exclaimed, "You said to that demon, 'Come on back in here Mr. Devil and put these seizures back on me!'" He then went on to share that the next day at the exact same time he was seized by that evil spirit, and in fear he was paralyzed, unable to move for several minutes. After preparing the room as before, I again commanded the evil spirit to manifest in the name of Jesus, but this time, it took 15-20 minutes before anything happened. But when the demon finally did manifest, the young student did not fall off the chair onto the floor as before; this time, he jumped out of the chair, angrily screaming two inches from my face. As you can imagine, this sudden burst of movement and screaming shocked me, but as best as I could I maintained my composure. I continued by telling the spirit that I was not afraid and that he had to leave the young man at once. Within seconds, the spirit came out with a loud shriek, and the young man fell limp in the chair.

After he gathered himself, we moved the furniture back into place, sat at the table together, and I spent the next 30 minutes or so teaching him how to stand in faith against further demonic oppression. Years later, after he had graduated and returned home, his pastor was in Boston doing ministry. During a time of fellowship, I mentioned the young man by name and asked how he was doing. His response gladdened my heart: the young man was married with children and one of the strongest leaders in his church. To God belongs the glory.

This taught me two basic truths: (1) The power in the name of Jesus; and (2) The fact that God will allow a spiritual father (pastor), by his faith in the power of the name of Jesus, and the authority of the Word of God, to cover a younger, weaker member of the Church. But the expectation is that the younger, weaker believer must become stronger in order to maintain the benefit of the ministry he receives. As the young man's spiritual father, I should have better prepared him for the advent of the evil spirit's return (cf. Matthew 12:43-45). He was better prepared after our second encounter and was able to maintain his deliverance and walk in victory.

The Word

The third of these three prayer basics you need to know is *the Word*. Knowing the authority of the Word will anchor in biblical truth what you believe and confess. An apostle of faith, Smith Wigglesworth said, "I am not moved by what I see. I am moved only by what I believe. I know this—no man looks at appearances if he believes. No man considers how he feels if he believes."[16] The psalmist wrote that God's Word is forever settled in heaven (Psalm 119:89 KJV), meaning it is the highest authority on earth—even higher than the laws and views created by people. Sometimes, even well meaning authorities can be misguided, not to mention those with a nefarious hidden agenda. For example, the high priest commanded the apostles to stop preaching in the name of Jesus, but the apostles chose to obey God rather than men.

> [27] *The apostles were brought in and made to appear before the Sanhedrin to be questioned by the high priest.* [28] *"We gave you strict orders not to teach in this name," he said. "Yet you have filled Jerusalem with your teaching and are determined to make us guilty of this man's blood."* [29] *Peter and the other apostles replied: "We must obey God rather than human beings!"* (Acts 5:27-29)

When the Word of God contradicts a law of humankind, faith requires that you "obey God rather than human beings" and then, with courage, prepare in love to suffer the consequences.

Believing and confessing biblical truth will minister to you in ways far beyond what you can ask or think, because truth spoken in faith opens spiritual, physical, and relational doors. When Jesus said, "Heaven and earth will pass away, but my words will never pass away" (Matthew 24:35), He was reminding you that the power of His Word is timeless. It does not matter what age of history you are in to claim its truth. When you exercise faith, God's Word always works! God's Word cannot fail!

The following disciplines will establish and equip you to become strong in your knowledge of the Word and, at the same time, undergird your faith. The disciplines follow the outline of Navigators' Hand Illustration (Figure 1, used by permission).

Navigators' Hand Illustration
Figure 1

1. <u>Hearing the Word</u>. The first discipline is *hearing* the Word. Position yourself with the mindset to hunger and thirst for a greater knowledge and understanding of Scripture. The psalmist wrote, "He sent out his word and healed them; he rescued them from the grave (Psalm 107:20). God's Word has the ability to heal you and make you whole—physically, mentally, and spiritually. It can even rescue you from death. Why would anyone in his or her right mind postpone or skip being influenced by an anointed teacher or preacher of the living Word of God? And in today's technologically advanced world, you are left without an excuse for not hearing the Word preached, taught, or read. You can have the Word read to you by your cell phone, tablet, or mp3 player. You can attend church via television, online live stream, or on DVD, just to name a few avenues available to you, besides actually attending a church service.

2. <u>Reading the Word</u>. You must develop the discipline of *reading* the Word. The benefit of setting aside a time daily, or as often as possible, to allow the Lord to speak to you through the Scriptures cannot be overemphasized. The psalmist wrote, "Open my eyes that I may see wonderful things in your law" (Psalm 119:18). One of the major ways God will speak to you is through His written Word, the Bible. The Scriptures pronounce a blessing to anyone who reads aloud and hears the words of prophecy (Revelation 1:3). Knowing this benefit should encourage you to spend some quality time in devotional reading through the books of the Bible, especially the epistles in the New Testament. Reading through the Bible—beginning with the book of Genesis and reading through

the Old Testament, or beginning with the book of Matthew and reading through the New Testament—is a worthy pursuit. It will strengthen your overall knowledge of the spiritual history within the Scriptures, the accounts of men and women of faith, what they said and did based upon the difficult and sometimes trying circumstances in their lives. You will gain a perspective of how their faith enabled them to stand strong with their confession, especially in the midst of threatening opposition (see, for example, the story of Shadrach, Meshach, and Abednego in Daniel 3).

A Confession of Faith: An Illustration

Some years ago, after hearing a sermon on the value of a confession of faith based on the Word of God and the leading of the Spirit in prayer, I began to confess to my wife that I was pregnant with 1,000 people—meaning I believed God was positioning me to grow a church of 1,000 people. One of the passages used in the sermon was, "Let us hold fast the profession of our faith without wavering; (for he is faithful that promised)" (Hebrews 10:23 KJV). At the time, I was the senior pastor of a small local church with fewer than 100 members. During the season of that confession, I was regularly reading through the Bible, and I came upon the story of the widow whose husband died leaving her and their two sons in debt (see 2 Kings 4:1-7). When the creditor threatened to enslave the widow's sons to repay the debt, she sought help from Elisha the prophet. Elisha asked her how he could help her by inquiring about what she had in her house. She responded that she had nothing, except a little oil.

Strangely enough, something happened as I read verse three: "Then he said, Go, borrow thee vessels abroad of all thy neighbors, even empty vessels; borrow **not a few**" (2 Kings 4:3 KJV, emphasis mine). Those words, "not a few," seemed to leap off the page as I read. I had what might be called an encounter with God as I read His Word. In that moment, I realized the level of the widow's faith could be measured by how many vessels she borrowed. The prophet said, "borrow not a few," and I remember as I was repeating the phrase "not a few" over and over again in my mind, the Lord spoke to me. "My son," He said, "It doesn't do you a bit of good in the world to have faith for a thousand people and only room for a hundred."

Since the widow could only fill the vessels she'd borrowed, if I truly had faith for a thousand people, my faith could be seen by my finding room for at least that many. For me, this was the beginning of a new level of faith talking and walking. But let's not forget, God spoke to me out of the discipline of reading the Scriptures.

3. Studying the Word. The discipline of *studying* the Word separates the adults from the children. Study will require segregating yourself from time-wasting events and people that sap the strength needed to dig into the truths of Holy Scripture. Spending time poring over biblical passages with reference aids[17] will create a familiarity with the truths of those passages that will speak to you during desperate times. Remember the Bible is a unique book of inspired writings; it is the record of saints who spoke as the Holy Spirit moved them (2 Peter 1:20-21). The Scriptures are the spoken words of God, and anyone who desires to pray with power must honor the Word. Real success in life is the fruit of being a doer of the Word (James 1:22). Doing the Word means living in obedience to its truth, and you can't obey what you don't know. Jesus taught the necessity of obedience in the parable at the end of the Sermon on the Mount. To obey and put the truth into practice is the key to experiencing the success of endurance and stability.

> *[24] Therefore everyone who hears these words of mine and **puts them into practice** is like a wise man who built his house on the rock. [25] The rain came down, the streams rose, and the winds blew and beat against that house; yet it did not fall, because it had its foundation on the rock. [26] But everyone who hears these words of mine and **does not put them into practice** is like a foolish man who built his house on sand. [27] The rain came down, the streams rose, and the winds blew and beat against that house, and it fell with a great crash.* (Matthew 7:24-27, emphasis mine)

The only difference between the two builders is what they did with what they heard. Many casually hear the Word of God preached or taught and leave the meeting without being influenced by its truth enough to change what they do. These are they who build their houses (lives) on sand and when the rains and the floods and the winds of life come against them, they literally fall apart; their lives fall apart *with a great crash* like a house with no solid foundation during a severe storm. But the ones, who hear the Word with a heart to obey it and practice its truth, are strengthened and sustained during the storms of life because their foundation of obedience is as solid as a rock. The same truth is taught in the Old Testament book of Joshua: "Keep this Book of the Law always on your lips; meditate on it day and night, **so that you may be careful to do everything written in it**. Then you will be prosperous and successful" (Joshua 1:8, emphasis mine). That which we learned from the parable in Matthew 7:24-27 was taught to Joshua, Moses' successor. He was taught the importance of putting into practice what he learned from the Word, the Book of the Law. Notice the wisdom of the gradual steps given to assist Joshua in remembering: (1) Keep the Book of the Law always on your lips—i.e. speak it to yourself and others; (2) Meditate on it day and night—think about the responsibility and the application of its truth and the possible outcomes of your obeying or not obeying. Why? Here's the reason for the steps—*"so that you may be careful to do everything written in it."* The steps fulfilled the purpose of engaging Joshua so he'd *remember*. The exhortation to perform all these operations—to hear, to read, to say, and to meditate on the Word—is so you will *remember* it so as to obey and do it. It is in the doing that the benefit happens. The doing can literally make the difference between prosperity and poverty, between success and failure. These fundamentals are universal: even the sagacious non-Christian Confucius outlined a similar progression when he said, "I hear and I forget. I see and I remember. I do and I understand."[18]

4. <u>Memorizing the Word</u>. The discipline of *memorizing* the Word will elevate you to a level of Scriptural proficiency many miss. Here's how to begin: invariably, you will come across Bible verses and passages that speak to specific needs in your life, and

you will want to commit those verses to memory. When this happens, write the verse on a 3x5 card: on one side write the verse, and on the other side write the reference. Always memorize the reference with the verse. Repeat the verse aloud, saying the reference before and after the verse. For example, you would say, "John three sixteen, 'For God so loved the world that He gave His one and only Son, that whoever believes in Him shall not perish but have eternal life.' John three sixteen." In addition, Navigators, a Christian organization emphasizing the primacy of discipleship, teaches you should give the Scripture reference a *topic*. For example, after thoroughly examining the passage to determine its meaning within its context, you should give the reference a topic, like "LOVE" could very easily be used as the topic to remind you of John 3:16.

Memory is like a muscle; the more you work it, the stronger it gets. The general rule of thumb about memory is to work on repeating the passage over and over again, breaking it down into small phrases, connecting them together, and doing this daily until you can say the entire reference verbatim without looking at the card. When you can say the passage from memory, then you are ready to repeat all three: the topic, reference, and passage every day for the next three weeks (21 days). This will drive it deep into your memory bank so you will never forget it. It is suggested you work on memorizing no more than three passages within this three-week period. I began Navigators' Topical Memory System (TMS) in 1965 while a freshman in college. Next to learning and practicing the fundamentals of prayer proficiency, memorizing Scripture has been the most influential discipline contributing to my spiritual growth than any other Christian discipline.

5. Meditating on the Word. The fifth discipline is *meditating* on the Word. In the sequence of the five, making meditation the last is wise, especially following the discipline of memorization. As you are memorizing a particular passage by repeating it over and over again (whether aloud or in your mind), what you are actually doing is meditating—chewing the cud, so to speak, turning it over and over in your mind—on the truth of that passage. This process drives that truth deep into the bone marrow of your spirit. The

psalmist David wrote, "I have hidden your word in my heart that I might not sin against you" (Psalm 119:11). The power of this memorizing and meditating process can cause immeasurable benefit to your walk with Christ and ministry in prayer for others. Always remember, God not only loves you to save you but also to use you to be an example for the salvation of others.

Meditation has become a lost art in the Church. Other religious groups, recognizing the value of meditation, have coopted its practice and benefits into their disciplines. But meditation is a biblical practice encouraged by the patriarchs, prophets, and psalmists thousands of years ago. In addition to Joshua 1:8, quoted above, perhaps the most familiar passage in which meditation appears is the first Psalm: "But his delight is in the law of the LORD, and in His law he **meditates** day and night" (Psalm 1:2 NKJV, emphasis mine). Incorporating meditation into your daily lifestyle will enable you to rise above the trappings of all kinds of sin, anxiety, and fear.

Additional benefits of biblical meditation include faith, peace, and a barrier to sin. Meditation produces faith since it includes repeating aloud a truth from the Word several times, or repeating it in your mind: "Faith comes from hearing the message, and the message is heard through the word of Christ" (Romans 10:17). It also produces a perfect peace, a serenity of spirit and freedom from the trappings of anxiety and fear, since it can fill your heart and mind with God's truth-filled promises (Isaiah 26:3; cf. also John 8:32). Finally, meditation forms a barrier against sin because it is a prelude to hiding the Word in your heart (Psalm 119:11).

Your Faith as a Prayer Warrior

Knowing what faith is and how it works is fundamental to being an effective prayer warrior. If we entitled this teaching as part of a college curriculum, it would be appropriately labeled Introduction to Faith 101. It is probably not possible to teach about *what* faith is without that teaching spilling over into *how* faith works, but I will try. Suffice it to say, the "HOW" section of this book will go into greater detail than this "WHAT" section.

An Atheist: The Necessity of Faith

A key Scripture indicating faith's necessity is in the book of Hebrews: "Without **faith** it is impossible to please God, because anyone who comes to him must **believe** that he exists and that he rewards those who earnestly seek him" (Hebrews 11:6, emphasis mine). We learn from salvation history that pleasing God[19] is important, and according to the text, you must have faith for "pleasing God" to happen. The requirement of believing in God's existence is added to faith's necessity in prayer. This is especially important in today's world where it's intellectually fashionable to proclaim you are an "atheist." It's really unfortunate if it's true someone actually does not believe God exists. In reality, it's quite possible the claim to be an atheist is only a claim with no basis in true belief. I remember Bob Harrington, the 'Chaplain of Bourbon Street,' saying, "There are no atheists in a foxhole or on a crashing plane." But if one's proclamation of atheism is genuine, that person is truly without hope according to Hebrews 11:6, and another passage dealing with the absence of "hope" comes to mind also:

> [11] ...*remember that formerly you who are Gentiles by birth...* [12] *...that at that time you were separate from Christ, excluded from citizenship in Israel and foreigners to the covenants of the promise, **without hope** and without God in the world.* (Ephesians 2:11-12, emphasis mine)

To be in a spiritual condition where prayer does not work because you do not believe in God's existence and therefore have NO faith in order to please God is sad. And the above text says that to be without God is to be without *hope*. Hal Lindsey is credited with saying, "Man can live for about forty days without food, and about three days without water, about eight minutes without air ... but only for one second without hope."[20]

An Agnostic

With respect to someone claiming to be an agnostic, they are in a different category than an atheist. By definition, agnostics are those who claim they do not know if God exists; they have no empirical evidence either for or against God's existence and because of that ignorance, they claim innocence. But here's the problem with that claim of innocence: (1) The hand of God can be seen in the order and majesty of creation (Psalm 19); but even if none of the classic arguments for the existence of God convince them (teleological, cosmological, ontological, etc.), there is a proof positive means; (2) If what the LORD spoke to Jeremiah is true (and it is), "You will seek me and find me when you seek me with all your heart" (Jeremiah 29:13), then those who claim ignorance about God's existence are actually playing an intellectual game with people and a rebellious game with God. They don't want to have faith and believe; they don't want to have a genuine encounter with God and have to change their pseudo-intellectual statements about atheism or agnosticism. In the final analysis, they are left without an excuse and are hopeless since they find it fashionable to refuse to believe and not test the truth of Jeremiah 29:13.

This will be dealt with in more detail later, but let me simply say — in the English language, the noun *faith* and the verb *to believe* are very different words, but in the Greek language of the New Testament, the words translated *faith* and *believe* are from the same root word. Therefore, to really *believe* means you have *faith*, and to have *faith* means you really *believe*.

The Importance of Scripture

Since faith is necessary, you need to know *how* faith comes. Again, this will be dealt with in more detail later, but let me summarize. Notice I entitled this section the "importance" of Scripture and not the "necessity" of Scripture. This is because faith comes from hearing God, not from reading about others who heard God. This is not to say that reading, studying, and knowing the Scriptures do not help increase your faith. Of course knowing the kinds of dealings

God had with others helps you understand how God will deal with you. But basically, your faith comes through having an intimate relationship with God; a relationship that may have begun with you hearing a sermon from the Word, but was developed as you sought God yourself as the ancients did. This important understanding is fundamental to strengthening your faith as you pray specifically for God to move in the various areas and directions of your life.

By no means am I trying to minimize the Scriptures' influence as an inspired resource for knowing God. My only attempt is to distinguish the knowledge of God, which the Scriptures most adequately give, from the growing of faith that comes from hearing God through an intimate relationship with Him.

There are a few monumental passages you must know. Let me give them to you in sections. First, the truth of Scripture's inspiration is key:

> *[16] All Scripture is God-breathed and is useful for teaching, rebuking, correcting and training in righteousness, [17] so that the servant of God may be thoroughly equipped for every good work.* (2 Timothy 3:16-17)

Along with that key verse for the Doctrine of Inspiration, you should add the words of Jesus about the authority of the Old Testament (see Matthew 5:17-18; 24:35); or the words of the psalmist (especially Psalm 119:89); or the combination of Genesis 1:1-2, 5, 9, 14, 20, 24, and 26 being compared with the words of Hebrews 11:3. The authoritative power of God's Word knows no equal. All you need do is *believe* what the prophets wrote—"For the mouth of the LORD has spoken" (Isaiah 1:20; 40:5, 58:14; see also Isaiah 34:16 and Micah 4:4).

Finally, the apostle Paul quoted from Moses in Romans 10 about the Word of faith. Notice first Deuteronomy 30:11-14,

> *[11] Now what I am commanding you today is not too difficult for you or beyond your reach. [12] It is not up in heaven, so that you have to ask, "Who will*

> *ascend into heaven to get it and proclaim it to us*
> *so we may obey it?"* [13] *Nor is it beyond the sea, so*
> *that you have to ask, "Who will cross the sea to get*
> *it and proclaim it to us so we may obey it?"* [14] *No,*
> *the word is very near you; it is in your mouth and*
> *in your heart so you may obey it.*

and then add Romans 10:6-11, 17,

> [6] *But the righteousness that is by faith says: "Do not*
> *say in your heart, 'Who will ascend into heaven?'"*
> *(that is, to bring Christ down)* [7] *"or 'Who will*
> *descend into the deep?'" (that is, to bring Christ*
> *up from the dead).* [8] *But what does it say? "The*
> *word is near you; it is in your mouth and in your*
> *heart," that is, the <u>message concerning faith</u> that*
> *we proclaim:* [9] *That if you declare with your mouth,*
> *"Jesus is Lord," and believe in your heart that God*
> *raised him from the dead, you will be saved.* [10] *For*
> *it is with your heart that you believe and are justi-*
> *fied, and it is with your mouth that you profess your*
> *faith and are saved.* [11] *As Scripture says, "Anyone*
> *who believes in him will never be put to shame."*
> *[Isaiah 28:16]...* [17] *Consequently, faith comes*
> *from hearing the message, and the message is heard*
> *through the word of Christ.* (Emphasis and paren-
> thesis mine)

What you need to guard against are the conclusions of some Bible scholars who have added to the doubt of the authenticity and authority of Scripture through the science of "Higher Criticism."[21] Some scholars question the authorship of various books of the Bible, and through an anti-supernatural bias they question the authenticity of some of the Old Testament and New Testament events,[22] and even delight in brandishing supposed contradictions. Unfortunately, these scholars are respected and lauded by the grad-uate university community and are unaware that their supposed research-based conclusions are part of the enemy's plan to discredit God's Word and, by so doing, hinder or even destroy the work of faith in the lives of believers. Another key New Testament passage about the Doctrine of Inspiration is 2 Peter 1:19-21.

> *[19] We also have the prophetic message as something completely reliable, and <u>you will do well to pay attention to it, as to a light shining in a dark place</u>, until the day dawns and the morning star rises in your hearts. [20] Above all, you must understand that no prophecy of Scripture came about by the prophet's own interpretation of things. [21] For prophecy never had its origin in the human will, but prophets, though human, spoke from God as they were carried along by the Holy Spirit.* (Emphasis mine)

Peter wrote "pay attention" to the inspired words of the prophets that will guide you like a "light shining in a dark place." By treasuring the inspiration of Holy Scripture, your faith in prayer and effectiveness in ministry are strengthened. Take heed to open your heart to the truth of all Scripture. Truth will grip your life and insulate you against dangerously false extreme teachings based on a few passages interpreted without the benefit of their immediate context, the context of the teaching of that particular epistle or writer, or the context of the systematic theological teaching of the Bible on that doctrine. Many have made a shipwreck of their faith and the effectiveness of their ministry in allowing pride to cloud their judgment of the obvious interpretation of the plain text. In the language of hermeneutics—the art and science of biblical interpretation—it is the difference between *exegesis*—leading out of the text the truth deposited there, and *eisegesis*—reading into the text the teaching you want to believe.

CHAPTER FIVE

WHAT DOES PRAYER EMPOWER YOU TO DO?

Power to See

FIRST, PRAYER INTIMACY WITH GOD GIVES YOU POWER TO SEE, DISCERN, and receive revelation knowledge. "Where there is no revelation, people cast off restraint" (Proverbs 29:18a) has become one of the watchwords of orthodox, full-gospel Christianity that seeks to influence the world with the gospel revelation of salvation through Jesus Christ, packaged in contemporary, revelatory words. Many times the message is encapsulated in a rhyming phrase surrounded by harmonious music, but make no mistake, the truth of Christian salvation—that salvation received by grace through faith (Romans 5:1-2; 10:9-10; Ephesians 2:8-9)—is the result of revelation which comes from God. Very simply, the Holy Spirit bringing revelation knowledge is part of the foundation of Christianity (1 Corinthians 2:9-12).

One of the ministries of the Holy Spirit is guiding believers into all truth (John 16:13). The prerequisite for the Spirit's guidance is your prayerful surrender to being *led*, *filled*, and *empowered* by the Spirit to do works of service (Acts 1:8; Romans 8:14; Ephesians 4:11-13; 5:18-19).

Being baptized, or filled, with the Spirit (Acts 1:4-5, 8; 2:1-4) is a requisite for ministry (Luke 24:49). As Jesus was praying during His Jordan River baptism, the Spirit descended on Him in preparation for His earthly ministry; an example to us.

> *²¹ When all the people were being baptized, Jesus was baptized too. <u>And as He was praying</u>, heaven was opened ²² and the Holy Spirit descended on Him in bodily form like a dove. And a voice came from heaven: "You are My Son, whom I love; with you I am well pleased."* (Luke 3:21-22, emphasis mine)

The other synoptic gospels do not mention that fact of Jesus *praying*. You need to pursue prayer that produces an intimacy with God the Holy Spirit that connects you to being "clothed with power from on high" (Luke 24:49). Luke records Jesus teaching that you should ask (pray) to receive the Holy Spirit: "If you then, though you are evil, know how to give good gifts to your children, how much more will your Father in heaven give the Holy Spirit to those who **ask** Him!" (Luke 11:13, emphasis mine) Prayer is an imperative, and the Holy Spirit is the Lord of the harvest! (Matthew 9:38) You must come to grips with your absolute need of the Spirit to do the work of the kingdom. Jesus told His disciples they could do "nothing" without Him (John 15:5), and I'm writing with similar emphasis—that without an intimate relationship with the wisdom, power, and guidance of the Holy Spirit, you can do nothing.

This does not mean you cannot experience a measure of success on your own, but for you to succeed in establishing a 21st-century, multigenerational, kingdom-minded church that the gates of Hades cannot overcome (Matthew 16:18), you will need intimacy with the Holy Spirit. The same goes for you who are employed in secular endeavors; you who seek to achieve the balance needed in your life as a mature believer desperately need the ministry of the Holy Spirit. Many succeed in business and fail in their personal lives with their spouse and children, or in their health and emotional wellbeing. Balance is key, and the Holy Spirit supplies the wisdom of His guidance to enable the balance that reflects what the

Bible calls, "prosperous and successful" (Joshua 1:8). This means you must treat prayer as an absolute necessity and prioritize it as an integral part of your preparation. Prayer must become a priority in your life above every organizational machination of ministry, family, or business. Prayer opens the door for the Spirit to bring revelation knowledge and visionary insight, along with the wisdom to achieve balance in all the affairs of your life. In fact, this key component of *balance* is fundamental to the abundant life Jesus referenced as part of why He came (John 10:10 KJV).

Definitions

The verb *to reveal* literally means to uncover, to disclose or make known or divulge meaning. Within the spiritual realm of God's kingdom, revelation only comes from God. That's why Simon Peter's words to Jesus, "You are the Christ, the Son of the living God," received the recognition, "Blessed are you, Simon son of Jonah, for this was not *revealed* to you by man, but by My Father in heaven" (Matthew 16:16-17, emphasis mine) Paul, in his ministry to the Corinthian church, taught there are things you cannot know apart from divine revelation.

> [9] *However, as it is written: "What no eye has seen, what no ear has heard, and what no human mind has conceived"—the things God has prepared for those who love Him—* [10] *these are the things God has* **revealed** *to us by his* <u>Spirit</u>*. The Spirit searches all things, even the deep things of God.* (1 Corinthians 2:9-10, emphasis mine; cf. also Acts 2:17; 4:19-20).

Prayer intimacy with God opens the door to revelation knowledge.

By definition, a vision from God is a supernatural occurrence where you see what God is saying about a situation or season in your future. A vision can occur while you are awake or asleep. When asleep, a vision is called a dream (Matthew 1:20; 2:13). Most of the time, your vision or dream's primary meaning is for you, and may include the presence of others, but their presence in the vision or dream is to assist you in understanding what God is saying to *you*. There are also prophetic visions or dreams God gives that have far-reaching meaning and implications beyond the individual dreamer. For example, the dream of King Nebuchadnezzar in Daniel 2 is such a dream.

It is vital you pay attention to what God is saying through your vision, for without the revelation vision brings, you cast off the restraint that wisdom brings with vision's obedience (Proverbs 29:18a). In essence, there are those who lack the wisdom that vision brings because they believe God no longer uses that means of prophetic guidance. There are others who also lack vision's wisdom because they are oblivious to God's guidance due to worldly involvements. Both are deficient in the wisdom needed for their personal growth and service to others because they fail to discipline themselves to pray and obey.[23] When prayer is undergirded with obedience to the Word of God and surrendered to the way and the will of God, that kind of praying brings the guidance of the Holy Spirit (Romans 8:14) who may use visions and dreams to pull you into your purpose.

An Apparent Exception

There are those involved in spiritual ministry who experience success because of their giftedness in personality, intelligence, and appearance without the benefit of prayer or the character development of a moral lifestyle. And though it may be true that a ministry can flourish during a gifted leader's lifetime, it will inevitably suffer and even perish for lack of prayer, the presence and guidance of the Holy Spirit, and vision that brings revelation knowledge. There is no escaping the consequences of ungodly, unwise behavior and decisions (cf. 1 Corinthians 3:12-15). By the power and ministry of the Holy Spirit using the Fivefold Ministry Gifts[24] to equip you, God enables true believers to prosper in works of service (Ephesians 4:12) that bring into reality the result of your praying, "Let Your kingdom come and Your will be done on earth as it is in heaven."

Power over Demons

Second, prayer intimacy empowers you with God's presence to rebuke and bind the enemy. Jesus taught, "How can anyone enter a strong man's house and carry off his possessions unless he first *ties up* ['binds' KJV] the strong man?" (Matthew 12:29 emphasis mine) You bind the enemy ("the strong man") in the name of Jesus (Luke 10:17; Acts 16:18), you carry off the possessions (bound souls) because you have the authority of the name of Jesus, the power of the Holy Spirit, all backed up by your praying, your surrendered life to the lordship of Christ, and the truth of the Word.

Prayer intimacy and proficiency enable you to use the name of Jesus with authority and not as a simple phrase at the end of your Christian prayer. Jesus said, "And these signs will accompany those who believe: *In My name* they will drive out demons..." (Mark 16:17, emphasis mine). Paul, in his letter to the Philippians, taught that at the name of Jesus every knee should bow, i.e. you have authority in three realms: in heaven (with God and angels), on earth (with people and even animals), and under the earth (with the devil and demons) (Philippians 2:10). This authority is not for sale; you cannot buy or barter for it. It only operates in the lives of genuinely committed believers who qualify to do this spiritual work by their faith.

All this is part of the spiritual warfare you are called to fight. In prayer, you are called to fight in faith against the enemy for the souls of men and women. Wisdom dictates you put on the armor of God and take your stand against the devil's schemes. Putting on the armor speaks of you consciously clothing yourself with Christ in every way as you go before the throne of grace to make your petitions known (Ephesians 6:18; Philippians 4:6-7; Hebrews 4:14-16). Paul's admonition reflects his acquaintance with prayer as warfare. You would do well to heed his admonition in order to achieve success in the warfare encounter we call prayer (Ephesians 6:10-18).

Power to Do Ministry

Third, prayer intimacy empowers you to do the work of ministry. For the mature believer who is a prayer warrior, ministry is part of his or her lifestyle. The psalmist called this matter of ministry as God showing you "the path of life": "You make known to me the path of life; you will fill me with joy in your presence, with eternal pleasures at your right hand" (Psalm 16:11). The joy and pleasure you experience in God's presence, at His right hand, is an enabling joy that strengthens you (Nehemiah 8:10) to do the work of the kingdom from your position in Christ (i.e. at the Father's right hand). Christ is seated at the right hand of the Father (Ephesians 1:20), and since you are in Christ (Ephesians 2:6) that's where you are seated in terms of your theological position. The primary work of ministry you are empowered to do is making disciples of all nations (the Great Commission, Matthew 28:19-20).

The Great Commission, the seeking and saving of the lost (Luke 19:10), in the mind of Christ included more than just preaching a message, calling sinners forward, praying with them, and sending them back into their dismal circumstances. The Great Commission mandate means saving the lost in every way: spiritually, emotionally, physically, educationally, mentally, financially, and in any other way not listed but could be included in the abundant life Jesus came to provide (John 10:10 KJV). This should remind you of the words Jesus read in the synagogue in Nazareth, inaugurating the beginning of His ministry as the Messiah: "The Spirit of the Lord is on me, because he has anointed me to preach good news to the poor. He has sent me to proclaim freedom for the prisoners and recovery of sight for the blind, to set the oppressed free, to proclaim the year of the Lord's favor" (Luke 4:18-19; cf. Isaiah 61:1-2). Therefore, the truth of the gospel includes the good news of the kingdom:

- For a poor person—good news is God can help you be productive and become a giver so you can reap provision for your family and no longer be poor;
- For a sick person—good news is God wills for you to be healed (Matthew 15:26; Psalm 107:20) and healthy

(Proverbs 4:20-22); then the good news is you can change your poor eating and drinking habits, exercise, and rest your mind and body from all fear and anxiety by prayerfully trusting the Lord (Proverbs 3:5-6);

- For a disenfranchised person — good news means the teaching of the Word, and the prayer-induced multiplication of changed lives demonstrating Christian truth can cause true justice and righteousness (Amos 5:24; 2 Corinthians 5:21) to work in society and in the courtroom so that you and your community are included in the dream[25] others are experiencing.

Make sense? Is this part of the message we receive from Christ that brings faith? (Romans 10:17) You'd better believe it is! Prayer should better prepare you to be used in the HERE and NOW in the affairs and circumstances that impact people's lives.

"Your kingdom come, Your will be done on earth as it is in heaven" (Matthew 6:10) means you should get your head out of the clouds longing for the "sweet by and by" and recognize you are called to be an agent of change in the "nasty now and now." San Antonio Spurs basketball player Tim Duncan has said, "Good, better, best. Never let it rest, until your good is better, and your better – best."[26] And while you are meditating on those wise motivational words, remember the serious judgment words of our Lord with respect to His realistic expectation of His covenant children:

> *[41] "Then He will say to those on His left, 'Depart from me, you are cursed, into the eternal fire prepared for the devil and his angels. [42] For I was hungry and you gave me nothing to eat, I was thirsty and you gave me nothing to drink, [43] I was a stranger and you did not invite me in, I needed clothes and you did not clothe me, I was sick and in prison and you did not look after me.'*

[44] *"They also will answer, 'Lord, when did we see you hungry or thirsty or a stranger or needing clothes or sick or in prison, and did not help You?'*

[45] *"He will reply, 'Truly I tell you, whatever you did not do for one of the least of these, you did not do for Me.'"* (Matthew 25:41-45; cf. 25:31-46)

Finally, faith-filled warfare prayer produces a power to do ministry because of your intimacy with Christ. Remember what was taught earlier and bears being repeated here, from Romans 10:17, "Consequently, faith comes from hearing the message, and the message is heard through the word [*rhema*] about Christ" (emphasis mine). The following illustration speaks of the importance of building spiritual intimacy with Christ and being open to listen.

A Word of Knowledge: An Illustration

I was standing on the stage of the Grande Ballroom of the Bradford Hotel in downtown Boston for one of the Sunday morning services of a new church my wife and I started in October 1982. Though we were small in number, we were large in the faith expectation that we would grow. We were at the end of our 11:00 AM service. I was standing on the stage looking out at a congregation of fewer than 100 adults and children, preparing to pray the benediction for the service's dismissal, when I heard a word—"arthritis."

When I heard it, I knew it was God speaking to me about someone, and so I said, "Before we dismiss, the Lord wants to heal someone here... of arthritis." And as soon as I uttered the word I'd heard, "arthritis," I saw two knees. And so I continued, "Arthritis, and it's in your knees." And as soon as I said, "It's in your knees," I saw someone straddling a toilet. And so I continued, "Before we dismiss, the Lord wants to heal someone here of arthritis, uh... it's in your knees, uh... and recently bending your knees was so painful you had to straddle your toilet. Come to the altar, the Lord wants to heal you." After hearing all the Lord had shown me, an older woman walked stiff-legged to the altar. I said to her, "You don't need me to lay hands on you; you're healed, just squat down and believe God."

She immediately tried to squat down, bending her knees, and she continued to go up and down, rejoicing and praising God for her healing. After church was dismissed, she went to my wife exclaiming, "Your husband is a man of God; no one knew I straddled that toilet." But of course God knew, and I believe He let me know all those specifics about her, not to embarrass her, but in order to build her faith to receive the healing she needed.

Your world needs you to be someone who prays, someone who is filled with the Holy Spirit, and someone who is open to being used of God to minister love and life through Christ to others. Those who know you may not need a miracle, but no one you know is complete without Christ. Being a prayer warrior prepares you with the love of the Father, the grace of Christ, and the intimate fellowship with the Holy Spirit that enables you to be used of God to minister life to others. The miracle begins with you caring enough to say, "Yes Lord! Use me." Finding your place of purpose in God's plan in the service of others is what it means to "test and approve what God's will is—his good, pleasing and perfect will" (Romans 12:2b).

Power to Walk in Purpose

Purpose is a benefit few believers truly experience because finding your purpose requires developing an intimacy with God through prayer that most believers have not done. Purpose is connected to the will of God; it is a matter of you finding your place in His plan. And since God knows why He created you, it is your prayer responsibility to discern His plan for your life. It's as though you are a significant piece of a large puzzle without which the puzzle makes no sense, but when that piece is added, the meaning of the puzzle is obvious to all observers. No one should live apart from purpose, but unfortunately, most people, even Christians, do. Prayer is the necessary missing part of the discipline you have to develop.

School

Everyone needs to be taught how to read, how to write, and how to do basic arithmetic. Those three were the main goals of education decades ago in my grandparents' day, but over the years educators saw the important need to teach subjects that added to the knowledge of the world in which students live: English literature, foreign language, geography, chemistry, physics, history, etc. When the higher education of college or university formed their curriculum, they required that every student take at least one class in the major disciplines for the purpose of seeing what discipline fit and what discipline you could do well in, with the view that you would choose to major in that discipline to pursue a career in that area. And you therefore graduated with a major in English, Mathematics, History, Sociology, Psychology, Chemistry, Physics, Medicine, the Law, etc.

But while all educational planning is good and necessary, many individuals end up pursuing a career in an area they do not like. I've counseled doctors who passed their exams with excellent grades, and who, based on their knowledge and ability as physicians, earned a living, but who could not bring themselves to love what they'd learned to do. I've pastored lawyers who graduated with honors from Law School and passed the Bar, but who, after practicing law, eventually quit to work in another field of endeavor. I've known teachers with a teaching degree who do not teach school. Need I say more? The issue is, after studying a specific area of expertise, graduating, and being employed in that field, they found that working in their trained area was not something they enjoyed doing, and they eventually quit.

Is there a solution to this dilemma? Yes! Developing a prayer life using the principles taught in this book will bring you to a place of spiritual intimacy with God as your Heavenly Father, and that intimacy will position you to receive revelation knowledge about your specific purpose. Purpose can be viewed two ways: (1) General Purpose includes growing in the grace and knowledge of Christ to become a mature believer God can use; (2) Specific Purpose includes God's calling and equipping you to do a specific work that agrees with your personality and innate gifts. The specific work may or may not be church related. Some think that the only call of God is to preach the Gospel, but God also calls doctors, lawyers, business persons, white collar and blue collar laborers who are overjoyed every day at the prospect to work with their mind and/or with their hands. And the secret to this joy is prayer intimacy with God.

From Pleasure to Purpose to Pleasure

One of the major schemes of the enemy is the lure and enticement of pleasure — sensual, sexual, drug related, ego related, or power related...well, you get the picture. Of course, the enemy's hold on many is the lie that the call to maturity in Christ includes abstinence from all pleasure. The truth is, mature Christians enjoy the wholesome pleasures of life all the time. We are just not deceived into believing we must violate the law of God or our relationship with Christ in order to have fun.

Let me explain. God created you to experience pleasure; He created sex for more than procreation but for the pleasure of intimacy within the boundary of the marriage covenant. Thus, it is not *what* is done but *how*. He gave you taste buds on your tongue and positioned your nose just above your mouth so that the dual pleasure of taste and smell heightens the enjoyment of taking in nourishment. Again, God wants you to enjoy your food. He created all the spices and herbs for our enjoyment, but eating should be for more than just enjoyment. It should also include the taking in of nourishment.

With all of the pleasure God created you to enjoy through your empirical senses, you were also created in God's image (Genesis 1:27) for the pleasure of fulfilling His purpose in your life. Remember Psalm 16:11: "You make known to me the path of life; you will fill me with joy in your presence, with eternal pleasures at your right hand." Notice the psalmist begins with the phrase, "You make known to me the path of life;" this is the psalmist recognizing the benefit of divine revelation that is ongoing. He didn't say "made known," indicating revelation that is in the past and completed, but "make known," thereby indicating revelation that is taking place as you walk the "path of life." Your growing understanding of God's purpose is discerned as you walk with Him; He literally fills you with joy in His presence. That joy is not only pleasurable, but remember joy carries a strength component revealed by Nehemiah: "Nehemiah said, 'Go and enjoy choice food and sweet drinks, and send some to those who have nothing prepared. This day is holy to our Lord. Do not grieve, for the **joy** of the Lord is your strength'" (Nehemiah 8:10, emphasis mine). What's neat about the joy component of prayer is that in addition to the emotional and psychological benefits, you also receive the spiritual benefit of strength—a powerful inner ability of resolve and purpose that stabilizes you so you cannot be shaken. This joy component is connected to prayer that ushers you into God's presence.[27]

The final phrase is, "...with eternal pleasures at your right hand." Understand Christ is pictured as seated at the Father's right hand (Ephesians 1:20), and you are "in Christ" (Ephesians 2:6). The meaning is the "eternal pleasures" you experience come from doing the will of God, given you are His "right hand." Remember, the Scriptures speak of God in anthropomorphic terms, meaning He is often described in ways that aren't meant to be taken literally but should be understood as speaking about God in human terms to help you understand Him from your human experience perspective. For example, in Genesis 2:2-3, Exodus 20:11, and Exodus 31:17, we are told that God rested from the work of creation, but it's not possible for God to tire, grow weary, or need sleep (Psalm 121:4; Isaiah 40:28). In Jeremiah 23:39 the LORD says, "I will surely **forget** you and cast you out of my **presence**," when it's not possible for the LORD to "forget" (Amos 8:7) or for anyone to be where God is not present (Psalm 139:7). It appears as though the LORD was grieved over the condition of the world (Genesis 6:6), and was grieved over making Saul king of Israel (1 Samuel 15:35). It seems the LORD changed His mind after hearing the desperate cry of his people (Psalm 106:45), because the prophet prayed (Amos 7:1-3), and because the people of Nineveh repented with fasting (Jonah 3:10). All this seemingly contradicts the teachings of Numbers 23:19 and 1 Samuel 15:29 that agree with Malachi 3:6 that says, "I the LORD do not change."

What does all this mean? I'm glad you asked! It simply means that our God is so far above us that in order to communicate effectively with us He must resort to speaking in human terms that reflect the normal, imperfect human condition. You must try to understand and make allowance for the fact that our *perfect* God is communicating to an *imperfect* world of people with finite understanding. Notice these prophetic words in the Old Testament book of Isaiah:

> ⁸ *"For my thoughts are not your thoughts, neither are your ways my ways," declares the LORD.* ⁹ *"As the heavens are higher than the earth, so are <u>my ways higher than your ways and my thoughts than your thoughts</u>."* (Isaiah 55:8-9, emphasis mine)

Also these apostolic words from John in the New Testament: "This is the message we have heard from him and declare to you: God is light; <u>in Him there is no darkness at all</u>" (1 John 1:5, emphasis mine).

Therefore, to be filled "with eternal pleasures at your right hand" means that our God does what He does with those who are aligned with and determine to do His will. If you are "in Christ," you are theologically seated at the right hand of God and are one of His children who are led to fulfill His will in the earth (Romans 8:14). Only those truly submitted to living in the center of God's will with the heart attitude, "Here am I. Send me" (Isaiah 6:8), receive the full inheritance as "heirs of God and co-heirs with Christ" (Romans 8:17), together with the benefit of "eternal pleasures at your [the Father's] right hand." In short, there is a *pleasure* that mature believers, especially prayer warriors, experience as they fulfill their specific purpose in following the will of God, and this pleasure is far beyond any physical sensory feeling possible in this carnal world by unsaved human beings. You are not only *at* the Father's right hand, but in the process of you obeying to do His will, you are in Christ and Christ is in you (Ephesians 2:6; Colossians 1:27), and you are filled with the Holy Spirit—in the sense of Christian work in the world, humbly you are the right hand of God, the righteousness of God in Christ (Psalm 16:11; 2 Corinthians 5:21).

When you, as a mature believer in Christ, determine to do the will of God in the world, you are in a place of peace (Romans 5:1), infused with the power of purpose (Acts 1:8; Romans 12:1-2), surrounded by God's protection (Luke 10:19), and rejoicing in the promise of prosperity (Joshua 1:8). You have the pleasure, the privilege of being *at* and *as* the Father's right hand in the lives of many.

THE WHAT OF PRAYER
(PART II)

Considering principles and practices

CHAPTER SIX

WHAT ABOUT PRAYER AND THE WILL OF GOD?

Finding God's Will

EVERY SERIOUS BELIEVER WHO HAS CONFESSED JESUS AS LORD AND believes He is raised from the grave needs to pursue knowing God's will for his or her life. For many believers, however, pursuing and knowing the will of God are a non-entity due to a couple of misconceptions. The first misconception is the belief that this level of longing or desire to know God's specific will for your life should only be expected in those with an apostle, prophet, evangelist, or pastor-teacher call on their lives (Ephesians 4:11). A typical response to the question, "Do you know God's will for your life?" might be, "Are you kidding? The only ones in the church who know God's will are the pastors." But knowing the will of God for your life is spiritual information accessible to every believer, not just those with a Fivefold Ministry call. The exhortation to present yourself completely as a "living sacrifice" to God, to refuse to conform to the dictates of this world's systems but to be transformed by renewing your mind, ends with you knowing the will of God for your life (Romans 12:1-2). And this is addressed to the body of believers.

The second misconception is the idea that finding the will of God is an arduous process that many have pursued but have failed. But the truth is, those who really want to know God's will for their lives always find it. Always! The key question is: do you really want to know it so you can follow it? Always remember, God knows your heart. Jesus taught in John 7:17, "Anyone who chooses to do the will of God will find out whether my teaching comes from God or whether I speak on my own." Seriously, this matter of choosing to do God's will is major, and unfortunately, rare. Many will say they want to know the will of God for their lives, but after numerous prayers, so-called, they testify to their inability to discern God's will. In essence, without saying it, they are actually revealing their lack of full surrender to *doing* that which they testify to seeking to know. God's will is only a mystery to those He knows will not hear, obey, and do it.

Higher Ground

Inherent in the psyche of believers who know the will of God and have an effective prayer life is the call to "higher ground." The old hymn's chorus says,

> Lord, lift me up and let me stand,
> By faith, on heaven's tableland,
> A higher plane than I have found;
> Lord, plant my feet on higher ground.[28]

In many respects, the prayerful plea of the hymn is seen in the intense longing of the apostle Paul expressed in Philippians 3:10-12:

> [10] *I want to know Christ—yes, to know the power of his resurrection and participation in his sufferings, becoming like him in his death,* [11] *and so, somehow, attaining to the resurrection from the dead.* [12] *Not that I have already obtained all this, or have already arrived at my goal, but I press on to take hold of that for which Christ Jesus took hold of me.*

Higher ground that includes a more intense identification with the resurrection power of Christ and His sufferings should become the pursuit of every believer that's pursuing and doing God's will. Where is this "higher ground" to be found? If there is a way to it, what is that way? What is that path? What challenges should you consider in this pursuit of true spiritual maturity in the will of God? What disciplines should you incorporate in your "higher ground" pursuit? Here again, let me use the passionate words of the great apostle Paul as a springboard,

> *13 Brothers and sisters, I do not consider myself yet to have taken hold of it. But one thing I do: Forgetting what is behind and straining toward what is ahead, 14 I press on toward the goal to win the prize for which God has called me heavenward in Christ Jesus.* (Philippians 3:13-14)

Notice with me three challenges we see in the words of the apostle that will strengthen the mettle of your determination to achieve the maturity of your full potential in doing the will of God.

1. <u>I do not consider myself yet to have taken hold of it.</u> You must never come to the conclusion, "I've arrived; there is nothing more I need to know or do." The *it* in Paul's statement has reference to what he wrote in the previous verse, *"I press on to take hold of that for which Christ Jesus took hold of me."* While Paul certainly became the apostle Christ called him to become, there was yet a *press* within him to take a better hold, a firmer grasp of that for which Christ Jesus took hold of him. Is not this the nature of the relationship God has with those who earnestly seek His face in prayer? Though Paul knew Christ and was in the center of God's will, yet there was a desire to know Him better; though he understood his call to be an apostle to the Gentiles, yet there was a desire to understand how to do what he was called to do better.

To find the *specific* will of God, the plan God has for you since eternity past (cf. Psalm 139:17-18), will require that you run with perseverance the race marked out for you (Hebrews 12:1), to press on toward the goal to win the prize for which God has called you heavenward in Christ Jesus, and, in prayer, never to stop running, never to stop pressing until you see Christ face to face. Part of knowing His will, as with Paul, is also the driving sense of "I have not arrived, I have not already obtained, I have not already been made perfect, there is still within me a 'press' for more of Christ." Though you may know the call of God for your life, yet the "press" within you can lead you in prayer to say as the apostle wrote, "I do not consider myself <u>yet</u> to have taken hold of **it**."

2. <u>Forgetting what is behind and straining toward what is ahead</u>. Every believer serious about finding and doing the will of God in pursuing the Spirit must come to the decision to forgive and forget. There is no one on the planet that has lived a perfect life, except Christ. You may have always had the best of intentions, according to you, but even if that's true, and it probably isn't, but let's say for the sake of argument that it is true, still all of us are surrounded by negative people in the world and in our families. Therefore, it's not possible to grow to an age of physical and mental maturity without carrying into your tomorrows some baggage. Recognizing the validity of this is the beginning of not allowing that baggage to limit and define you.

You cannot effectively go forward before you recognize the impact of the baggage in your past. Paul said, "Forgetting what is behind and straining toward what is ahead." Do you notice the two actions? The first half is negative in nature because it requires that you pull away from that which is behind you. Paul said, "Forgetting what is behind…" In many respects, there can be no forgetting without *forgiving*. A synonym for *forgive* is the word *release*. Those who refuse to forgive genuinely do not release the person(s) or the circumstance(s) of their past; instead, they hold onto it, binding it to their future attitude, perceptions, actions, and reactions. It is why a young boy who hates the fact his mother is beaten whenever the father comes home drunk will oftentimes grow up to drink and abuse his wife just as his father did. If you don't forgive and release, you can end up binding that misbehavior to yourself and see it repeated in the next generation. It's what is meant by the Scripture, "The parents have eaten sour grapes and the children's teeth are set on edge" (Jeremiah 31:29). The answer—forgive fully and then forget, meaning do not allow the negative past to affect the potential of your present and future. And if ever you recall that past difficulty, say, "In the name of Jesus, I forgive and release that person, situation, or circumstance that hurt me, and I determine to walk in full deliverance from its negative effect in my future. Amen!" This may even include forgiving yourself. Amen?

The second half is positive in nature because it encourages you to *strain toward what is ahead*. It reminds you of the exhortation in Hebrews to run with perseverance the race marked out for you (Hebrews 12:1b). Many allow the mistakes of their past, or even the mistakes of family in their past, to bind them to the burdensome baggage of regret or negative habit patterns that weigh them down and preclude the meaningful growth that enables the embracing of eventualities in their future with a positive perspective. Here is your remedy — *strain with faith and confidence toward your future by knowing and doing the will of God*.

Many have asked me in counsel, "What should I do now since I do not yet know God's will for my life?" My response has always been, "When you don't know what to do, do what you know to do." Do you know to love? Then love others with a pure heart, fervently (1 Peter 1:22 KJV). Do you know to be kind? Then be kind. Do you know to serve? Then serve (Matthew 20:26-27). The revelation and insight needed to discern the will of God will eventually appear before you like lighted steps on an upward path. Amen?

3. I press on toward the goal to win the prize for which God has called me heavenward in Christ Jesus. The phrase Paul uses here of "pressing on toward" is basically the same as the earlier phrase, "straining forward toward…" There is no significant difference between "pressing" and "straining." Both indicate the attitude of serious pursuit. In the former, Paul pictures himself as "straining" toward what is ahead. When you've come to a place of repentance where you truly change and, in the process, put behind you the negative practices and associations of your past, your "straining" toward a future in Christ is always positive. And if you are praying and seeking to fellowship with strong believers who are a genuine source of encouragement and support to your continual growth,

you are on a significant path that says your "straining" was a wise decision.

This phrase, "I press on toward the goal," provides the specific future the apostle envisions and the sense he has of being called "heavenward" in his press toward the goal. You should not become confused by Paul's word "heavenward." All our callings are "heavenward." It does not mean Paul was despairing of his mission on earth. He was a committed servant with a heart to be in the center of God's will—serving others and seeing those won to Christ becoming mature believers who can join in the all-important sense of being called heavenward in our earthly ministry pursuit.

As with Paul, so it is with you. Your heavenward goal where your potential will be maximized is achieved through an intimate relationship with God in prayer. He will guide you by His Spirit into the center of His will for your life. This matter of God's will is not minor because it encompasses you seeking God's face with all your heart to find your place in His plan (Jeremiah 29:11).

Confidence in Knowing God's Will

Understand that the *general* will of God for you is to be saved, to trust the shed blood of Jesus for your personal eternal salvation. You should know you are saved and be prepared to testify to that fact. You should know *generally* that God expects you to be saved enough to reach out to save others (Proverbs 11:30 KJV). The apostle Peter agreed, "He (God) is patient with you, not wanting anyone to perish, but everyone to come to repentance" (2 Peter 3:9b, emphasis mine). Therefore, the general desire of God is for the salvation of the lost. Christ came into the world to fulfill this purpose of salvation—to seek and save the lost (Luke 19:10). He did not come to condemn anyone but to save everyone who believes (John 3:16-17; cf. Romans 1:16-17). After you make Jesus Christ the Lord of your life: believing He died on the cross for your sins according to the Scriptures, was buried, and was raised from the grave for your justification according to the Scriptures (Romans 10:9-10; 1 Corinthians 15:3-4), you are saved and have fulfilled the general will of God for your life.

The Specific Will

Truthfully, God expects *every* mature believer to seek His face in prayer for His will. Seeking His hand for provisions or desires is not the same as seeking His face for your place at His table of service. Paul said it best on the Damascus Road, "'Lord, what wilt Thou have me to do?'" (Acts 9:6a KJV) This author, who has been a faithful shepherd of a local church in New England, is saying that knowing the will of God for your life is as basic as knowing your sins are forgiven and that you are a saved, maturing believer. Knowing God's will for your life is tantamount to being conversant in the ABC's of spiritual maturity. The will of God is part of the initial prayer pursuits of born again believers serious about pleasing the Lord in every possible way.

You need to be mature enough in your prayer life to discern God's specific will for your life—to know your place in His plan. An integral part of that plan is for you to cover in prayer those who you are among. One of the most powerful passages concerning providing a prayer cover for others is found in the Old Testament book of Ezekiel: "**I looked for someone** among them **who would** build up the wall **and** stand before me in the gap **on behalf of the land so I would not have to destroy it, but I found no one**" (Ezekiel 22:30, emphasis mine). Notice in the text three truths about the need for mature believers:

- God is looking for *someone among them*. God, speaking in the first person, says, *"I looked for someone,"* meaning the work requires a spiritually mature person. Specifically, the first qualification is to be *someone among them*. You must see yourself as a connected person who maintains a relationship with family and friends. Being mature and connected qualifies you to do the two things outlined in the text.
- To *build up the wall* means to surround the *"them"* (family and friends) with the truth of God's Word. Those you are *among,* those you are connected to, should be covered and protected by the truth you share with them (cf. Isaiah 26:1). You should seek to become knowledgeable enough to share

with or even teach those you are among basic Christian truth (cf. John 8:31-32; 2 Timothy 2:15; 1 Peter 3:15).

- To *stand before me in the gap* means to intercede in prayer on behalf of others, those you are *among*. This praying needs to become part of your daily devotional routine. Since the enemy does not take days off, neither should you. Therefore, as a warrior, you are called to grab a weapon and stand a post. The weapon is the sword of the Spirit, the Word of God. Your post as an intercessor is in the "gap" between the person(s) you are "among" and the Lord. You covering them in prayer, by name and by need, can actually make the difference between life and death. This is not minor; it is a major warfare responsibility desperately needed in today's complicated world. It's a responsibility only mature, Spirit-filled believers that study the Scriptures can fulfill.

Of course the Lord does not want to destroy the land as is stated at the end of the text (cf. 2 Peter 3:9). The reason God is *looking* for you who are *among them* and connected to them is to qualify you to be one who can *build up the wall* (witness, share, teach) and *stand before Him in the gap* (pray for them by name and by need) so that those who are protected by your prayer covering will not be destroyed by the wrath that is to come (1 Thessalonians 1:10). Make sense? Then let me hear you prayerfully say, "Yes Lord, use me to pray and to teach those I am among."

CHAPTER SEVEN

WHAT ABOUT PRAYER AND CHRISTIAN UNITY?

Christian Unity

THOUGH JESUS PRAYED FOR UNITY (JOHN 17:20-23) AND BIRTHED A united Church on the Day of Pentecost, that united Church was called to minister to a divided world whose influences gradually affected the Church's view of unity. Those beginning years of the Church found believers together in simple Christian fellowship where they submitted to leadership and shared everything in common.

> *⁴² They devoted themselves to the apostles' teaching and to fellowship, to the breaking of bread and to prayer. ⁴³ Everyone was filled with awe at the many wonders and signs performed by the apostles. ⁴⁴ All the believers were together and had everything in common.* (Acts 2:42-44)

But as the Church grew in Jerusalem, persecution prompted a diaspora of believers fleeing Jerusalem for Judea and Samaria after the martyrdom of Stephen (Acts 7:54-8:1). Afterwards, Saul of Tarsus, one of the chief exponents of the persecution in

Jerusalem (Acts 9:1-2; Galatians 1:13-14) was converted (Acts 9). Subsequently, he went first to Arabia, then to Damascus (Galatians 1:17), and after three years he went to Jerusalem and spent fifteen days with Peter and also saw James, the Lord's brother. It must have been during these beginning years, the apostolic call of God on Saul's life was beginning to manifest where he was no longer known as Saul of Tarsus but as the apostle Paul. Afterwards, he went to Syria and Cilicia where his ministry as an apostle obviously flourished (Galatians 1:18-21) because after 14 years, Barnabas, knowing Paul's gifts, sought him out to bring him to Jerusalem (Galatians 2:1; cf. Acts 12:25-13:3). I've given you this overview of history ending with the apostle Paul because the Holy Spirit used him in his writing as a powerful exponent of Christian unity.

True Christian Unity

Many scholars put the epistle of Paul to the Galatians as his earliest projected epistle written about AD 50.[29] Paul is clearly upset that the Galatian church adopted a theological perspective contrary to the Gospel of God's grace. Even his salutation lacked the normal warmth of praise and thanksgiving for them that is common in other epistles. At the outset, he begins his critique,

> *[6] I am astonished that you are so quickly deserting the one who called you to live in the grace of Christ and are turning to a different gospel— [7] which is really no gospel at all. Evidently some people are throwing you into confusion and are trying to pervert the gospel of Christ. (1:6-7)*

I trust you will take the time to familiarize yourself with the error Paul exposes concerning the difference between being justified by faith versus being justified by the works of the Law. Paul's condemnation of those teaching this error was so intense that he consigned being "eternally condemned" to them,

> *[8] But even if we or an angel from heaven should preach a gospel other than the one we preached to you, let them **be under God's curse!** [9] As we have already said, so now I say again: If anybody is preaching to you a gospel other than what you accepted, let them **be under God's curse!*** (1:8-9, emphasis mine)

The epistle to the Galatians raises a key biblical distinction often lost in modern attempts at ecumenical unity: while pushing toward Christian unity, the process must never include the compromise of essential doctrinal truth. Angered by how unsettled the Galatian church was by these false teachers, Paul wrote,

> *[11] Brothers and sisters, if I am still preaching circumcision, why am I still being persecuted? In that case the offense of the cross has been abolished. [12] As for those agitators, I wish they would go the whole way and emasculate themselves!* (5:11-12)

For Paul, theological disagreement about what someone needs to do to receive salvation was serious enough to require separation. Paul treated the disagreement as divisive: "Those people are zealous to win you over, but for no good. What they want is to alienate you from us, so that you may have zeal for them" (4:17, emphasis mine).

Agreement over *essential* sound doctrine should precede attempts at Christian unity. In other epistles, Paul consistently warns the churches concerning those causing division over essential doctrinal truth. For example, in Romans 16:17 he warns the church "to watch out for those who cause divisions and put obstacles in your way that are contrary to the teaching you have learned." In 1 Corinthians 1:10 he appeals to believers in the name of our Lord Jesus Christ to "...agree with one another in what you say and that there may be no divisions among you, but that you be perfectly united in mind and thought." In 1 Timothy 4:16, Paul exhorted his spiritual son, "Watch your life and doctrine closely.

Persevere in them, because if you do, you will save both yourself and your hearers." The clear sense is that this is essential doctrinal truth for salvation. To be divisive about essential doctrinal truth for salvation, according to the apostle Paul, was grounds for separation from the fellowship as in Titus 3:10, "Warn a divisive person once, and then warn them a second time. After that, have nothing to do with them."

Basic to a discussion of doctrinal soundness is distinguishing between doctrines that are essential to Christian faith and doctrines that are not. True Christian unity recognizes *unity's* value to the strength of kingdom ministry, but also that *unity* is neither *true* nor *Christian* apart from agreement about essential doctrinal truth.

Reconciliation and Unity

Pursuing the ministry and the message of reconciliation (2 Corinthians 5:18-19) should be enough to create unity within the local church setting, but even there, unity can be an elusive commodity if pride and a failure to forgive are allowed to muddy the reconciliation waters. Unity is often the product of humility and forgiveness. Forgiving a wrong done to you, though difficult, is not impossible if you remind yourself: (1) you are forgiven; and (2) the benefit of being forgiven is connected to you forgiving others (Matthew 6:14-15). Jesus emphasized the absolute must of forgiving others in the parable of the man that was forgiven a multimillion-dollar debt but who refused to forgive his fellow steward of a hundred-dollar debt (Matthew 18:23-35). Accordingly, your willingness to forgive is not an option if you are a genuine Christian and understand you are forgiven. And to the words of Jesus in the Sermon on the Mount, being willing to forgive and be reconciled with your brother must precede prayer (offering your gift at the altar, Matthew 5:24-25).

How to Begin a Discussion about Unity

Please allow me to deal with this "how" portion here instead of throwing it into the HOW in section five. Again, I'd be one of the first to agree that unity in the Church is part of the assignment we've received from the prayer of Christ in John 17, and that unity in the Church is not real if it is not Christian. So let's begin to structure a basic biblical perception of unity from the Father's perspective. Do you understand that God has already established a unity with His children by the Holy Spirit? Paul wrote about it in the epistle to the Ephesians,

> *³ Make every effort to **keep** the unity of the Spirit through the bond of peace.   ⁴ There is one body and one Spirit, just as you were called to one hope when you were called; ⁵ one Lord, one faith, one baptism; ⁶ one God and Father of all, who is over all and through all and in all.* (Ephesians 4:3-6, emphasis mine)

Let us examine the obvious truths from statements in the text:

   1. "Make every effort to keep the unity of the Spirit through the bond of peace." Genuine unity already exists for those who are truly Christian. You needn't create it; you have it through the Spirit who binds us together in His peace. You simply need to believe and embrace what you've been given by virtue of your living relationship with Christ. The Holy Spirit does this work of uniting us and we must make every effort to *keep* that which the Spirit provides. Remember, "The Spirit himself testifies with our spirit that we are God's children" (Romans 8:16).
   2. "There is one body and one Spirit..." The unity of the Church, the Body of Christ, is biblical truth. Though people create denominational divisions, you must not allow that to separate you from the praying, fellowshipping, and working together needed for kingdom work to be done in the power of the one Spirit. The indwelling presence and power of the Spirit enables mature believers to focus on God's agenda—the salvation of the lost and the establishment of righteousness in the earth (Luke 19:10; Matthew 6:33).
   3. "Just as you were called to one hope when you were called..." Even the one "hope" to which we've all been called, unites us. Paul

prayed in Ephesians chapter one, "I pray also that the eyes of your heart may be enlightened in order that you may know the hope to which he has called you..." (Ephesians 1:18a). Of course that *hope* is the hope of eternal life (John 3:16-17), but it also includes the *hope* connected to believers maturing and being refined through the fiery trials of life to become God's instruments of love and light in a hate-filled dark world (Romans 5:3-5). The *one hope* anchors and unites us to our destiny purpose in Christ (Hebrews 6:17-19).

4. "One Lord, one faith, one baptism; one God and Father of all, who is over all and through all and in all." Paul, in this statement, had an attack of the truth of oneness. There is no room for another idea, given the agenda expressed in Christ's prayer (John 17). It says unequivocally—if you justify division, you're on the wrong side of this issue. You must push past the barriers people have created and determine to work collaboratively with Christian brothers and sisters beyond denominational divisions. Unity is key! John Wesley, wrestling with the issue of unity and understanding its importance, was famous for quoting a slogan created by St. Augustine that served as a starting point for reconciliation discussions with other Christian brethren:

In essentials, unity;
In non-essentials, liberty; and
In everything, charity.

Paul's exhortation to "make every effort to keep" this unity is a subtle hint of how vital unity's existence is to the success of the Church's mission whether universal or local. We desperately need to "keep" this God-given unity in full recognition of the great benefit mentioned in Christ's prayer—"so that the world may believe that you [the Father] have sent me" (John 17:21c).

Examining the subject of essentials would be the place to begin a discussion about unity. I will not spend time outlining what the essentials are, given that discussion needs to occur with faithful, godly leaders who, with their whole hearts, love Christ, His Church, and our mission. That which falls outside of being essential Christian beliefs will fall into the non-essential category where "liberty" is allowed. Hopefully, you are mature enough to allow for "liberty" in non-essentials. Unfortunately, history tells us some are not emotionally or psychologically mature or balanced enough to make the distinction between that which is essential and that which is non-essential. Thus, the continual need to bathe the work of the Church in prayer.

The only remaining criterion for this discussion of unity to be complete is for the leaders involved to "love one another deeply, from the heart" (1 Peter 1:22; cf. 1 Corinthians 13 and 2 Corinthians 5:14-15). May the plague of pride, the cult of competition, and the stubbornness of sectarian separation in every major city dissolve in the tolerant, loving atmosphere created by your praying local church.

CHAPTER EIGHT

WHAT ABOUT PRAYER AND KINGDOM MINISTRY?

Christ, the Foundation for Kingdom Ministry

JESUS STATED EMPHATICALLY HE WOULD BUILD HIS CHURCH UPON WHO He is (His person) and upon what He came to do (His work). He is "the Christ, the Son of the living God" (Matthew 16:16 KJV). He "came to seek and to save the lost" (Luke 19:10), "and to give his life as a ransom for many" (Matthew 20:28).

Jesus of Nazareth is both Lord and Christ (Acts 2:36 KJV; Philippians 2:10-11). As the prophetic King who was promised (Zechariah 9:9; cf. Matthew 21:4-5), who is the King of kings and the Lord of lords (Revelation 19:16), Jesus is the King of the kingdom of God. By definition, the kingdom of God is the rule of God in the earth since creation. The kingdom has progressed through various phases to this end-time phase called the Church Age. Though some scholars refuse to see the Church prophesied in the Old Testament, the Church is there in typology and undeniable prophetic predictions. As the coming of the Messiah, the Christ, the anointed One, was predicted in Old Testament prophecy, so it goes without saying that the Church, the Body of Christ, was predicted and can be seen.

This end-time phase of the kingdom of God is no accident; the Church, the redeemed of the world—both Jews and Gentiles, bound and free, male and female, old and young, all sectors of society—are included prophetically (see Genesis 3:15, 12:1-3, 22:18; cf. also Galatians 3:16); God in His infinite wisdom established the nation of Israel as His covenant people through Abraham, Isaac, and Jacob (Israel). Through the twelve tribes of Israel, God put them in the land He promised to Abram (Genesis 13:14-15); Judah became the tribe and King David's lineage became the family through which the Christ would come (Genesis 49:10; 2 Samuel 7:11-13; Revelation 5:5). The "forever" nature of the kingdom to be established by the anointed One, the Messiah, is prophesied again and again (Isaiah 9:6-7; Daniel 2:44; Luke 1:32-33). Israel becoming a "light to the Gentiles" (Isaiah 49:6; Luke 2:32) is, of course, connected to the New Covenant (Jeremiah 31:31-34; Luke 22:20; Hebrews 8:8-13), and this end-time kingdom, the Church (Gk. *ekklesia* – "called out ones") includes both Jews and Gentiles from every tribe, nation, and people group (Genesis 12:3 "all peoples on earth"; 22:18 "all nations on earth"; Galatians 3:28-29 "... you are all one in Christ Jesus. If you belong to Christ...[you are] heirs according to the promise"). Therefore, as you understand the salvation purpose of the kingdom, you pursue ministry recognizing it begins with your fervent, faith-filled prayer, "Thy kingdom come, Thy will be done in earth as it is in heaven" (Matthew 6:10 KJV).

Make Disciples

The basic call of the Great Commission is to care enough to spend the quality time with those you are among (family and friends) for the purpose of *influence*. The need is to touch them for Christ and influence them to become mature believers. That's what a disciple is, a mature believer. Your level of spiritual maturity can be measured by your commitment to the work of the kingdom. Are you willing to be transparent and seen as trustworthy in your character so that others will feel drawn to have a relationship with you—a relationship where your lifestyle and words will influence them to respect and honor truth enough to desire the change truth brings?

That which Jesus did so well is what you are called to do. Let us not forget the assignment Jesus gave His disciples in one of His post-resurrection appearances, "As the Father has sent me, I am sending you" (John 20:21). And remember, included in the call to *do* is the call to *be*. Your example in the decisions you make, the responsibilities you shoulder, and the people with whom you fellowship goes a long way in making the kind of impression needed for the influence of your words to create change. Jesus effectively reproduced Himself in the lives of eleven of His twelve disciples by His person, His work, and His words.[30] The "What Would Jesus Do?" movement focused predominately on the task of making moral decisions, but the ultimate "What Would Jesus Do?" question should lead you, along with moral excellence, to be one who disciples others—where the priority of reproducing the mature life of Christ in others is obeyed.

Hearing that discipleship call and understanding the priority of that kingdom mission is what separates mature believers from babes in Christ. Actually, the Great Commission is Jesus, the Head of the Church, giving you an assignment—the mission of making disciples of all nations. And though you may be married with children, have a job, a business, or a career, and recognize a social responsibility to family and friends, bottom line: you must find a way to prioritize God's mission. This prioritization begins with you taking seriously this matter of prayer consistency and effectiveness.

Remember, Jesus is the One building His Church both locally and universally. He knows exactly what's needed and whom He can use. The most important way for you to align yourself with the Lord is through prayer. Since prayer time is not wasted time, make time to begin your day in building intimacy with the Father through prayer. He knows your name, who you are, the gifts you have, and the path you are on. In fact, He knows more about you than you can remember about yourself, but your relational need for prayer is to increase your knowledge of God so that you grow in your understanding of His ways (Psalm 103:7; Proverbs 10:29a). Your full surrender to the Lord your Shepherd will result in Him making you lie down in green pastures (nourishing you), leading you beside quiet waters (refreshing you), and restoring your soul (forgiving and cleansing you) as He guides you in paths of righteousness for His name's sake (Psalm 23:1-3).

In the process, there are two passages of Scripture, one from the Old Testament book of Isaiah and one from the New Testament epistle to the Romans, that speak together about discerning the truth from teachers revealed through experiences fraught with adversity, affliction, and suffering. The amazing thing is how God can use that which would tend to press you down to open your eyes to see that which is causing you to be lifted up:

> [20] *Although the Lord gives you the bread of **adversity** and the water of **affliction**, your <u>teachers will be hidden no more</u>; with your own eyes you will see them.* [21] *Whether you turn to the right or the left, your ears will hear a voice behind you, saying, "This is the way; walk in it."* (Isaiah 30:20-21, emphases mine)

> [3] *Not only so, but <u>we also</u> <u>glory in our sufferings</u>, because we know that <u>suffering produces perseverance;</u>* [4] *<u>perseverance, character; and character, hope</u>.* [5] *And hope does not put us to shame, because God's love has been poured out into our hearts through the Holy Spirit, who has been given to us.* (Romans 5:3-5, emphasis mine)

First, Isaiah the prophet teaches that the Lord uses adversity and affliction to open your eyes to see events, circumstances, and people as *teachers* who point you in the direction where you hear the Lord's voice behind you confirming the way you are to go. Then, Paul the apostle connects the influence of you rejoicing in *sufferings* because they produce *perseverance* that produces *character* that produces *hope* that allows God to pour His *love* into your heart by the gift of the Holy Spirit.

Both passages are teaching the same truth—God uses the occurrences of *life* to guide you into a path where your walking, acting, reacting, and living result in you prayerfully hearing His voice as your life overflows with the *love* you can only receive from the gift and ministry of the Holy Spirit. Let us pray…

> Father, thank You for the wisdom of Your ways with us. We are grateful for Your longsuffering that gave us space to repent and mature in faith to become useful in Your kingdom. We say, "Yes!" to Your Spirit guiding us into all truth and delivering us from every deceptive snare of the enemy. Keep us, we pray, pliable in Your hands so that we can be the effective examples and leaders others will follow. Thank you Lord, in Jesus's name we pray. Amen.

THE WHY OF PRAYER

*Considering the rationale behind why God is
calling His people to pray*

CHAPTER NINE

WHY SHOULD YOU PRAY?

LET ME SHARE SOME BASIC ASSUMPTIONS I AM MAKING ABOUT YOU: the first being that you are a believer who at some point in your spiritual journey repented, confessed Jesus Christ as the Lord of your life, and believed that God raised Him from the dead (Romans 10:9).[31] My second assumption is you believe it is true that you reap what you sow, and at the end of your life you will stand before God where your life will be judged (Galatians 6:7-9; 2 Corinthians 5:10-11). Though we all come to faith from different backgrounds and circumstances, yet there is a commonality in all of our journeys.

Four Reasons Why

There are four basic reasons why it's important you should consider learning to pray more effectively. Please forgive me if these are review for you, but it never hurts to be reminded of the basics every once in a while. Prayer is important...

1. <u>Because Jesus prayed</u>. Prayer is something Jesus did very well. Can you wrap your mind around the fact that Jesus, the Son of the living God, your Savior, spent a lot of time in prayer? Doubtless, you also comprehend the impractical truth that Jesus, being full of wisdom, would not have wasted time with an unnecessary practice. It must be that Jesus prayed often because He had to. This then gives weight to the obvious rationale that if Jesus had

to pray, you have to pray. If prayer was important enough and necessary for Him, it is important enough and necessary for you. The Bible teaches Jesus began His days in prayer: "Very early in the morning, while it was still dark, Jesus got up, left the house and went off to a solitary place, where He prayed" (Mark 1:35).

Prayer for Jesus was usually private, but there were a few significant events where others witnessed Him praying. For example, when He was baptized by John the Baptist in the Jordan River—

> *[21] When all the people were being baptized, Jesus was baptized too. And as **he was praying**, heaven was opened [22] and the Holy Spirit descended on him in bodily form like a dove. And a voice came from heaven: "You are my Son, whom I love; with you I am well pleased."* (Luke 3:21-22, emphasis mine)

A common occurrence was Jesus would pray in private and his disciples would be with Him. Luke writes about one of these occasions Jesus questioned His disciples,

> *[18] Once when Jesus was **praying** in private and his disciples were with him, he asked them, "Who do the crowds say I am?" [19] They replied, "Some say John the Baptist; others say Elijah; and still others, that one of the prophets of long ago has come back to life." [20] "But what about you?" he asked. "Who do you say I am?" Peter answered, "God's Messiah."* (Luke 9:18-20, emphasis mine)

And at the occurrence of the Transfiguration, Luke wrote that Jesus,

> *[28] ...took Peter, John and James with him and went up onto a mountain to **pray**. [29] As he was **praying**, the appearance of his face changed, and his clothes became as bright as a flash of lightning.* (Luke 9:28-29, emphasis mine)

We could go on and on about the pervasive quality of Jesus's prayer life, but perhaps the most significant proof of its power was its impact upon His disciples. What must it have been like to live with One who lived in constant contact with His Father? His prayer life could not go unnoticed. The prayer connection with the Father together with the anointing of the Holy Spirit (Acts 10:38) supplied the power over sickness, disease, and infirmity, over demonic forces, and over death itself. His prayer life also enabled a wisdom in answering the questions of accusers or inquisitors. It's no wonder His disciples asked Him to teach them to pray (Luke 11:1). He then taught them what we know as The Lord's Prayer.

2. <u>Because Prayer is Commanded</u>. We are exhorted by Jesus and the apostle Paul to pray. Can you wrap your mind around the fact that God is commanding or exhorting or encouraging you to pray? What is the rationale for this command? Why is the omniscient God of all creation, the One who knows everything there is to know about you, even your thoughts before you think them (Psalm 139:1-4), requiring prayer from you? The answer is simple: God does not need you to pray, YOU NEED YOU TO PRAY. The Father is commanding you to pray because prayer strengthens your relationship with Him. You actually grow in faith and in your understanding of God's ways, how He works, in response to your specific prayers and petitions. Prayer provides the intimate connection you desperately need with your Heavenly Father who is your ultimate resource.

Therefore, Jesus, in the Sermon on the Mount, did not say "*if* you pray" but "*when* you pray" and "*when* you fast," indicating that prayer and fasting would be part of the normal spiritual practice of the mature believer (Matthew 6:5, 16, emphasis mine). Jesus, in the Gospel according to Luke (18:2-8), taught a parable about the importance of praying in faith. Luke uses these introductory words: "Then Jesus told His disciples a parable to show them that they should <u>always pray</u> and <u>not give up</u>" (Luke 18:1, emphasis mine). The parable contrasts an "unjust judge" (v. 6), who "neither feared God nor cared what people thought" (vv. 2, 4), responding to a "widow," who repeatedly came before him with her "plea, 'Grant me justice against my adversary'" (v. 3), with a just "God" who is determined to "bring about justice for his chosen ones who cry out to him day and night" (v. 7).

My interpretation of the <u>unjust judge not fearing God</u> is: he was not particularly religious or moral; maybe he had no thought or fear about one day standing before the Great Judge of all the earth. My interpretation of the <u>unjust judge not caring what people thought</u> is: the judge was in his position for life; he did not have to concern himself with being re-elected to the bench; he was not some political appointee who had to answer to some superior person or committee. No decision he made on the bench would or could be overturned by some appellate court. His decision in a case could not be scrutinized with the possibility of him being impeached and removed from the bench. His rulings were final.

Then, my interpretation of <u>the widow</u>: I believe Jesus used a widow in this parable, this fictional human story used to teach a valuable spiritual lesson, because a widow was one of the weakest free humans in ancient civilization. The only ones weaker than a widow in ancient civilization were slaves who were not free. In ancient times, women were indeed second-class citizens with very few rights in terms of sociological standing or economic strength. They could, however, achieve benefit by marriage where their husband could protect and provide for them, but this woman lost that benefit because she was a *widow*.

Jesus pictures in the parable a woman who is a widow, in all of the weakness her ancient civilization piled on her, standing before an unjust judge who neither feared God nor cared what people thought, and the judge finally grants her justice after her repeated, insistent, coming. Unspoken is the *faith* of this widow—she firmly believed that she could be more determined to get justice than the judge's determination to deny justice. He said, "Because this widow keeps bothering me, I will see that she gets justice, so that she won't eventually wear me out with her coming!" (Luke 18:5)

Again, Jesus contrasts this unjust judge's response to the constant coming of the widow before him with the just response of God to His "chosen ones" (male or female, slave or free, old or young, rich or poor, black or white) that cry out to Him day and night. He concludes in the contrast, "He will see that they get justice, and quickly" (v. 8a). Jesus ends the parable with the words, "However, when the Son of Man comes, will He find faith on the earth?" (v. 8b) Clearly, the meaning of this final sentence is, will God's people exercise the kind of *faith* demonstrated by the widow in the parable? In other words, you must not stop praying in faith when the answer you seek is delayed. Our God is not an unjust judge. His will is to answer you "quickly," but there may be circumstances that require you "not [to] become weary in doing good" (Galatians. 6:9). God's timing is best and always for your good. Let it be said that when the Son of God comes, He will find faith in you. You will be one of those stalwart warriors holding on to the horns of the altar, so to speak, praying and thanking God for what He has promised. Keep on Believing! This hymn by Frank C. Huston was a source of encouragement to me on numerous occasions of waiting in faith.

> Sometimes the shadows gather, and mists obscure the way;
> Sometimes, the clouds grow heavy, and darken all the day.
> How precious to remember our Father's loving care,
> That He still loves His children, and He answers prayer.
>
> *Refrain*
> Keep on believing, God will answer prayer;
> Keep on believing, never despair
> Tho' you be heavy laden, and burdened down with care,
> Remember God still loves you and He answers prayer.
>
> Sometimes, the way is dreary, we seem to walk alone,
> Forgetting that the Father keeps watch above His own.
> How many needless sorrows the faithless have to bear,
> For, God still loves His children, and He answers prayer.
>
> O soul, weighed down with sorrow, beneath a heavy load,

Remember God will help you, however rough
the road.
His grace is still sufficient for every load of care,
God ever loves His children, and He answers prayer.[32]

The epistle to the Hebrews teaches that Jesus is our "Great High Priest." Thus, your mediator, the One who stands before God the Father on your behalf, is not just a man (as were the descendants of Aaron the high priest in Israel), but also the Son of God. He is not only your mediator but also your advocate (1 John 2:1-2 KJV). Understanding that truth should result in you being bold and confident in prayer, knowing that your Savior who was here in the flesh sympathizes with your weaknesses.

> *[14] Therefore, since we have a great high priest who has ascended into heaven, Jesus the Son of God, let us hold firmly to the faith we profess. [15] For we do not have a high priest who is unable to <u>empathize with our weaknesses</u>, but we have one who has been tempted in every way, just as we are—yet he did not sin. [16] Let us then <u>approach God's throne of grace with confidence</u>, so that we may receive mercy and find grace to help us in our time of need.* (Hebrews 4:14-16, emphasis mine)

So the apostle exhorts you to approach the throne of grace with confidence remembering the person and work of Christ in His earthly life and ministry and His present mediatory function as your Great High Priest. The source of this *confidence* is twofold.

The first source of *confidence* is the knowledge of what the Father accomplished on your behalf through Christ's death on the cross and resurrection from the tomb. Literally, He "disarmed the powers and authorities, he made a public spectacle of them, triumphing over them by the cross" (Colossians 2:15). So your confidence is strengthened by the knowledge that demonic powers and authorities have been <u>disarmed</u> as a result of the cross. God made a public spectacle of the enemy by the sacrifice of Christ on the cross. So the enemy is not only disarmed (powerless to harm you—cf. also Luke 10:19) but a public spectacle (embarrassed). Paul, in worshipful terms, exclaims,

> ...*¹² and giving joyful thanks to the Father, who has qualified you to share in the inheritance of his holy people in the kingdom of light. ¹³ For he has rescued us from the dominion of darkness and brought us into the kingdom of the Son he loves, ¹⁴ in whom we have redemption, the forgiveness of sins.* (Colossians 1:12-14)

This first source of confidence is not only for what God has done to the demonic forces through the cross, but His elevation of believers: rescued from the dominion of darkness, brought into Christ's kingdom of light, redeemed, and forgiven. Hallelujah!

The second source of *confidence* is the faithfulness of your walk. Bear in mind, theologically, you are not saved by works, but when you really repent and experience salvation's transformation enough for others to notice, you emerge as someone zealous to do good works (see Matthew 5:16; Ephesians 2:10; Titus 2:14). Though your works do *not* save you, yet being a person of integrity with a desire to do good works helps to insulate you against the enemy's attempts to accuse you (Revelation 12:10). The devil's desire is through false accusation to prompt doubt in your heart and, in the process, weaken your faith in prayer. But your godly character, along with good works that have ministered love and life to others, serve to insulate and strengthen your *confidence* for believing prayer (cf. 1 John 3:21-22).

Jesus called this the new birth, being "born again" (John 3:3). It is not unrealistic to expect a change in the lifestyle of those who have genuinely encountered Christ, and, as believers who are experiencing victory in their walk, they will also have a *confidence* in prayer that is connected to their transformed lifestyle. This confidence is based upon what God has and is doing in them because they are believers, as opposed to an arrogance based upon what they feel they have accomplished on their own.

The apostle Paul, on several occasions, exhorted believers to be faithful in prayer. He exhorted the Ephesians to "put on the full armor of God...[and] pray in the Spirit on all occasions with all kinds of prayers and requests" (6:11, 18a); to the Philippians he wrote, "Do not be anxious about anything, but in every situation, by prayer and petition, with thanksgiving, present your requests to God. And the peace of God, which transcends all understanding, will guard your hearts and your minds in Christ Jesus" (4:6-7); he exhorted the Colossians, "Devote yourselves to prayer, being watchful and thankful" (4:2-5); and in his first epistle to the Thessalonians, he commanded them to "pray continually" (5:17). Please do not take any of this lightly. These apostolic admonitions of Paul carry the weight of one who was an example worth following. An exhortation to the Philippian church powerfully illustrates this truth: "Whatever you have learned or received or heard from me, or seen in me—put it into practice. And the God of peace will be with you" (Philippians 4:9).

3. Because Prayer Changes You. The third reason why prayer is important is because prayer changes you. You cannot take the time to prioritize talking to someone every day without building relational intimacy. Experientially, those who discipline themselves to delight in the Lord's presence and daily seek His face in prayer will find themselves transformed by the intimacy they discipline themselves to develop. The Greek word *metamorphoo* is translated by the English word "transform." Paul used it to describe what happens to those who spend quality time in the Lord's presence. "And we, who with unveiled faces contemplate the Lord's glory, are being **transformed** into His image with ever-increasing glory, which comes from the Lord, who is the Spirit" (2 Corinthians 3:18, emphasis mine).

Though the word "prayer" does not appear in the passage, yet the contextual application is obviously about those who experience transformation in God's presence while praying. Its context reminds you of the experience of Moses in God's presence (Exodus 33:7-34:35) where he met with the LORD face to face in the tent of meeting and was called to chisel two tablets of stone and take them to meet with the LORD on Mount Sinai. Moses was there with the LORD forty days and forty nights without eating bread or drinking water, and when he returned to the camp, his face was radiant because he had spoken with the LORD. As prayer literally changed the face of Moses making it "radiant," even so your spiritual countenance is transformed by the power of God's presence as you worship and pray.

The same Greek word is also found in Paul's letter to the Romans,

> *¹ Therefore, I urge you, brothers and sisters, in view of God's mercy, to offer your bodies as a living sacrifice, holy and pleasing to God—this is your true and proper worship. ² Do not conform to the pattern of this world, but be **transformed** by the renewing of your mind. Then you will be able to test and approve what God's will is—His good, pleasing and perfect will.* (Romans 12:1-2, emphasis mine)

Both passages speak of the change you experience as you surrender unconditionally to God's will and purpose for your life. You *reflect the Lord's glory* as you open wide your heart *(unveiled faces)* to God's will and purpose, and are *transformed into His likeness with ever increasing glory.* When your surrender is unconditional it mirrors the *spiritual act of worship* and results in you refusing to *conform any longer to the pattern of this world.* You then experience being *transformed* by your mind being *renewed* as you align yourself with God's *good, pleasing, and perfect will.*

The result of unveiled, open-faced, mature believers in a corporate setting of worship and prayer is that their general lives and wellbeing reflect His glory in such a way that it ministers without words to others they touch. This is what corporate worship and prayer services are all about (see Acts 4:23-31). Corporate worship and prayer is at its best when believers are transformed in God's presence and they impact those who are part of their community.

A Season of Transformation. During a season of prayerful introspection, I heard the Lord say, "You don't pray enough." My concern was for the health and growth of my church along with the personal need to have a consistent devotional life. Concurrent with my desire to be a stronger prayer warrior was the call of God that His house was to be a "House of Prayer" according to Isaiah 56:7. Knowing this meant establishing a daily Early Morning Prayer (EMP) meeting in my church caused hesitation on my part, given my inconsistent prayer life. But the more I prayed, the more I heard the same words as if they were an echo bouncing off the walls in the corridors of my mind, "You don't pray enough," and I knew the Lord was calling me to establish my church as a House of Prayer.

It had always been my plan to begin an EMP meeting, but believing I needed first to become more consistent in my own prayer life, I delayed starting. However, because of the promptings of the Spirit, I pushed my own un-readiness aside and added EMP to our weekly order of services.

To my utter amazement, I found that opening my mouth to announce these new meetings for prayer gave me the strength of consistency I'd not expected. And what amazed me more in my success is I'd actually taught the truth that open confession can strengthen your ability to be steadfast. The principle is found in Revelation 12:11, "They triumphed over him [the enemy] by the blood of the Lamb and by the word of their testimony; they did not love their lives so much as to shrink from death." In disciplining myself to pray without an open confession I was about 70-75% faithful, but after I announced EMP to the congregation, that addition of accountability pushed me to be 100% faithful overnight.

Now before we go further, notice in the above text three criteria for overcoming the enemy: the *first* is being a believer who's washed by the blood of the Lamb, meaning your sins are forgiven and you are saved (Ephesians 1:7; 2:8-9); skipping the *second,* the *third* is being committed enough to Christ that you would die before you would deny your faith. Then with the first and the third criteria in place, all you need to do is open your mouth to testify, announce, confess—that's the *second,* the action that creates the accountability with those who have heard the words of your mouth.

When I opened my mouth to announce I would be present in EMP, that word of testimony snatched me out of hiding and set me in a place where all could see my stand and my determination to be consistent and follow through with what I'd said. The last thing any of us ever want to be is a talker and not a walker. Therefore, my prayer life was undergirded by the "word of my testimony." Testimony made me observable and somewhat accountable to those present in EMP (Mondays-Fridays 5-6 AM and Saturdays 7-9 AM). Leaders must lead, and so, in those beginning years from 1986-1991, winter, spring, summer, and fall, I was at my post in the early morning hours leading my church in prayer.

Little did I realize how much partnering with others in prayer would enable my own ability to become consistent in prayer and impact and change me; and I also had not discerned fully the impact that EMP would have on the culture of my church. It's no wonder Jesus quoted Isaiah 56:7 at the cleansing of the temple: "'It is written,' He said to them, '"My house will be called a house of prayer," but you are making it "a den of robbers"'" (Matthew 21:13). When we began praying together in tandem daily for our church leaders, other local churches' leaders, public and private school teachers and administrators, social service agencies, and the police and politicians in our community, it provided an intercessory covering that released a power over our city's inhabitants—a power we actually witnessed in Boston.

Many organizations and individuals have taken credit for what is known historically as the "Boston Miracle," where in the mid-1990s for over two years there were no teenage homicides.[33] During that period, hundreds gathered regularly in EMP from 5-6:00 AM and from 6-7:00 AM Mondays through Fridays praying systematically for various aspects of our city's life. No one group or person can take credit for the "Boston Miracle" because in truth, it was a collaborative effort where the Justice Department, police, social service agencies, street workers, pastors, and churches came together to solve the problem of gang violence. The part that prayer played (ours and others') I believe, was the spiritual removal of the adversarial forces that precluded the coming together in agreement needed to provide workable solutions. And for Jubilee Christian Church, beyond those community benefits, we witnessed the impact EMP had and still has on the atmosphere of our Sunday worship services.

There is no way to calculate the overall long-term benefits that this prayer discipline has brought to our church and our community since 1986 in transformed lives. Only God knows how many youth were saved from gang violence, how many marriages were saved from separation and divorce, how many crimes were solved or governmental decisions were made for the common good because people prayed.

One of the faithful prayer warriors during that initial season (1986-91) was a believer old enough to be my grandmother by the name of Mother Mae Gadpaille. She was a former school-teacher who, with a compassionate, no-nonsense approach to teaching, used the Montessori Method and started the first Montessori School for African American youth in Boston's inner-city. Her favorite passage I'd hear her quote was Psalm 92:10-15,

> *[10] You have exalted my horn like that of a wild ox;*
> *fine oils have been poured on me.*
> *[11] My eyes have seen the defeat of my adversaries;*
> *my ears have heard the rout of my wicked foes.*
> *[12] The righteous will flourish like a palm tree,*
> *they will grow like a cedar of Lebanon;*
> *[13] planted in the house of the LORD,*
> *they will flourish in the courts of our God.*
> *[14] They will still <u>bear fruit in old age</u>,*
> *they will stay fresh and green,*
> *[15] proclaiming, "The LORD is upright;*
> *He is my Rock, and there is no wickedness in him."*

Mother Gadpaille always respected me as her pastor, but because of her age and the way she'd been raised, she would not hesitate to speak her mind of counsel if she saw something she thought needed correcting. God help me if Mother Gadpaille arrived at our place of prayer before me. We met on the second floor of a narrow, three-story storefront the church purchased at auction for $7,000, in the Grove Hall neighborhood of the Roxbury/ Dorchester section of Boston.[34] I can hear her chastening me now,

"Pastor, I remember my mother saying to me, 'It's better to be an hour early than to be a minute late.'"

Of course, my respectful reply would always be, "Yes ma'am, I'll do better." And many a winter morning I would rise early to shovel out my car so as to beat Mother Gadpaille to our place of prayer. I can't remember her ever missing, and she'd have to shovel her own car out. Honestly, many a dark morning leaving the house around 4:30 AM I remember saying to myself, "Why did I start this EMP meeting? What was I thinking? I shouldn't have opened my big mouth." There were always other believers there but none more faithful than Mother. As I look back over those beginning years I spent praying with her, I understand now that the Father, knowing how much I needed to develop into a warrior in prayer, gave me the gift of Mother Gadpaille. She's with the Lord now and I'm still praying because her faithful attendance caused a warrior prayer anointing to be birthed in me. Thank you Father for the gift of that tough teacher, Mother Mae Gadpaille.

4. <u>Because Prayer Releases God's Power</u>. The fourth basic reason prayer is important enough to prioritize is prayer spoken in faith releases a power beyond any earthly form of energy in the world. In Ephesians chapter 3, Paul closes out his prayer with an oft-quoted doxology,

> [20] *Now to him who is able to do immeasurably more than all we ask or imagine, according to his power that is at work within us,* [21] *to him be glory in the church and in Christ Jesus throughout all genera-tions, for ever and ever! Amen.* (vv. 20-21)

That really says it all! This understanding about the power of God released significantly as a result of prayer, though basic, does not influence all who are believers to pray. In spite of the simple nature of this truth, many set out to do and accomplish spiritual works without the power of the presence and will of God invited by heartfelt prayer.

Do you remember Jesus strongly urged His disciples not to leave Jerusalem but to wait until they were clothed with power from on high? (Luke 24:49; cf. also Acts 1:4-5) Some, whether pastors or businesspersons, seek to build the kingdom without praying for God's helpful wisdom and guidance, and some gifted individuals have actually succeeded in doing noteworthy work in their own strength. But they miss the full meaning of what Jesus meant about building His Church, "...and the gates of Hades [death] will not overcome it" (Matthew 16:18), whether it's the Church or the business entrepreneur or anyone else who is a saved part of the Church, God's kingdom-builders need to be cognizant that they cannot do the job God wants done without Christ. Jesus is not just building for today but for generations to come. So the church is to be vibrant and alive to support the propagation of truth for generations, and not just while you are alive and well. You cannot do multigenerational work without Christ; therefore, prayer is not optional, it's necessary.

This spiritual work of building God's kingdom is reserved for those who fully understand that Christ is doing the real work of grounding the next generational leaders in truth, so you are called as the leader today to stay connected with Him in the process. He will use your gifts and abilities, but He is the Builder who is to receive all the glory and credit. If you get connected and stay connected to Him in prayer, you can accomplish your potential through His power, and with His help and guidance, pass the ministry on to the next generation. The song poet wrote,

No matter how hard goes the battle of life,
God's children need never despair;
His conquering grace giveth peace 'mid the strife,
There is wonderful pow'r in prayer.

Chorus
Wonderful pow'r,
A wonderful pow'r in prayer;
For it moveth the arm that moveth the worlds,
There's a wonderful pow'r in prayer.

We know that the roses not always will bloom,

> The skies will not always be fair;
> But go to the Father to brighten the gloom,
> There is wonderful pow'r in prayer.
>
> Perhaps you are seeking a soul far astray;
> That name to the mercy-seat bear;
> The Shepherd Himself will go with you today,
> There is wonderful pow'r in prayer.
>
> Thro' all the swift changes that come to us here,
> Till white robes of glory we wear,
> We'll look up to Jesus for comfort and cheer,
> There is wonderful pow'r in prayer.[35]

Allow me to close this last reason why prayer is so important with the words of Jesus in His discourse in John 15. In verse five He said, "I am the vine; you are the branches. If you remain in me [in prayer] and I in you, you will bear much fruit; apart from me you can do nothing."

For you who are pressed to change your world—like me you are someone who desperately wants to hear the approbation of Christ, "Well done, good and faithful servant!" There is a press within your spirit to live a balanced life and to run with perseverance this Christian race by living by the Spirit and not gratifying the desires of the sinful nature (Galatians 5:16), by loving deeply as Christ loved (John 13:34-35), by continually praying in faith (1 Thessalonians 5:17), and by ministering a word of faith (Romans 10:8) based upon the gospel (Romans 1:16-17) to save, teach, and disciple others (Matthew 28:19-20; 1 Timothy 4:16). Let me encourage you to make your calling and election sure (2 Peter 1:10 KJV) by strengthening your intimate relationship with Christ through prayer. Make every effort to seek His face before your major decisions that place you on a path in a specific direction. Segregate seasons where fasting and prayer for God's wisdom and your sensitivity to His guidance is part of your spiritual culture, and you will find, as I have, that the Lord will, in the process of leading and guiding you into all truth, protect you even from the negative effects of decisions that are not the best. Let us pray...

Father, I'm asking You to move significantly in the lives of those who surrender fully to the truth they are learning from this section of the book. I'm praying that You will guide them by Your Spirit to establish multigenerational ministries and businesses that will represent by precept and example the righteousness of Your kingdom, and that will support and teach truth that will disciple multiple generations for Your glory, in Jesus's name. Amen.

CHAPTER TEN

WHY IS PRAYING WITH POWER SO DIFFICULT?

T HE KIND OF PRAYING THAT MOST PEOPLE DO IS NOT DIFFICULT. I DARE say, if questioned under oath in a courtroom to give specific testimony of answered prayer, the majority of Christians, even those who go to church regularly, could not give the details of how they prayed and how they know their prayer was answered specifically. You see, I'm not talking about the general prayers that most Christians pray; prayers so non-specific that to claim it was answered could validate the claimant as being guilty of fantasy fiction. What I'm talking about is the kind of faith-filled praying where you hold on to the horns of the altar, so to speak, until the specific answer comes to your specific requests; a prayer where the specificity of your request is so detailed and the answer so on point that the devil himself is forced to say, "Amen."

The majority of Christians are not praying those kinds of prayers, because those kinds of prayers are *difficult*, and many are not willing to go the extra mile and make the center-of-the-will-of-God kind of adjustments in their lives to develop an intimacy with God where He quickly moves on their behalf. Let me give you five reasons why praying with power is so difficult.

Five Reasons

1. <u>Praying with power is difficult because of the independent nature of humankind</u>. The creation narrative of Genesis 1 has God creating humankind in His own image; meaning people, male and female, have the license (like the angelic beings) to choose what they will or will not do, whom they will or will not obey. A person can choose to be connected to God by faith or to be disconnected by unbelief and doubt. One can simply choose to do their own thing and live their own life independent from God. Of course, this desire can be prompted and/or nurtured by the worldly influences of education and the culture, but many determine, by their own volition, to live their lives without God's influence. The poem "Invictus" exemplifies this independent nature of humankind.

Out of the night that covers me,
Black as the pit from pole to pole,
I thank whatever gods may be
For my unconquerable soul.
In the fell clutch of circumstance
I have not winced nor cried aloud.
Under the bludgeonings of chance
My head is bloody, but unbowed.
Beyond this place of wrath and tears
Looms but the Horror of the shade,
And yet the menace of the years
Finds and shall find me unafraid.
It matters not how strait the gate,
How charged with punishments the scroll,
I am the master of my fate,
I am the captain of my soul.[36]

Did the author of this poem ever repent of his independence and commit his life to the lordship of Christ? I don't know, and I am not his judge, but the anger underlying the words shout, "I am my own person; I rule myself and make my own decisions; I am subject to no one." Biblical salvation begins with you repenting of the sin of unbelief (cf. John 16:8-9) and surrendering your independence to trust the lordship of Jesus Christ to receive "abundant life" (John 10:10 KJV; see also Romans 10:9-10).

2. <u>Praying with power is difficult because mature prayer warriors have failed to disciple the young</u>. Unfortunately, prayer has been treated like a spiritual discipline the average Christian believes those who are truly born again will learn without help. It's almost unimaginable that as important as prayer is to our spiritual growth and strength to accomplish God's purposes we have not done a better job of training young converts in the rudiments of prayer. This will be dealt with in more detail later, but let me simply outline here some prayer basics:

- *The need to understand the process of being discipled into prayer proficiency.* John, in his first epistle, mentions three groups: fathers, young men, and children (2:12-14). The underlying proposition is that the <u>fathers</u> pour into the <u>young men</u> and the young men and fathers pour into the <u>children</u>. You need to have this understanding and bear this responsibility of teaching those you influence who are younger, whether in age or experience. You may impress someone from a distance, but to impact him you must get close.

- *The need to teach the qualifying criteria to climbing the holy mountain and standing in the holy place (Psalm 24:3-4).* These criteria are (a) clean hands, (b) a pure heart, (c) does not lift up his soul to an idol, and (d) does not swear by what is false.

- *The need to show the importance of praying alongside of a prayer warrior.* An apprentice plumber, for example, cannot become a journeyman plumber without working alongside a journeyman plumber. Even so in the area of prayer proficiency—you need to begin praying with someone who really knows how to pray in faith with power in order to develop that area of spiritual strength in your life.

3. <u>Praying with power is difficult because living by faith and learning to ignore the empirical senses is not easy</u>. Though learning to "live by faith, not by sight" (2 Corinthians 5:7) is not easy, it

is possible. Of course, "not by sight" does not mean you pay no attention to your empirical senses—sight, sound, smell, taste, and touch; the awe of a beautiful multi-colored sunset can still take your breath away, or the smell of fresh cut grass or flowers can still bring delight, or the aroma of delicious food cooking on the stove will still make your mouth water. No, your head is not in the clouds oblivious to the sights, smells, and sounds around you; nor is your ear deaf to the wise counsel of friends in your pursuit of living by faith.

To live or walk by faith has to do primarily with you following the will of God for your life and overcoming those worldly and sometimes demonic influences or obstacles that might delay or distract you. In the process, there will arise challenges where the only solution is one of faith, and you will find yourself forced to pray and seek God and not people. Of course, there will be those situations or trials where you will seek both God and individuals. You may, for example, prayerfully go to the doctor and use the medication prescribed, but that does not mean you are not living by faith; it just means your faith is in God using the doctor or the dentist. Make sense?

But understand, dear friend, there are conditions or circumstances where no doctor, lawyer, banker, or counselor can help you—a circumstance like the one King Jehoshaphat faced when three nations (Ammon, Moab, and Mount Seir) assembled to attack Judah (2 Chronicles 20:1-28). The king, with his people, prayed, "Our God, will you not judge them? For we have no power to face this vast army that is attacking us. We do not know what to do, but our eyes are on you" (2 Chronicles 20:12). This is a prime example of the response of faith. It's where you refuse to allow the circumstances to dictate your response. The king's response was one full of faith, and one fully aware of the devastating threat of the vast army: he gathered the people and prayed. Walking by faith does not mean you don't know or are unaware of the circumstances surrounding you. Yes, sight is there, but you do not let what you see or feel force you into a fearful or negative response. In faith, Jehoshaphat prayed. That's faith in action.

The result of the collective faith of King Jehoshaphat, the men, women, and children of Judah, and those living in Jerusalem was a miraculous victory of deliverance where no Israelite had to fight.

> *[14] The Spirit of the LORD came on Jahaziel...a Levite...as he stood in the assembly. [15] He said: "This is what the LORD says to you: 'Do not be afraid or discouraged because of this vast army. For the battle is not yours, but God's... [17] You will not have to fight this battle. Take up your positions; stand firm and see the deliverance the Lord will give you, Judah and Jerusalem. Do not be afraid; do not be discouraged. Go out to face them tomorrow, and the Lord will be with you.'"* (2 Chronicles 20:14-15, 17, emphasis mine)

Hearing this, the people worshipped, and as they worshipped their enemies were defeated (vv. 22-24). The amazing victory was the result of a collective prayer of faith, a prophetic word, and corporate, exuberant worship.

The apostle Paul would say we overcome while "we fix our eyes not on what is seen, but on what is unseen. For what is seen [physical reality] is temporary, but what is unseen [spiritual reality] is eternal" (2 Corinthians 4:18, emphasis mine). The older, mature believers in my home church would say, "God has never lost a battle, and He can do anything but fail." To that I say, AMEN!

4. Praying with power is difficult because the world makes being spiritual into something weird and undesirable. One of the unfortunate realities is that unsaved people, and even some unspiritual believers, misunderstand the attitude and actions of mature Christians. Charges like "you are too religious" or being branded as ignorant or superstitious are unfair accusations that are being used as tools of the enemy to unsettle mature believers who pray. Do not let this deter you, especially if your faith has achieved a balance and a success that can be seen. Recognize this simple truth: the enemy is angry. It is understandable that no forward-thinking person wants to be branded as unintelligent, ignorant, or superstitious, but

recognize the truth of the words of Jesus, "You will be hated by everyone because of me..." (Matthew 10:22), and, "If the world hates you, keep in mind that it hated me first" (John 15:18).

Having said that, let me also admonish you not to allow the critical attitudes or words of others push you into reacting negatively. Your Christian commitment is to portray the righteousness of the kingdom of God, not to be judgmental or critical of those God has called you to influence and disciple. You are prayerfully to stand for truth and to speak the truth in love (Ephesians 4:15) and let the Holy Spirit do His work. In addition, remember what Jesus taught, "Do not give dogs what is sacred; do not throw your pearls to pigs. If you do, they may trample them under their feet, and turn and tear you to pieces" (Matthew 7:6). The meaning is, do not share your faith stand with everyone; keep your mouth shut if unspiritual believers or unsaved persons are present. Amen?

Finally, another trick of the enemy deserving of mention is the tendency of some believers to become too liberal or too legalistic. Remember, you are saved by grace through faith and *not* by works (Ephesians 2:8-9). Being too liberal will remove you from the Faith that's anchored in biblical truth, and being too legalistic will lead you to add to the basic biblical tenets of salvation issues like dress apparel, adornments, hair styles, etc. that belong in the *non-essential* category.[37] Common sense dictates you cannot scale a fish until you catch it. Your job is to catch them with your love, with wise responses to their questions, and with your productive life. Then, in the process of discipleship, teach the truth of the Word and allow the Lord to remove their scales that would preclude their effective growth and witness.

5. <u>Praying with power is difficult because the enemy confuses the meaning of praying with power</u>. Please understand the spiritual reality that the devil is fighting to keep you ignorant (Hosea 4:6). He does not want you learning how to pray with power, and after reading this book and coming to an understanding of procedural prayer truth, he will do everything in his power to stop you from praying through distractions, interruptions, overcrowded schedules, and the like. But be encouraged and remember what Jesus

said, "Now that you know these things, you will be blessed if you do them" (John 13:17).

Praying with power is for all believers in whatever meaningful occupation they hold. Praying with power means you are someone whose prayers include three necessary ingredients.

- *Praying in line with the will of God.* This includes praying the promises in Scripture. God's words indicate His will just as your words indicate your will. This praying the will of God can also include praying in line with the Spirit's guidance (Romans 8:26-27); guidance based in the principles of Scripture but not necessarily specifically stated. For example, I prayed for a church building using five criteria the Spirit led me to outline: (a) a building large enough to seat 1000 people; (b) a building with a parking lot; (c) a building accessible to public transportation; (d) a building on a main street; and (e) a building in a part of the city where anyone would feel safe. Of course, none of those particulars are spelled out in Scripture, but the Spirit led me in my praying for those criteria, and we received all five.

- *Praying from the position of a committed Christian whose lifestyle is one that includes godly character and holiness.* Jesus taught an important principle: before you can straighten out others, you must first straighten out yourself. Not only do you need to be a Christian, but you also need to exemplify the lifestyle of a committed believer. Notice this word in the Sermon on the Mount,

> [3] *"Why do you look at the speck of sawdust in your brother's eye and pay no attention to the plank in your own eye?* [4] *How can you say to your brother, 'Let me take the speck out of your eye,' when all the time there is a plank in your own eye?* [5] *You hypocrite, first take the plank out of your own eye, and then you will see clearly to remove the speck from your brother's eye."* (Matthew 7:3-5, emphasis mine)

Obvious moral failure will hinder your effective sharing of the truth with others. Additionally, there are those passages that speak against you petitioning God from a position of uncleanness. The psalmist wrote, "If I had cherished sin in my heart, the Lord would not have listened" (Psalm 66:18). And from Psalm 34,

> *[15] The eyes of the LORD are on the righteous, and his ears are attentive to their cry; [16] but the face of the LORD is against those who do evil, to blot out their name from the earth.* (vv. 15-16)

Of course, God hears all prayers, but these passages tell us God will not hear the prayers of the wicked, meaning God will not answer their prayers. And an unrepentant Christian who justifies the practice of wrongdoing through manipulative rationalization also falls into this category.[38]

- *Praying recognizing faith is warfare and may take time to become sight.* As you wait for faith to become sight, your responsibility is to fight the good fight of faith through a good confession (1 Timothy 6:12), and not to become weary in doing good as you wait for your "due season" to manifest (Galatians 6:9 KJV). Remember, to have faith means you believe with all your heart. As you determine to stand upon the solid foundation of the truth of Scripture, the enemy will fight you. Expect this warfare, and gird up the loins of your mind (1 Peter 1:13 KJV) to stand in faith, clothed with the full armor of God (Ephesians 6:10-18), knowing you are more than a conqueror (Romans 8:37-39) because the battle has already been won (Colossians 2:15).

Four Categories of Knowledge

There are four basic categories of knowledge proficiency.

First, there are those who know and know that they know. Everyone falls into this category in some areas of life. You know how to do something and you know that you know and your positive confession of that knowledge is not a matter of arrogance but simply a statement of fact. For example, I know how to operate a motorcycle.

Next, there are those who know but do not know that they know. Most of us also fit into this category. Usually, it has to do with you believing you can't do something until you are forced to try to do it and you succeed. You then move from category two to category one.

Third, there are those who do not know and know they do not know. Every sane person realizes he or she is ignorant in some areas of expertise. You know you cannot fix your television, tune up your car, or program your computer, so you find someone to do those things for you. Then there is category four...

Finally, there are those who do not know and do not know they do not know. These poor mortals make fools of themselves with ignorant statements and actions because the phrase, "I don't know," is not part of their vocabulary.

Unfortunately with respect to praying with power, many believers fall into this fourth category. Since they don't know the specific biblical principles or criteria for prayer proficiency and they think they do know, they go through the motions of shaking the prayer wires or tapping the prayer tubes, hoping to get a picture on their prayer TV without much success. And since their prayer practice is not grounded in solid biblical principles that strengthen their praying in faith, and they continue to do what everyone around them does with little or no results, they console themselves with the thought that this is what prayer practice is in the *normal* Christian life. But while that may be true, you do not have to be like the *normal* Christian who really does not know how to pray. Prayer is not an empty practice where your so-called faith never becomes sight. Praying with power is the right of every mature believer (James 5:16b).

The truth is, the average local Christian church does not have many, if any, prayer warriors who by faith put a demand on the resources of heaven. It's like the account of Jesus on His way to Jairus' house to heal his daughter. The text says,

²⁴...A large crowd followed and pressed around him. ²⁵And a woman was there who had been subject to bleeding for twelve years. ... ²⁷When she heard about Jesus, she came up behind him in the crowd and touched his cloak. ... ²⁹Immediately her bleeding stopped and she felt in her body that she was freed from her suffering. ³⁰At once Jesus realized that power had gone out from him. He turned around in the crowd and asked, "Who touched my clothes?" (Mark 5:24-30)

The incredulity of the disciples at Jesus's question (v. 31) is because everyone was touching Him. But the woman in question touched Him differently—her touch was one of *faith*. Her touch put a demand on His ability to heal her. *Father, teach us how to touch You in faith with our prayers, in Jesus's name. Amen.*

CHAPTER ELEVEN

WHY DO I PRAY IN THE EARLY MORNING?

Introduction

A GREAT CLOUD OF WITNESSES, THOSE COMMENDED FOR THEIR FAITH, surround you (Hebrews 12:1), and their memory should encourage you in two ways: (1) you can persevere and achieve by faith because they did; and (2) you are connected to them because they are made perfect as some of the promises made to them are or will be fulfilled in you (Hebrews 11:39-40). It's important that you see your connection to salvation history, the truth that predecessor saints who are with the Lord are actually fulfilled by your success. Your success is dependent upon a strong prayer life that brings revelation knowledge, strengthening your faith to minister more effectively to those around you.

Your faithfulness in prayer also strengthens your confidence in your vertical relationship with the Father, and at the same time, when you agree in prayer with a partner, it strengthens your horizontal relationship with them. Agreement-praying can create what I call a prayer-mode attitude, where even though the season of prayer has ended, you still have a spirit of prayer throughout the day so that when a need arises, you are always ready in your prayer-mode to cry out to the Father. This is what the apostle meant when he exhorted the saints to "pray continually" (1 Thessalonians 5:17).

Hebrews 12:1 exhorts every believer to "run with persever-ance the race[39] marked out for us." Never stop running your race! Don't be distracted or detoured from your course. Keep praying and keep running even when you don't understand all that the Lord is doing to lead you. Grab hold of believing faith and let it spur you on to a greater level of faithfulness in praying and serving. There are some things you will not understand until you get to the other side, but please know you are connected to the "great cloud of witnesses" who have finished running their earthly course and are now in the grandstand, prayerfully cheering you on to victory. Stay in prayer-mode, practicing the presence of God, standing in faith, and experiencing God's promises for yourself and others as you rise early to pray.

The Copycat Reason

This first reason for praying in the early morning takes into account the biblical teaching that serious believers prayed in the early morning; you should purpose to pray like they prayed (see, for example, Psalm 63:1 KJV; Proverbs 8:17 KJV; Isaiah 26:9; Mark 1:35).

Could it be that the sages and prophets of old knew something about prayer you don't? Many fail to pray effectively. This is true. But is it possible that some of your failure is time-related? Should your prayer time compete with work, eating, or socializing? Surely Jesus exhorted, "Seek ye first the kingdom of God" (Matthew 6:33 KJV). Is He implying you should prioritize prayer in your daily schedules?

"Make time!"

While struggling to *find* time to pray, I heard the Lord say, "Make time." To *find time* means securing some time in between other important events. The problem with prioritizing worldly responsibilities above prayer is that those responsibilities, regard-less of how important they are, tend to squeeze your time for prayer into virtually... no time.

To *make* time means that prayer is prioritized as an important event, and instead of trying to *fit* it into your busy schedule, make the other important events fit into your prayer schedule. That's how you *make* time. A leader once told me that early-morning-prayer threw off his day. His mornings began with aerobic and anaerobic activities and prayer was an unscheduled interruption. Well, of course I understand the importance of physical exercise and being "in shape," but to place its importance above prayer is to misunderstand the real source of your power, and as quiet as it is kept, physical health is not the source of the power you need.

Clearly, you make time for what you want to do. My contention is that prayer time should be on the schedule and not relegated to when you find time. Why not set a time when nothing else is happening? For most of us, that time is early morning. Jesus was busier than any two executives put together, yet He made time to pray. If He had to pray during His earthly ministry, and He was (and is) the Son of God, you have to pray. Jesus prayed early in the morning (Mark 1:35). When do you pray? Of course, I'm not saying that prayer must be early in the morning in order to be effective. At times Jesus prayed at night—sometimes all night—but early-morning prayer has advantages.

The Watch-winding Reason

Understanding this aspect is difficult for the younger generations who have never known of wristwatches without batteries, but in generations past, most if not all wristwatches were wound, and the tension of a spring ran the watch, not a battery. By winding it in the morning, the spring was tight making the inner workings of the watch less susceptible to damage during the normal bumps or jolts of the day. Prayer serves to wind your spiritual wristwatch, making it tight to withstand the various "bumps" of your day, and those unexpected difficulties don't upset you because the strength of your early-morning-prayer life has tightened your spiritual spring.

Recently, while encouraging believers in my fellowship to adopt an early-morning-prayer habit, I coined the phrase "prayer DNA." The apostle Paul exhorted the church in Thessalonica that praying continually is a part of God's will for believers in Christ Jesus (1 Thessalonians 5:16-18). Most believers would consider the exhortation to "pray continually" undoable in this modern world. In fact, pastors have said to me, "Praying continually is unrealistic given my ministry responsibilities and schedule." But I'm saying you should not misunderstand the apostle's meaning. Paul is not teaching you to spend every waking hour on your knees. You "pray continually" within the context of worship. You start your day in God's presence by winding your spiritual prayer-watch early in the morning. As you faithfully prioritize prayer in the mornings, you will develop a prayer DNA where praying becomes a part of who you are and what you regularly do, and you will grow into praying continually. Of course, this growth does not happen overnight and there are no shortcuts, but when you understand the miracle of worship and you start your day with it, miraculous power and guidance are released.

The psalmist said, "Yet You are holy, O You who are enthroned upon the praises of Israel" (Psalm 22:3 NASB). As your day begins with praise where the presence of God is invoked, according to the Psalm, His presence is "enthroned," meaning He comes with authority to rule in your circumstances. In a very practical sense, you are practicing the presence of God in your spirit, and it matters not where you are or what you are doing. Various events may take place around you and you may work under intense pressure, but when you start your day by setting your heart to seek the Lord in worship and praise, the songs of His glory can fill your heart, translating into continual prayer, relieving the pressure, and depositing peace.

The psalmist called this a "path of life" in Psalm 16:11; the revelation of this path begins with worship, bringing you into God's presence where there "...is fullness of joy" (NASB). Paul taught there is a glorious, transforming strength released in His presence (2 Corinthians 3:18), and Nehemiah taught the joy of the LORD produces strength (Nehemiah 8:10). Doubtless, Nehemiah understood the benefit of rejoicing before the LORD in everything you put your hands to do (Deuteronomy 12:18). This is the attitude the believer needs to adopt in order to pray continually. Where the joy of the Lord enables you to meditate upon the law of the Lord day and night (Psalm 1:2), where you make melody in your heart to the Lord with psalms, hymns, and spiritual songs (Ephesians 5:19), and where you remain in an attitude of worship and prayer throughout your day beginning early morning. The psalmist ends Psalm 16:11, "...with eternal pleasures at your right hand" (NIV). In New Testament terminology, Christ is seated at the Father's right hand (Ephesians 1:20) and since we are "in Christ" (Ephesians 2:6), we are seated at the Father's right hand. Thus the "eternal pleasures" translate into the joyful experience of doing the will of God. This joy in His presence strengthens you to do His will, resulting in a pleasure, a fullness of life, an achievement of purpose and destiny related to beginning your day with early-morning prayer. Praying continually is achievable. Begin by winding your worship and prayer-watch early.

> Sow a belief, you reap a thought;
> sow a thought, you reap a confession, a prayer;
> sow that confession, that prayer, you reap an agreement;
> sow that agreement, you reap a habit;
> sow that habit, you reap a DNA;
> sow that DNA, you reap a destiny.

The Firstfruits Reason

This reason says the first hours of the day are the best. It follows the firstfruits reasoning: the children of Israel gave a firstfruits offering, the firstfruits of the harvest (Exodus 23:16). The tithe is supposed to be the firstfruits of your income, not the dregs of what's left over. In other words, the tithe on $100 is not just $10, but the *first* $10. In the same way, giving God the beginning of your day is different from giving Him the end; it says you prioritize your relationship with Him to seek His presence early, rather than late. Will God accept whatever time you give Him? Of course, but the beginning time is when you are most alert and fresh, when you are at your best. That's what "firstfruits" is all about—giving God your best. It's what Stephen Covey calls Quadrant Two thinking.

Quadrant Two Thinking[40]

Prayer is a Quadrant Two event. In the book by Stephen Covey, *First Things First*, he divides up the things you do into four areas or quadrants:

1. **IMPORTANT** **and** **URGENT**	**2.** **IMPORTANT** **but** **NOT URGENT**
3. **NOT IMPORTANT** **but** **URGENT**	**4.** **NOT IMPORTANT** **and** **NOT URGENT**

Stephen Covey's Four Quadrants
Figure 2.

All of us are strongly influenced by the call of urgent things. They have a sort of emergency ring to them demanding our immediate attention. In quadrant thinking, urgent things fall into two categories: important and not important. Of course you must do the urgent and important things as soon as possible.

Necessity requires your diligence in properly handling with care those important emergencies, however the urgent but not important things, that's another story. Those things may be important to someone else, but not to you. You may need to learn that "no" is a success word. You may also need to learn how to delegate to others what is urgent but not important for you to do.

Also, all of us, because of the weakness of our flesh, are strongly influenced to spend time in the quadrant labeled: NOT important and NOT urgent. This is where you "chill;" where you may pass the time with television or an interesting novel. You're not doing anything productive, just, as they say, "maxing and relaxing."

But the area most often neglected is Quadrant Two; the area where important, vital things need our attention and time, but they are not urgent or pressing. To do them, however, will necessitate a discipline found only in what is called "Quadrant Two thinking." This is the thinking of one who plans and prepares to be used in the future. It is the disciplined thinking of one who knows most of the problems of tomorrow find their solutions in the preparation of today. Quadrant Two thinkers are aware it is necessary they discipline themselves to do the not urgent important things in preparation for seeing their dreams become reality. For example: a leadership retreat, devotional reading of the Bible, a brain-storming session with the heads of every department in the firm, an appreciation luncheon for those who worked behind the scenes on an important project, etc. The practice of these kinds of things with this kind of thinking actually prepares you to do other things better. Praying in still moments and hours of the morning falls into this area of *important but not urgent.*

The No Distraction Reason

This reason comes from the understanding that most people are asleep in the very early morning hours. Praying later in the day or evening can mean competing with the telephone, unexpected visitors, and common urgencies. There is a stillness in the early morning hours that's special and sacred. The LORD sought to teach Israel to seek sustenance from Him in the early morning hours. This is the meaning of the manna. This bread provided by God was to be gathered in the morning before the heat of the sun melted it (Exodus 16:21). Later, in the commentary of the Exodus account in Deuteronomy, we are told the lesson being taught, "He humbled you, causing you to hunger and then feeding you with manna, which neither you nor your ancestors had known, to **teach you** that man does not live on bread alone but on every word that comes from the mouth of the LORD" (Deuteronomy 8:3, emphasis mine). To prioritize seeking the Lord's face in early morning hours sets you apart from those who pray later in the day. In obedience to the implication of the word about the "manna," we find strength to survive and prosper. The psalmist and Isaiah knew of it (Psalm 63:1 KJV; Isaiah 26:9 KJV), of course Jesus knew of it (Mark 1:35), and the song poet knew of it:

> I come to the garden alone
> While the dew is still on the roses
> And the voice I hear falling on my ear
> The Son of God discloses.
> And He walks with me and He talks with me
> And He tells me I am His own
> And the joy we share as we tarry there
> None other has ever known.[41]

Rising early to pray when there are no distractions, "while the dew is still on the roses," before the sun creeps over the eastern sky; going alone to the garden to pray becomes a "joy" that brings strength (Nehemiah 8:10) because the Lord meets him there, and speaks to him as they walk together in the garden. It's Early Morning Prayer (EMP) at its best.

The Best-Smartest-Most-Alert-Hours-of-the-Day Reason

This reason recognizes early morning as the best time to make an appointment with God because you are your smartest, your mind is alert making you more receptive than at any other time of the day. Why shouldn't you take advantage of all those positive strengths? Why wait until mid-morning when your body is completing the digestion of breakfast or working hard to prepare for lunch? Being burdened with the pressures of the decisions your day's activities require, or concerned about the prospective opportunities presented by the current events can distract you from an unhindered prayer focus. In the process you're aware that while prayer is always appropriate, it would have been better if you'd sought the Lord early with worship, fellowship with Him, and intercession as your focus. His strength prepares you better for the pressures of the day when you seek Him early.

Do you believe God can prepare you for your day? Of course your answer is "yes," and I believe it is the reason wise men and women of old prayed in the early morning hours. Daniel prayed three times a day and was always prepared for the trying events of his day. The prayer lives of men like Martin Luther, John Wesley, George Whitfield, George Mueller, and Hudson Taylor all testify of the wisdom of revelation received in prayer while their minds were at their sharpest.

Some of you are so intelligent, even at times when you are tired and slow you are still faster than the rest of us. But is that an adequate excuse? Sounds like the man who praised his uncle who lived to be a nonagenarian smoking two packs of cigarettes and drinking a fifth of hard liquor daily. My response was, "Well, how long could he have lived if he'd taken better care of his obviously strong body?" Life is full of exceptions that violate the rules. Wisdom says you don't use the exceptions to excuse stupid decisions. Can you be a strong Christian without having a strong scheduled prayer time? Of course it's possible, but my sense is you'd be the exception, not the rule. The evidence of Scripture is that the men and women of God in both testaments distinguished themselves by the time they spent in prayer. That's the rule. Can you build a strong church without teaching your people to pray? I doubt it, but maybe you are counting on being the exception, not the rule. Can you achieve abundant life success that's spiritual, physical, relational, and financial without prayer? Again, I doubt it, but again, maybe you're hoping on being one of the exceptions, not the rule.

In one of my early-morning best-smartest-most-alert-hours-of-the-day prayer times, I heard the Lord say, "Son, when you pray, you open a door for Me to work behind the scenes in your life." I rejoiced at this revelation pulling me into being more prayerful around issues confronting me, members of my family, leaders and members in my church, etc. In the midst of my rejoicing, I heard Him speak again, "And when you don't pray, you open a door for the enemy to work behind the scenes in your life." Frankly, that was a scary thought for me. I've not always been a prayer warrior.

There were those seasons when I was trying to get to a level of prayer consistency and proficiency and much of my prayer time was spent crying out of my failure rather than establishing in faith the dominion of His kingdom by the authority of His Word.

Prayers prayed from a position of weakness are different than prayers prayed from a position of strength. I've wondered how my life has been influenced by my own prayerlessness, and what doors were opened in my life because of it. I thank the Lord for His perseverance with me and now rejoice over this mature place of prayer effectiveness the Spirit has led me to see. The Lord ended by saying, "It is up to you which door you want opened." Let us pray:

> Father, You have opened my eyes to see the advantageous truth of Early Morning Prayer, and I am grateful. From this moment, I determine my gratitude will know no bounds in the prayer effectiveness of demolishing demonic strongholds to rescue the bound and the lost. Because of Your guidance, I now rejoice in a confident strength of knowing who I am in Christ, what I have as an heir of God, and what I am called to do for Your glory as one who prays. Thank you Lord in the name of Jesus. Amen.

THE WHO OF PRAYER

Considering the matter of qualifications

CHAPTER TWELVE

WHO QUALIFIES TO PRAY EFFECTIVELY?

Those Committed to Godly Character

DO YOU HAVE A PROBLEM WITH THE WORD QUALIFIES? WELL, YOU shouldn't. It is used to indicate there's a difference between the prayer of a sinner, the prayer of a "lukewarm" believer, and the prayers of mature believers who know how to pray. Of course God hears and is fully aware of all prayers, but the major difference is *faith*. When a sinner believes the gospel of the death, burial, and resurrection of Christ (1 Corinthians 15:1-4), repents, and confesses the lordship of Christ over his life (Romans 10:9), God hears his prayer and saves him.

However, the expectation of the Father is that this newborn *child* in the kingdom will grow in grace and in the knowledge of Christ (2 Peter 3:18). When he does not grow, over time he becomes a "lukewarm" Christian (Revelation 3:16), one who exercised faith to be saved but who has little or no faith to do anything else. God saves you to use you to help save others (Matthew 28:19-20; John 20:21). These words spoken by Christ to His disciples are also for you and me. In essence, the Lord is saying, "I will not do this work of winning and discipling the world without you, and you cannot do this work without Me." There's an old Holiness Christian expression I remembered hearing in church,

It is faith alone that saves,
but that faith that saves is not alone.

As a new convert, I understood the meaning to be that if you are really saved, you will live right. But another interpretation of the phrase is the influence others have on your initial faith and growth. The "faith that saves is not alone" means the faith you received came through a mature believer's faithful lifestyle and witness.

The Influence of Godly Authority

You must not treat lightly the matter of *influence*. In large measure you are who you are because of the influence you received during your formative years, and it's unfortunate that this works in both positive and negative ways. This influence in many respects is subliminal, meaning that without knowing it you were being shaped by the surroundings and atmosphere created by the person(s) who raised you during your formative years. Of course, those who influenced you may not have been persons you should emulate, and hopefully, for God's sake, you had some additional people in your life whose influence was positive.

Parents

While faith comes into play in all circumstances of prayer, there are instances where the faith of the one praying can override the lack of faith of the one receiving. This is especially true in the nuclear family where saved parents provide a faith covering in prayer over the lives of their submitted children. Children born into the Christian home of parents who are mature believers follow the teaching of Proverbs 22:6, "Train up a child in the way he should go, even when he is old, he will not depart from it" (NASB).

Training includes teaching them: to repent and believe the gospel, to honor and obey the truth of the Scriptures, to pray, to walk in forgiveness, to love, and to honor their parents and elders. With the proper perimeters of love, balance, and discipline in place, parents need not fear raising children who love the Lord, walk in righteousness, and are saved; these parents believe the truth of Acts 16:31, "They replied, 'Believe in the Lord Jesus, and you will be saved—you <u>and your household</u>'" (emphasis mine).

The Compliment of a Friend

Some years ago when all of our eight children were young and living at home with us, we entertained a visit from my best friend from high school. We both majored in three sports during our high school matriculation and were very close. After I received Christ a few months following graduation, my first outreach was to my friend by inviting him to my church; my hope was that the same truth that gripped me would grip him, but it didn't happen. He traveled from Philadelphia to visit me in my home in Boston where I'd been a senior pastor for about 15 years. During our visit and sharing together for several hours, he articulated his assessment of my parenting style. He said, "It's plain to see that you have brainwashed your children."

Of course I understood he meant his assessment as a criticism of my parenting, but I decided to counteract his criticism by treating it as a compliment, "Hey man, thank you for your wise insight into what Yvonne and I agreed to do with our children." I then continued by saying, "I'm glad you recognize that this world is no friend to families and is especially destructive to the lives of the young, and that Yvonne and I are busy trying to insulate our children against the deceptive practices and images of the world." In conclusion, as he was in the process of leaving I asked, "Is it your belief that our world is neutral and that the evils of our world are not doing everything they can to corral the young into their web of wicked practices with the intent of gaining their adherence?" He offered no response to my question, and years later when I visited him in Philadelphia he was living alone in a rooming house, stoned on heroin.

Pastors

Anyone with an ounce of discernment can see the demonic plan at work in our world—lowering morals, redefining marriage and family, so-called politically correct thinking, drug and alcohol addiction, sexual addiction and perversion, the proliferation of pornography and violence, and corruption at almost every level of society all over the world, etc. It is a plan to lead the younger, unsuspecting generations into a future without God or faith. Into that spiritual conflict God has placed the *family* of godly fathers and mothers teaching their children by precept and example (Deuteronomy 6:4-9), and the *church* of mature believers, Sunday school teachers, and pastors as spiritual guides called to counteract the lies of the world with the truth of the gospel.

The major, most time-consuming job of the pastor is to pray, study the Word, and prepare to minister in the pulpit and to individuals. He preaches, counsels, and encourages those who are under his watchful care with the view of preparing them to win and disciple others. Along with the sacerdotal functions of baptism and communion, he has the extremely important responsibility of discerning and discipling the ones under him who are called of God to pastor. All this must be balanced with the responsibilities of being a husband, father, community leader, and good citizen. And while the call of the pastor is important, it must not take precedence over the responsibilities of his personal life and wellbeing and the oversight and care of his family.

Many pastors do not prioritize their work in their parish above their work in the community. While the social and even the political work of the community deserve the pastor's attention, they should not be prioritized above the major work in the church God has called him to pastor. The pastor is the major professional in the local church who is called of God to equip the believers to do ministry. The words of the apostle Paul in Ephesians bring this call to responsibility to center stage,

> [11] *It was he who gave some to be apostles, some to be prophets, some to be evangelists, and some to be pastors and teachers,* [12] *to prepare God's people for works of service, so that the body of Christ may be built up* [13] *until we all reach unity in the faith and in the knowledge of the Son of God and become mature, attaining to the whole measure of the fullness of Christ.* (Ephesians 4:11-13)

The Need for Faithful Examples

Let's not forget the illustrative words of Jesus in the Sermon on the Mount that we quoted earlier in the book. It is at best foolish, or at worst hypocritical, for you to think you can get the speck of sawdust out of your brother's eye while at the same time you have a plank of wood sticking out of your own eye (Matthew 7:3-5). Thus, being an example others can see qualifies you to be someone others will listen to. Don't be guilty of exhorting a group of friends to be faithful in paying their debts when you owe someone in the group money that is long overdue. God's expectation is truth will be heard not only from the words of your mouth but also more importantly from the words emanating from your life (1 John 3:18).

In this matter of a need for faithful examples, God expects you to be a prayer example worth following. Now we come to the full treatment of Psalm 24:3-4, briefly mentioned earlier and addressed in greater detail here.

> *³ Who may ascend the hill of the LORD? Who may stand in his holy place? ⁴ He who has clean hands and a pure heart, who does not trust in an idol or swear by what is false.*

Notice the outline of the two verses is simple: the question, and the answer. The question (v. 3) asks who is qualified to "ascend the hill of the LORD" and "stand in his holy place?"— i.e. who qualifies to be a spiritual priest, one who intercedes in prayer for others? The answer (v. 4) outlines four expectations of a spiritual priest God uses.

1. Clean hands. Someone who is effective in praying for others must have "clean hands," i.e. outward observable righteousness. Many Christians pray without the success of God's intervention into their circumstances because there is some unrighteous act (perhaps even more than one) that's blocking the path to their faith access (Romans 5:2). Don't get me wrong, I'm not encouraging you to go on a witch-hunt for some sin you are unaware of committing. That's the accusation of the enemy. No, this is something

that you know full well what it is, and the guilt you ignore is hindering you from taking a faith stand against the wrong to make it right. The psalmist wrote, "If I had cherished sin in my heart, the Lord would not have listened" (Psalm 66:18). And John wrote, "If we claim to have fellowship with him yet walk in the darkness, we lie and do not live out the truth" (1 John 1:6). A believer whose prayers are answered is one walking free from guilt and walking in *fellowship* with the Father.

2. <u>Pure heart</u>. God expects someone who seeks to be effective in prayer for others to have a pure heart; a righteous, faith-based relationship with Him. Remember when Samuel went to the house of Jesse to anoint one of his sons to become the next king of Israel:

> *⁶ Samuel saw* [the eldest son] *Eliab and thought, "Surely the LORD's anointed stands here before the LORD." ⁷ But the LORD said to Samuel, "Do not consider his appearance or his height, for I have rejected him. The LORD does not look at the things people look at. People look at the outward appearance, but <u>the LORD looks at the heart</u>."* (1 Samuel 16:6-7, emphasis mine)

People can put on a Christian appearance like a garment and act in a spiritual way in church, convincing many of their sincere relationship with Christ. But the real story is the Lord's judgment that cannot be fooled by outward acts and appearances. The Lord judges the genuine spiritual state of their heart. There is a centuries-old adage,

> You can fool all of the people some of the time
> and some of the people all of the time,
> but you cannot fool all of the people all of the time.

I add to that statement, you cannot fool God any of the time. That's because God can look at your heart. God's expectation for one who stands in the place of a spiritual priest to intercede in prayer for others is that their heart is pure and in right standing with God.

3. <u>Does not trust in an idol</u>. God expects His spiritual priests to prioritize their relationship with Him. The first of the Ten Commandments is, "You shall have no other gods before me" (Exodus 20:3). This should not only include the gods represented by idols from other world religions, but also prioritizing a personal relationship, a practice, a business, an investment portfolio, money, property, or social position above God and His kingdom can be considered *idolatrous*. Priority is key! In New Testament terms, this would mean to seek *first*[42] God's kingdom and His righteousness. The resulting truth is that whatever you place above God can bring you into an idolatrous state where the effectiveness of your prayers will be hindered.

4. <u>Does not swear by what is false</u>. Not swearing falsely says that you are a person whose character is above reproach. Such a person could be described by words like integrous, honest, truthful, trustworthy, just, fair, and righteous.

Finally, you must see these four criteria as prerequisites for the ministry of a spiritual priest—those who intercede in prayer on behalf of others. Their confident faith is strong because they know they have qualified themselves by their determined discipline to adhere to these criteria in order to be an effective spiritual priest in their prayer life. A major cry of their heart is, "Here am I; use me!"

Who Qualifies?

It may be that some of you view these criteria as insurmountable obstacles to prayer proficiency. You may even be saying to yourself, "Given how far I have to go and how much I need to change, this will take me forever." But let me encourage you with a simple truism spoken by Dr. Edwin Louis Cole, the founder of the Christian Men's Network Worldwide.

> Change is not change until it is change! ... Men can think about change, pray about change, promise to change, imagine what change is like, decide to change, but it's never change until it is change. Too many men give themselves credit for their intentions

but not their actions. They judge others for their actions, but themselves for their intentions.[43]

Let me encourage you dear friend; you can begin to make change part of your reality!

Start by Strengthening your Change Muscle

1. <u>Change who you spend time with</u>. While negative, world-ly-minded people may be in your life, determine to limit the time you spend with them, and decide to maximize the fellowship you need to have with believers.

2. <u>Change what you read</u>. Discard all pornographic books, pictures, tapes, and discs; delete all pornographic websites; establish an accountability relationship with a mature believer whom you ask to question you regularly about what you are reading or watching.

3. <u>Change what you do during the first moments of your day</u>. As you dress to prepare yourself for your day, change from listening to the news (television, radio, iPad), to listening to worship songs and music. Instead of reading the paper, get up early enough to have a 15-30 minute time with the Lord: pray, read your Bible, and review the verses you are memorizing (if you're not memorizing any verses, start today[44]).

4. <u>Change what you do on your weekend nights (Fridays and Saturdays)</u>. Instead of spending time and money attending some club or party with non-spiritual friends, plan to visit with some believers who may be gathering for Christian fellowship. As a new convert, I found there were always homes, usually where a young married couple in our church lived, and several of us would gather with them around food, fellowship, and fun. Those informal times of fellowship with each other not only strengthened our relationship with other growing believers, but it helped maintain a sense of accountability. We always knew where everyone was. No one could slip away into the practice of darkness without the group making a concerted effort to pull him or her back into the light. And it enriched the Sunday church fellowship because we were together

in church and ended singing hymns together and discussing the pastor's sermon.

These are just four simple changes you can make to hasten developing the attitude and spirit of the mature, strong believer you recognize and admire in others. Let us pray.

> Father, thank You for the unseen support You are providing for these who are growing in the grace and knowledge of prayer proficiency. I stand with them as they venture forward with a sincere heart to put the truths they are learning into practice. I bind the enemy that would seek to hinder their progress toward being the prayer warrior You will for them to be and their family and friends need for them to be. Encourage their hearts, I pray, as they continue to run with perseverance this prayer race, in Jesus's name. Amen.

CHAPTER THIRTEEN

WHO ARE THOSE COMMITTED TO KNOWING THE WORD?

Knowledge of the Word

LET'S LOOK AT THE PRAYER IMPORTANCE OF YOU BEING SOMEONE WHO knows the Word, or as I have often said, "is Worded." There is no substitute for knowing the Scriptures, and there is no better way of gaining a superior knowledge of biblical truth than through study that includes memorization. Some of this is covered in the teaching of Chapter 4 of this book. Remember the five fingers illustration from Navigators with the words *hear, read, study, memorize,* and *meditate* written on the fingers grasping a Bible? While that presentation was thorough enough for you to gain a basic grasp of the Word, in this chapter, you will learn the importance of studying the Scriptures *theologically.*

The Theological Knowledge of the Word

Gaining a deeper theological understanding of the Word will strengthen your faith and your effectiveness in prayer. Becoming a prayer warrior whose prayers are honored by God and feared by the devil will require discipline in the theological study of Scripture. In this section, we will only summarize each doctrine, but my recommendation is that you go further on your own to strengthen your mastery of these major doctrines.[45] We will consider the seven doctrines of the faith in this order:

1. Theology   –   The Doctrine of God
2. Christology   –   The Doctrine of the Person of Christ
3. Soteriology   –   The Doctrine of Salvation
4. Pneumatology –   The Doctrine of the Holy Spirit
5. Anthropology –   The Doctrine of Humankind
6. Ecclesiology   –   The Doctrine of the Church
7. Eschatology   –   The Doctrine of Last Things

Studying the Scriptures theologically will give you a better grasp of the teachings or doctrines of the Bible, and that grasp will enhance your teaching ability. Remember what Paul wrote to Timothy, "Watch your life and doctrine closely. Persevere in them, because if you do, you will save both yourself and your hearers" (1 Timothy 4:16).

1. The Doctrine of God. (Theology) The Scriptures presuppose the existence of God (Genesis 1:1), and they teach it is possible to know God (1 Corinthians 2:9-14) because God has revealed Himself in three major ways: (1) In creation (Psalm 19; Acts 14:17; Romans 1:19-20); (2) In the Scriptures (Psalm 103:7); and, (3) In the Lord Jesus Christ (John 1:18; Hebrews 1:1-2). The Scriptures teach it is foolish to doubt God's existence or to refuse to believe God has a right to your allegiance (Psalm 14:1). At issue in this is the necessity of *faith*. According to Hebrews 11:6, both faith and believing are connected to your ability to connect and commit to God. Those who refuse are at risk, according to the teaching of Scripture.

2. The Doctrine of the Person of Christ. (Christology) The Scriptures teach that Jesus of Nazareth was and is God (John 1:1), the Creator (John 1:3; Colossians 1:16-17; Hebrews 1:1-2). On several occasions, Jesus received worship from men (Matthew 14:32-33; 28:9, 17; Luke 24:52; John 9:35-38) and God instructed the angels to worship Him (Hebrews 1:6). Jesus is called the Son of God (Matthews 16:16), the great God and Savior (Titus 2:13), the

mighty God and everlasting Father (Isaiah 9:6-7), and the Almighty (Revelation 1:8).

3. The Doctrine of the Work of Christ. (Soteriology) The Scriptures teach that God loves the world of mankind and sent Jesus to be the atoning sacrifice (Savior) for our sins, and He offers eternal salvation as a gift to all who believe (John 3:16-17; Titus 2:11; 1 John 2:1-2). Those who receive Christ and the gift of salvation (John 1:12; Romans 6:23) are all who exercise faith and believe (Ephesians 2:8-9). The proof their saving faith is genuine is that the Holy Spirit baptizes them into the Body of Christ, the Church (1 Corinthians 12:13), and by the power of the gospel, they begin to walk in righteousness by faith from first to last, from beginning to ending (Romans 1:16-17). Salvation is the hope of the righteous.

4. The Doctrine of the Holy Spirit. (Pneumatology) The Scriptures teach the Holy Spirit is the third person to the Godhead we call the Trinity (2 Corinthians 13:14). The Holy Spirit is a person, not a force. He speaks (Acts 28:25), teaches (John 14:26), intercedes for us according to the will of God (Romans 8:26-27), can be grieved (Isaiah 63:10; Ephesians 4:30), and resisted (Acts 7:51). All of these are attributes of personality. The Holy Spirit is God. He possesses the attributes of deity: He is called God (Acts 5:3-4; John 1:12-13; compare with 3:6-8); He is eternal (Hebrews 9:14), omnipotent (Luke 1:35), omniscient (1 Corinthians 2:10-11), and omnipresent (Psalm 139:7-13); He is creator (Genesis 1:2), sovereign (1 Corinthians 12:6, 11), and He imparts the new birth and baptizes new believers into the Body of Christ (John 3:3, 8; 1 Corinthians 12:13).

5. The Doctrine of Humankind. (Anthropology) The Scriptures teach God created two people in His image, after His likeness, male and female (Genesis 1:26-27), and placed them in a garden called Eden. The origin of sin in the human race, called "The Fall" (Genesis 3), was committed by Adam and Eve in the Garden of Eden and resulted in a fourfold curse (Genesis 3:14-19): (a) the serpent (v. 14), (b) the woman (v. 16), (c) the man (vv. 17-19); and (d) the ground (vv. 17b-18). In the midst of the catastrophic drama created by the fall, God predicted the victory of a man over the serpent's

progeny as there being enmity between the seed of the serpent and the seed of the woman (Genesis 3:15). The seed of the woman crushes the serpent's head and the serpent bruises His heel. This prophecy is the first biblical prediction of the coming Messiah, the anointed One who would triumph over Satan. The New Testament book of Hebrews contains a passage that summarizes perfectly the how and why of the mission of Christ (the Messiah):

> [14] *Since the children have flesh and blood, he too shared in their humanity so that by death he might destroy him who holds the power of death—that is, the devil—* [15] *and free those who all their lives were held in slavery by their fear of death.* [16] *For surely it is not angels he helps, but Abraham's descendants.* (Hebrews 2:14-16)

Consider also Paul's teaching about the "disarming" of the devil and making him an open spectacle by the cross (Colossians 2:15) and the victory through suffering Christ achieved over the devil in the messianic prophecy of Isaiah 53.

6. The Doctrine of the Church. (Ecclesiology) The Scriptures teach the Church, the called out ones,[46] the Body of Christ (1 Corinthians 12:27), the redeemed, just to mention a few of the names, is being built by Christ. The primary mission of Jesus was to give His life as a ransom for many (Matthew 20:28), and concomitant with that mission was the incarnation, the Word being made human flesh, the Christ, the anointed One. So He began His ministry in Nazareth where He grew up by reading from the prophecy of Isaiah in the synagogue on the Sabbath,

> [18] *The Spirit of the Lord is on me, because he has anointed me to preach good news to the poor. He has sent me to proclaim freedom for the prisoners and recovery of sight for the blind, to release the oppressed,* [19] *to proclaim the year of the Lord's favor.* (Luke 4:18-19; cf. Isaiah 61:1-2a)

After reading that prophetic passage, Jesus then announced, "Today this Scripture is fulfilled in your hearing" (Luke 4:21), and for the next three-plus years He preached good news to the poor, healed the sick, cleansed the lepers, cast out demons, raised the dead, and in the process trained twelve disciples. It was in one of their times with Him that He questioned, "Who do you say I am?" and Simon Peter answered, "You are the Christ, the Son of the living God" (Matthews 16:13-20, esp. vv. 15-16).

After Peter's confession, Jesus told His disciples, "On this rock I will build my **church**, and the gates of Hades will not overcome it" (v. 18, emphasis mine). This is the first of only three places in the Gospels where the word *church* is used. The "rock" upon which the church is built is the revelation that Jesus of Nazareth is the Christ, the Son of the living God. After His crucifixion and resurrection, the disciples were commissioned to, "Go and make disciples of all nations..." (Matthews 28:19); approximately 120 of them (Acts 1:15) waited for the promise of the Father (Acts 1:4-5), and on the day of Pentecost they were all together in an upper room and were filled with the Holy Spirit (Acts 2:1-4). From that initial, explosive, supernatural event, the Church was birthed with about 3000 being added to their number that day (cf. Acts 2:1-41).

7. <u>The Doctrine of Last Things</u>. (Eschatology) The Scriptures teach the Second Coming of Jesus (John 14:3; Acts 1:10-11; 1 Thessalonians 4:15-5:11; Titus 2:12; Hebrews 9:28; Revelation 1:7) as a single event, and the General Resurrection of the dead as a single event (Daniel 12:2; John 5:28-29; Acts 24:15) to take place on the last day (John 6:39, 40, 44, 54; 11:24). Jesus descends with clouds on the last day, the resurrection of the righteous and the wicked occurs on the last day, judgment is made on the last day, and eternity begins. The song poet James Hill in 1955 wrote,

What a day that will be when my Jesus I shall see,
And I look upon his face,
The One who saved me by his grace;
When He takes me by the hand,
And leads me through the Promised Land,
What a day, glorious day that will be.

There'll be no sorrow there, no more burdens to bear,
No more sickness, no more pain, no more parting over there,
But forever I will be with the One who died for me,
What a day, glorious day that will be.[47]

The importance of having a systematic theological under-standing of the major doctrines of the Scriptures should not be minimized. I've actually been in church services where speakers have castigated doctrinal preaching saying, "I'm not here to preach doctrine; I'm here to preach the Word." But you cannot preach the Word without teaching something from the Scriptures. A doctrine is simply a *teaching* from Scripture. I understand that those preachers were probably trying to say that they were not there to bring about some sort of doctrinal controversy, but if you are the pastor or you have been invited by the pastor of the church to preach, the expec-tation is that you will preach that which pertains to sound doctrine. But by all means, let us be clear—you cannot preach or teach the Word without communicating *doctrine*.

Knowing the Position of Being *In Christ*

In addition to the theological (doctrinal) knowledge of the Word, you need a positional knowledge that includes the power of you being *in Christ*. For you to stand in faith against the devil's schemes you need to arm yourself with a theological understanding of Scripture and the powerful advantage you have over the enemy because of the position God gives you *in Christ*. It is a strategic war-fare prayer position; one with which you must become intimately familiar.[48]

Knowledge of the Word of Faith

The subject of faith will be covered with more depth in Section Six—HOW, but let's take a brief summary look at *faith* as we con-sider the question, who qualifies to be used of God in prayer? Faith is at center stage when it comes to prayer, especially the prayers of mature believers. There is no getting around the necessity of believing what God says before you actually see the promise become a reality. If you can see what you are praying for, you do not need faith. The faith realm is where you are being sure of what you hope for and certain of what you do *not* yet see (Hebrews 11:1), and mature believers have testified with confidence for generations that they "live ["walk" KJV] by faith, not by sight" (2 Corinthians 5:7). Faith is not a luxury but a necessity.

Years ago, cars were sold stripped down to just the necessities needed to drive it from point A to point B. You could pay to add a radio, air conditioning, leather seats, power steering, power brakes, etc., but they were considered luxury extras or additions that did not come standard with the car, and the car would still run without those extras. But the dealer could not sell you a car without the engine. The engine is a necessary part of the car without which the car would be of no use. Faith is the engine of the believer's prayer life. Without it, you actually cannot please God (Hebrews 11:6), and your praying would be a useless exercise.

Also, faith comes by hearing, and hearing by the **Word** of Christ (Romans 10:17). Faith comes from hearing the Lord speak; it is why building intimacy with the Lord in prayer is so necessary. Faith is a heard word!

Finally, faith is seen as a shield used to extinguish all the flaming arrows of the evil one (Ephesians 6:16). This presence of a spiritual shield of faith that is part of the armor of the prayer warrior indicates the fierce fight the enemy will wage against you to stop you from praying. But as you are grounded in the truth of what you *believe the Scriptures say and promise*, your faith will extinguish the flaming arrows of doubt the enemy will shoot as you pray through in travail and intercession. More will be taught about this important subject of faith in the HOW section of this book. Let us pray...

> Father, open the eyes of those reading this book with open hearts. Give them insight into the truth of Your Word that will set them free from every lie and deceptive snare of the enemy. Bring them to a place of spiritual maturity and strength as they pursue becoming hearers and doers of Your Word, in Jesus's name. Amen.

CHAPTER FOURTEEN

WHO ARE THOSE COMMITTED TO KNOWING GOD'S WAYS?

DAVID WROTE IN PSALM 27, "TEACH ME YOUR WAY, LORD; LEAD ME IN a straight path because of my oppressors" (v. 11). For mature believers, knowing the way or ways of the Lord is as old as the Bible. David recognized the need to be taught, to receive divine revelation. There are things you cannot know apart from divine revelation (Matthew 16:17; 1 Corinthians 2:9-10). There is truth you will never understand or apply properly without the uncovering and the guiding that only God can provide. Thus, the prayer of David— LORD, teach me—needs to become your prayer. Here again, the necessity of believing prayer is seen. Whatever your station: male, female, old, young, churchman, businessman, white-collar, blue-collar—you need to pray for guidance, "Lord, show me Your ways." Let's look briefly at some of the *ways* the Lord teaches us in order to bring us to maturity where we can be used.

The Way of Perseverance

In the New Testament book of Hebrews it says, "You need to persevere so that when you have <u>done</u> the will of God, you will receive what he has promised" (Hebrews 10:36, emphasis mine). Implied is that you can do the will of God for a season, quit before you are "done," and not receive what God has promised. But *perseverance* enables you to continue going forward until you receive what God has promised, where your faith becomes sight. Another text corroborating Hebrews 10:36 is, "Let us not become weary in doing good, for at the proper time we will reap a harvest if we do not give up" (Galatians 6:9). So underlying the press to persevere is the belief that you will reap a harvest if you don't give up.

Paul includes perseverance as part of the progression believers follow to deeper levels of maturity in the New Testament book of Romans,

> *¹ Therefore, since we have been justified through faith, we have peace with God through our Lord Jesus Christ, ² through whom we have gained access by faith into this grace in which we now stand. And we rejoice in the hope of the glory of God. ³ Not only so, but we also rejoice in our sufferings, because we know that* **suffering** *produces* **perseverance;** *⁴ perseverance,* **character;** *and character,* **hope.** *⁵ And hope does not disappoint us, because God has poured out His* **love** *into our hearts by the Holy Spirit, whom he has given.* (Romans 5:1-5, emphasis mine)

The first two verses set up the progression of verses three to five. Several beginning benefits occur in your life by faith: you are justified, your sins are forgiven, and you are declared righteous before God; you have peace with God—warfare, guilt, and condemnation cease (Romans 8:1); you are able to gain access to God's grace, the power of God's favor (2 Corinthians 12:9); and you can stand rejoicing as you look forward to the future hope of the glory of God. These first two verses are foundational to the New Testament teaching about salvation by grace through faith. Basic in them is the truth that faith accesses grace and not the other way around. When you have faith, you believe with all of your heart, you are declared righteous (justified), and you receive the assurance of "peace with God through Christ." Further, through Christ you gain access by faith into grace that strengthens your ability to "stand" and "rejoice in the hope of the glory of God." Amen?

Next, verses 3-5 outline the increasing benefits experienced by those who continue moving forward toward prevailing truth. It begins with "rejoicing in <u>sufferings</u>." Sounds odd to rejoice in sufferings, but when you understand the benefits of persevering—or staying-the-course—that underline the text, it makes sense. This truth is also taught by the apostle James,

> *² Consider it **pure joy**, my brothers, whenever you face trials of many kinds,³ because you know that <u>the testing of your faith produces perseverance</u>.⁴ <u>Perseverance must finish its work</u> so that you may be mature and complete, not lacking anything.* (James 1:2-4, emphasis mine)

Sufferings produce perseverance. Some have prayed for their road to be devoid of suffering, but this progression clearly teaches that God does not shield you from all suffering because suffering can become the father of perseverance. An old word of encouragement is appropriate here: "A good start is not always a good finish." Not only should you be encouraged to press forward in perseverance to what is promised, but you should also take into account that, as a believer who is filled with the Holy Spirit, you already possess strengths God has given that should enable your perseverance.

The development of perseverance produces <u>character</u>. The Greek word translated "character", *dokime*, means "tested trustiness, experience, proof, trial."[49] With respect to this progression, the text outlines how character is developed—it can be traced to the ability to endure with rejoicing trials of suffering that allow you to produce perseverance that in turn produces character—strength of genuineness that's been proven in the fires of testing.

Then this strength of character produces <u>hope</u>. So much can be said about the necessity of hope. Hope is connected to faith (Hebrews 11:1). Hope is "an anchor for the soul, firm and secure;" because hope's anchor is God's presence, hope "enters the inner sanctuary behind the curtain" (Hebrews 6:19). And in Romans 5,

Paul writes, "Hope does not put us to shame, because God's **love** has been poured out into our hearts through the Holy Spirit, who has been given to us" (v. 5, emphasis mine). So then, hope produces an opened heart to the Holy Spirit who pours out His love.

So sufferings produce perseverance, perseverance produces character that produces hope, and hope produces love as the Holy Spirit is poured out into your heart. That progression is an inspired formula for success, a formula of which you need to be aware in order to follow each level of the progression to the end where the balanced strength of love fills your heart as you pray.

The Way of Believing

Jesus opened the door of salvation for all by His sacrificial death on the cross, and because He was "the Lamb who was slain from the creation of the world" (Revelation 13:8b), His sacrifice not only covers the New Covenant believers but the Old Covenant believers as well. We in the Church look back in faith at what Christ did to save us; they looked forward in faith from the perspective of the prophetic promises God gave them (see, for example, Hebrews 11:8-16).

The apostle Paul exhorted, "For the grace of God that brings salvation has appeared to all men" (Titus 2:11). Though the depravity of humankind is real, yet the truth of God's grace being dispensed from the cross has appeared to all people as far back as Adam and Eve whom God covered with the skins of animals. Grace is seen in that sacrifice of innocent animals for Adam and Eve through to the Old Testament sacrificial system where bullocks, lambs, and goats were sacrificed and their blood shed on the brazen altar in Jerusalem to cover the sins of the people. All this prefigured Christ's shed blood on the cross (cf. Isaiah 53), and thousands of years later, looking forward to the last person born in human history, Christ died to open the door of salvation to all of lost humanity.

Jesus told Nicodemus, a godly member of the Sanhedrin Council, that he must be born again (John 3:3). And that conversation made clear that salvation is only for those who believe (John 3:16). Genuine believing is where eternal salvation is either received or rejected. Jesus said, "Whoever is not with me is against me, and whoever does not gather with me scatters" (Matthew 12:30).

> [16] *[The gospel] is the power of God for the salvation of everyone who <u>believes</u>: first for the Jew, then for the Gentile.* [17] *For in the gospel a righteousness from God is revealed, a righteousness that is by faith from first to last, just as it is written: "The righteous will live by faith."* (Romans 1:16-17, emphasis mine)

Therefore, since believing is necessary for salvation, what does it mean to believe? Some believe the gift of eternal salvation is given because you joined the church, shook the preacher's hand, and submitted to water baptism. A person joining a church may not be taught to believe and commit with all their heart; they may simply jump through a few religious hoops to gain membership where no genuine commitment or behavioral change is expected or required. But it is not unrealistic for God to expect your commitment to the lordship of Christ to be evidenced by change. In fact, that's what the word *repent* literally means, and repentance was a fundamental teaching of the apostles (Acts 20:21). Unfortunately every church does not teach the necessity of repentance and faith evidenced by a lifestyle change.

Dietrich Bonhoeffer was a Lutheran pastor in Germany during the rise of Adolf Hitler and the Third Reich. He personally witnessed the silence of many Christian pastors and leaders as Hitler initiated genocidal atrocities against the Jewish people. Bonhoeffer's commitment to Christ would not let him be silent or justify the silence of others. He coined the phrase "cheap grace" in his book, *The Cost of Discipleship*, to describe the grace of his Christian contemporaries:

> Cheap grace is the preaching of forgiveness without requiring repentance, baptism without church discipline, Communion without confession, absolution without personal confession. Cheap grace is grace

without discipleship, grace without the cross, grace without Jesus Christ, living and incarnate.[50]

Cheap grace is no grace at all; the grace that brings biblical salvation comes as the result of repentance and faith.

Though the grace of God that brings salvation has appeared to everyone, everyone is not saved. And though the text says, "all are justified freely by his grace" (Romans 3:24), grace is not cheap. Little-to-no confidence should be given to anyone who says they've repented, confessed Jesus as the Lord of their life, and they believe Jesus is risen from the grave, yet there is no witness of the heart change the Spirit brings in the new birth. The Holy Spirit has not baptized everyone into the Body of Christ who claims to be saved (1 Corinthians 12:13; cf. also Acts 2:47b).

Being saved is a lifestyle commitment to the lordship of Christ where the Spirit enables you to live in *peace* and in *holiness* (Hebrews 12:14). *Peace* is the extension of being justified by faith (Romans 5:1) where you receive peace with God (vertical) through faith in Christ, and that peace extends into your relationships (horizontal) with others, i.e. peace with everyone, if possible (Hebrews 12:14; Romans 12:18). *Holiness* includes shunning ungodliness and worldly passions (cf. Galatians 5:19-21; Ephesians 5:1-14), and living a self-controlled, upright, and godly life in this present age (Titus 2:12). The goal is that you might "become the righteousness of God in Christ," a mature believer who's an example and witness God can use to lead the lost and the bound out of darkness into God's light (compare Luke 4:18-19 and John 20:21 with 2 Corinthians 5:21; Philippians 4:9; Colossians 1:11-14).

The Way of Conditions and Promises

Scripture is replete with the promises God has made to His children, and while it is impossible for God to lie (Numbers 23:19; Hebrews 6:18) there appear to be promises He has made that have not been kept. But when you understand God's ways, like the *way of perseverance,* you learn the necessity of *waiting* for your "due season" (Galatians 6:9 KJV) where the promise will be fulfilled.

Another truth about God's ways is *The Way of Conditions and Promises*. Promises are not unconditional. If the specific conditions that qualify you to believe and receive the promise are not stated, they may be implied. It's part of knowing God's ways. Therefore, the promise was not kept because the conditions were not met.

I'm aware that some theologize a world in which no one is able to obey God or seek His face. But from where I sit, it does not make sense to me that God would command or exhort you to do something you cannot do. You've been created in the image of God and despite depravity, you have the ability to choose—you have free will. Here are just a few of the numerous exhortations and admonitions in the Scriptures that God expects you to obey.

- Joshua, the successor of Moses said, "...Choose for yourselves this day whom you will serve...But as for me and my household, we will serve the LORD" (Joshua 24:15).
- From the prophet Isaiah, "You will keep in perfect peace those whose minds are steadfast, because they trust in you" (Isaiah 26:3).
- Also from Isaiah, "Seek the LORD while he may be found; call on him while he is near. Let the wicked forsake their ways and the unrighteous their thoughts. Let them turn to the LORD, and he will have mercy on them, and to our God, for he will freely pardon" (Isaiah 55:6-7).
- Jesus said, "Ask and it will be given to you; seek and you will find; knock and the door will be opened to you. For everyone who asks receives; the one who seeks finds; and to him who knocks, the door will be opened" (Matthew 7:7-8).

It makes no sense for God to expect you to do something you cannot do and then for Him to judge and punish your disobedience. Listen! If God through His Word commands or exhorts you to do something, you can do it. If you don't, it's because you decided not to.

Wake Up and Pay Attention

The conditions that are stated or implied in the text must be recognized and obeyed in order to qualify for the promise. You will hear a believer quoting the promise part of a verse to encourage other believers to trust the Lord, but if the particular verse or verses within the immediate context spell out conditions connected to the promise, those conditions should be quoted along with the promise for the encouragement to achieve the necessary results. For example, you could exhort someone who is going through a difficult season, "Remember, the Bible says in Romans 8:28, 'In all things God works for your good,' so you be encouraged." But the full text not only gives the promise, it also gives the conditions for the promise to be actualized: "And we know that in all things God works for the good of those who love him, who have been called according to his purpose" (Romans 8:28). The promise of God causing all things to work for your good has two conditions: (1) You must be one who loves the Lord (see Deuteronomy 6:4-5, *The Shema Yisrael*). (2) You must be called according to His purpose, meaning you must be a believer who is growing in the grace and knowledge of Christ (2 Peter 3:18). This includes growing in your knowledge of the Word, strength in faith, prayer, and ministry to others according to His purpose—the will of God for the lost, the sick, the bound, and the imprisoned (cf. Luke 4:18-19; Matthew 25:31-40). The promise that God will cause things to work together for your good is not a promise to the weak, carnal, or lukewarm Christians, but to the strong, praying, committed, mature believers who are endeavoring to touch others for Christ.

The Way of Faith, Foolishness, and Presumption

Simply stated: faith in prayer is exercising believing trust in the truth of God's Word, either written (Scripture) or spoken (a prophetic word or an inward witness of God's Spirit, both of which do not contradict the truth of Holy Scripture). Your trust is that the Word you've either read or heard is true and worthy of your confidence. Paul said, "Faith comes from hearing the message, and the message is heard through the word of Christ" (Romans 10:17). Faith does not come from the casual reading of Scripture or the casual hearing of a message preached. Faith comes as you prayerfully read or listen to a message with the intent to hear the word of Christ concerning your dilemma or circumstance. Being desperate is not necessary, but oftentimes faith comes on the heels of an intense situation fraught with desperation. Basically, to pray in faith means you base your prayer upon a promise in Scripture.

Foolishness in prayer is to importune the throne of grace for a desire or a need without having any basis in Scripture for your requests. There must be a promise, a leading of the Spirit through a dream or a vision, something upon which to anchor your faith. Your prayer is not of faith but is foolish without the foundation of an inspired or confirming Word. It would be as though you travelled by plane to a distant city hoping to meet with an important businessperson without an appointment, without the knowledge that their schedule would accommodate you, or even without the knowledge that the person you hope to see is even in town. That would be foolish! Don't you agree? Well then, why would you pray with uncertainty concerning God's will to provide or guide you in a specific direction? Praying from the position of your feelings, wants, desires, and needs with no sense of God's promise or plan, and where doubts arise and fears overwhelm, is a formula for foolishness, not faith.

Presumption is where faith has a basis in biblical truth, but the one praying has disqualified him or herself from receiving what God has promised. An excellent example of presumption is Jesus in the wilderness, at the beginning of His earthly ministry, being tempted by Satan. In Matthew 4, the second temptation is Satan taking Jesus to the pinnacle of the temple saying, "If you are the Son of God...throw yourself down. For it is written: 'He will command his angels concerning you, and they will lift you up in their hands, so that you will not strike your foot against a stone'" (v. 6). But Jesus did not respond to Satan tempting him to be presumptuous. He answered him, "It is also written: 'Do not put the Lord your God to the test'" (v. 7). It would have been presumptuous for Jesus to expect God to send angels to save Him when intentionally throwing Himself off the pinnacle of the temple was avoidable. This is applicable today—it is presumptuous of a believer to pray for healing from high blood pressure, for example, while he refuses to discipline his eating habits, or it would also be presumptuous for you to pray for God to protect you from harm while driving intoxicated.

The Way of Submission to Authority

So many have misunderstood the truth of being under authority. An important passage is the account of the centurion in Matthew 8 whose servant was sick so he asked Jesus for help. When Jesus asked, "Shall I come and heal him?" the centurion objected, saying,

> [8] *"Lord, I do not deserve to have you come under my roof. But just say the word, and my servant will be healed. [9] For I myself am a man under authority, <u>with soldiers under me</u>. I tell this one, 'Go,' and he goes; and that one, 'Come,' and he comes. I say to my servant, 'Do this,' and he does it."* (Matthew 8:8-9, emphases mine)

Jesus commended the centurion's great faith to His followers and spoke a word of confirmation about the healing of the servant to the centurion (v. 13).

Notice the centurion *defined* himself as "<u>a man under authority</u>" meaning there were military or political leaders to whom he was submitted. They could order him to come and go according to their will and he obeyed them as "a man under authority." Then the centurion *described* himself as a man with authority, "<u>with soldiers under me</u>," and he proceeded to describe his authority over his soldiers and over his servant, all who obeyed him as those under his authority.

Also noteworthy is the insight the centurion reportedly gained from his faithful military service. He understood the power of words spoken with authority. He honored and obeyed the words from superiors, and his subordinates honored and obeyed his words.

And after observing Christ, he recognized that the same honor and obedience he experienced in the military realm, Christ was experiencing in the spiritual realm of healing and deliverance. He could see achievement in both realms initiated by words spoken by someone with authority. He recognized Jesus had authority to speak words that achieved results, just like he knew he had authority to speak words that achieved results. Jesus called the centurion's perspective "great faith" (Matthew 8:10).

Those who recognize the privilege and power of being under authority rejoice at that revelation, especially when the one they are submitted to is a godly example worth following. Unfortunately, there is almost always an example of leadership gone tragically wrong that creates hesitation in the minds of those called to following the biblical pattern of submission to authority. One such example of leadership gone tragically wrong is Jim Jones. Jonestown is the name associated with the Peoples Temple where the Americans who followed Jim Jones died from an apparent mass suicide, where over 900 followers were possibly forced to drink cyanide-laced Kool-Aid, November 18, 1978, in a remote commune in northwestern Guyana.[51]

Another example of leadership gone tragically wrong is David Koresh, the leader of a religious commune called the Branch Davidians outside Waco, Texas in 1988. He attracted largely vulnerable and insecure people to his so-called "flock." He reportedly "married" as many as 19 women, including a 13-year-old girl, fathered at least 12 children, and became an absolute dictator over his followers. Koresh gradually built an arsenal of firearms amounting to 11 tons of firepower. It all ended tragically as the FBI sieged the commune for 51 days without a negotiated settlement. The FBI lost patience and attacked the commune, fire broke out, and by the time they were able to break in and put out the fire, they found David Koresh along with 75 followers dead (including 25 children, 12 his own).[52]

History records unfortunate accounts of broken people, who were ignorant of the character traits of true leaders and the necessity to discern them, being susceptible to the lure of charismatic leaders. Sadly, many accounts ended tragically. To protect yourself or provide counsel to someone you know and love, notice these basic admonitions:

- You should be open to the counsel of godly leaders whom you know love you and whose judgment you respect.
- You should have a relationship with a pastor or older believer whose knowledge of the Word you respect.
- You should take the time to measure a prospective leader or pastor by some basic standards of moral character and integrity.

Had the followers of Jim Jones or David Koresh used the above three admonitions to measure those leaders they would have resigned following them long before tragedy struck.

The Way of Spiritual Leadership

The crucial truth of Christian unity has been dealt with in Chapter Seven: What About Prayer and Christian Unity, but here we will address the subject of unity from a leadership point of view.

Given the world's desperate need for ministry-effective churches, it is unfortunate that leaders don't do a better job of sharing successful strategies and innovative ideas with one another. Is it a spirit of competition that has deceived many spiritual leaders into building their own spiritual worlds oblivious to what others are doing in their worlds? Don't the spiritual leaders realize that for the truth of unity to materialize, leaders must lay aside their egos and reach beyond their denominational division to unite in ministry with others? God's powerful favor and yoke-breaking anointing is the result of a hard-fought and sought after *unity* across cultural, racial, generational, male/female, and denominational barriers. Your prayer should be, "Lord, pour out upon me hunger for Your anointing of Christian unity needed in my area."

Unity is a benefit for which Christ Himself prayed:

> [20] *My prayer is not for them alone. I pray also for those who will believe in me through their message,*
> [21] *That all of them may be one, Father, just as you*

162

are in me and I am in you. May they also be in us
<u>*so that the world may believe that you have sent me*</u>.
(John 17:20-21, emphasis mine)

This prayer initiates a call for mature spiritual leaders to love Christ and His kingdom enough to pray in agreement with Christ for unity—to honor the scriptural admonitions about unity enough to work for unity by pushing past the various denominational and social barriers to unite with other believers in order to strategize how to fulfill the prayer of Christ practically.

A major part of Christian unity is theological, meaning division is based upon what is believed, and what is believed is rooted in the understanding of biblical truth. But foundationally, the Scriptures teach that Christian unity is not a condition we must *obtain* but a condition we must *maintain*. Paul wrote,

> *[3] Make every effort to **keep the unity** of the Spirit through the bond of peace. [4] There is one body and one Spirit, just as you were called to one hope when you were called; [5] one Lord, one faith, one baptism; [6] one God and Father of all, who is over all and through all and in all. (Ephesians 4:3-6, emphasis mine)*

The unity strategy of true Bible-believing Christians is to wear their denominational labels loosely and determine, "through the bond of peace," to reach their hands in full fellowship to other believers who are 'blood-washed' (Revelation 7:14), remembering: In essentials, unity; in non-essentials, liberty; and in all things, charity. Can I get an amen?

Hearing Spiritual, Innovative Words

Traditionally, many have locked themselves into using methods that worked in the past but are not working now. They console themselves by believing that what worked for Grandma will work today and continue trying with little success. But you must realize that those *old* methods were actually *new* and innovative years ago, and that today you must seek God through prayer and corporate multigenerational leaders' discussions to discover the current *new* methods that effectively communicate truth to this generation just as our predecessors did to theirs. Many of them pushed past the critical words of their old-school counterparts, "We've never done it that way before," and encouraged themselves with the success they envisioned as they employed innovative methods they believed were heaven-sent.

Pastor Samuel G. Hines was the keynote speaker of the 1980 National Inspirational Youth Convention (NIYC) of the Church of God in St. Louis, MO. The Convention leaders chose the theme "Tell the Generations Following" because the Church of God Reformation Movement began in 1880, and they sought a theme that looked forward as the Church celebrated its centennial history. In the midst of all of the praise lauded over the success of the founding fathers of our Church Movement, Pastor Hines said something in his sermon I will never forget, "If we are to do today what our founding predecessors did in their day, we must hear what God is saying to us today just as they heard what God was saying to them in their day." Leaders who deeply respect and honor the roots of their predecessors must see themselves as called to make the same kind of difficult methodological decisions their leaders made in their day. In reality, this is what it really means to honor the "traditions of the elders." Jaroslav Pelikan said, "Tradition is the living faith of the dead. Traditionalism is the dead faith of the living."[53]

Some years ago when my children were small, my wife and I drove them to an amusement park in a neighboring state. This is before GPS in cars and on cellphones, and we got lost. Driving into a small town to find someone who could give me directions, I saw an older man exiting a General Store and inquired how to get to the well-known amusement park in the area. I remember distinctly; he tilted his head back a little while he rubbed his cheek and chin with his hand and finally answered, "You can't get there from here." He then gave me directions to another location, saying, "When you get there, ask someone for directions to the amusement park. The directions from there are much easier than from here." I took his counsel, drove to the place he directed us, asked for directions to the amusement park, and arrived at our destination with no further difficulty. The reason for giving you this true story is the words of the older man before he gave me directions. He said, "You can't get there from here."

His initial words struck me as odd, but I understood him to mean that getting to where I was going was not easy from that location. While I paid attention as he directed me to a place where I was to find someone else to direct me to where I was finally trying to go, my spiritual mind was racing. "How true are those words," I thought, "concerning going to a mature place in God from a place of doubt, lack of discipline, ignorance of the truth of Scripture, prayer-lessness, or continual moral failure." If approached by someone desiring to be used of God while they live in guilt from any of the aforementioned weights or sins (Hebrews 12:1 KJV), the appropriate response should be, "You can't get there from here." They should be directed to another place where repentance, faith, prayer, and the study of the Word are taught along with the important discipline of accountability. It should be that from the maturing strength of that new place they could legitimately ask how to be used of God in a significant way. Make sense?

Of course, the goal is always to bring you to seek first God's kingdom and His righteousness (Matthew 6:33), to take seriously the Great Commission of making disciples of all nations (Matthew 28:19-20), and to see yourself as following in the ministry steps of Jesus, "As the Father has sent me, I am sending you" (John 20:21b). Those ministry steps include being anointed with the Spirit to proclaim good news to the poor, to proclaim freedom for the prisoners and recovery of sight for the blind, to set the oppressed free, and to proclaim the year of the Lord's favor (Luke 4:18-19). This truth is needed in the church, in the workplace, in your business, in the home with your family, and in your community.

None of these motivational and directional truths shared here will bring about competent multigenerational ministry apart from understanding fully that the call to ministry must be undergirded with the call to prepare. Real success, even real potential success will require real change in you, beginning with prayer proficiency, being grounded in essential doctrinal truth (1 Timothy 4:16), and being disciplined enough to balance the spiritual, physical, social, relational, and financial aspects of life in such a way as to support the primary focus of the kingdom (Matthew 6:33; Romans 14:17-18).

Be What You Teach

James M. Kouzes and Barry Z. Posner, in their book *The Truth About Leadership*, take 30 years of research experience to outline what may be called "old school truths" or principles that have worked for eons. Their eighth truth, "You either lead by example or you don't lead at all,"[54] epitomizes the essence of *being* what you *teach*. Again let me emphasize—you cannot give what you do not have, you cannot teach what you do not know (by experience), and you cannot take me where you've never been.

Today, many leaders have a worldly, competitive view of life where the possession of money and things shape their perspective of success, but as a true spiritual leader, you must see the world and your work or ministry in it through *kingdom eyes*. You must see the revelation of building the multigenerational, multicultural kingdom Jesus predicted He would build in His Church (Matthew 16:18) as that for which your secular or spiritual work exists. Because of the spiritual influence of this *kingdom perspective*, some business leaders in the church are experiencing extraordinary success from integrity-based solutions where honesty and integrity dominate how they conduct their business in the world. Though they are *in the world*, they are not *of the world*.

Stephen R. Covey in his book, *The 7 Habits of Highly Effective People*, teaches the same truth of integrity-based living in his principle-centered approach to solving personal and professional problems. Living a life grounded and guided by principles anchored in biblical truth actually enables you as a believer to understand how faith works. You actually gain access by faith into a grace that glorifies God (Romans 5:1-2), and that faith is connected to vision from revelation knowledge (Proverbs 29:18). Habakkuk 2:1-3 outlines three things you prayerfully need to oversee in order to achieve success that is multigenerational:

1. You need to have a God-given vision or revelation of what you are called of God and gifted by grace to achieve.
2. You need to write down, in plain language, the revelation and share it with those working with you who can ask questions in a non-threatening atmosphere, so that in agreement they can buy into the revelation God has given.
3. You need to become the living embodiment of the vision, the revelation, so that those reading the vision and running with you can gain encouragement that the vision will surely come to pass because they see it in you.

To achieve the *first* will require an intimate relationship with the Lord, one that is established and maintained by prayer, where you hear His voice (John 10:3-4) and are submitted to following the guidance of the Holy Spirit (Romans 8:14).

To achieve the *second* will require a commitment to teach and disciple those around you. In addition, it certainly will require the prayerful ability to distinguish the faithful workers and followers from the pretenders who are only out for themselves. Remember: you can impress others from a distance, but to impact them you must come close.

Finally, to achieve the *third* will require the discipline to run faithfully with perseverance the race set before you (Hebrews 12:1-2). It's a disciplined determination to see beyond the immediacy of today into the possibilities of the tomorrows in the lives of future generations. It asks the question, "What needs to be true of me today in order for that tomorrow reality to have a firm foundation upon which to build truth into the lives of the next generation?" It's the epitome of the words of Habakkuk 2:3, "For the revelation awaits an appointed time; it speaks of the end and will not prove false. Though it linger, wait for it; it will certainly come and will not delay."

Being a transparent example others can buy into, a tangible, living embodiment of the revelation God gives, is one of the most important motivations those who are connected to you need to see.

Actually, one's leadership at this level can make the difference between success and failure in the realm of multiplying the truth you see into the hearts and lives of those around you. By all means, you must not fail in this matter of seeing yourself, as the apostle Paul says, "...called to be..." (1 Corinthians 1:2). As Paul summarized his ministry work, "I laid a foundation as an expert builder, and someone else is building on it" (1 Corinthians 3:10b), so you should strive to achieve the same level of kingdom faithfulness.

Pray to Stay Connected

Have you ever noticed that most ticket stubs with a perforated section have a warning printed near the perforation: "Void if detached." It always reminds me of the importance of staying connected to maintain value. Many in the church world or in the world of business can be too eager to get involved in the work without the in-depth understanding needed to achieve the expected results. You don't want to run ahead of yourself and prematurely become disconnected from those who are called and equipped to guide you into the work of ministry or business with a mature grasp of *what* you are called to do; you should prayerfully stay connected so you can ascertain the important *why* and the all-important *how*. The road "less traveled by...that has made all the difference" in Robert Frost's poem, The Road Not Taken, is reminiscent of those who patiently search for the best path and go the extra mile in search of the full understanding of the *way* of truth that brings lasting significance. Staying connected can be seen as a road not always taken. With a spirit of independence, many go off into mediocrity and even into failure because they unwisely detached themselves from their roots. Unfortunately, without knowing it, many are demonstrating a subtle form of disrespect where they fail to honor their roots as they refuse to stay connected.

A Connected College Freshman

When my oldest daughter left home for college in a southern state and city, she called me about where she should go to church.

"You've not only been my dad all my life," she said, "but also my pastor, and for the first time in my life, I will need to look for a pastor. What do I look for?" My response over the phone became a document I've shared with other parents faced with the college condition of helping their child measure the spiritual worth of a leader before joining his flock. I've added it here for your benefit.

The Selection of a Shepherd

The union between a pastor and his people is much like the union between a husband and wife. The marriage really works well when mutual love and respect is at its core. And to avoid unnecessary conflict, there needs to exist an understanding of roles. According to God's plan and design, we all have our roles to play, and the recognition of this truth creates an atmosphere for order that's productive.

In terms of spiritual authority, most of us must decide to whom we will submit at least once in our lives. Pulling oneself out from under the authority of a leader is always difficult. As in a marriage, divorce is problematic, and the confusion that is left in its wake has caused many an innocent child to despair of submitting to authority. The choice of spiritual leadership is so important you will need the spiritual wisdom that's an answer to prayer (James 1:5) and anchored in the truth of God's Word. In addition, you will need good common sense. Common sense (which is not very common) dictates that you "look before you leap."

The one whose responsibility it will be to watch over your soul must be respected enough by you to rebuke and correct you without you running for cover. If you run from him at the first sign of correction, it will nullify the benefit that God has ordained for him to be to you (Hebrews 13:17). You cannot be open to God's government and, at the same time, casually remove yourself out from under the protective covering of that government at the first sign of correction. He of whom it is said, "The government will be on his shoulders" (Isaiah 9:6), is the One who has delegated authority to pastors, and these men are gifts to the local church (Ephesians 4:8, 11) and have the responsibility to shepherd God's flock (Acts 20:28). As shepherds, their major duties fall into two categories: *feeding* and *leading*. They can do neither well if they are not respected. God desires to lead us all into green pastures, but first, His order is that we come together.

Your development into a strong believer who is equipped for God's service will depend, in large measure, upon whom you are submitted to in pastoral authority. This is not a time to leave the selecting to others, especially if by virtue of their own negative lifestyles they have disqualified themselves. You must take prayerful care in the examination of the character of this one to whom you will entrust the watch-care of your most precious possession — your soul. The following are the questions you should ask yourself about the pastor to whom you are prayerfully preparing to submit.

1. Is he a man of godly character, one whose lifestyle of holiness and personal integrity are without question? (1 Timothy 3:2, 7) A wise expression states, "More is caught than is taught." It means, he cannot impart what he is not. If you are going to follow him, you must make sure he is, in reality, a man of God. Is he more than just some brother who went to seminary or someone whose father left him the church? Is this person who stands before you to proclaim the truth of God's Word walking in the light of that truth, and does he love the God of that truth with all of his heart? Do you sense he has clean hands, and a pure heart, is free from idolatry, and all falsehood? (Psalm 24:3-4) Accept nothing less.

2. What is the quality of his relationship with his wife and children? (1 Timothy 3:4-5) Are these relationships stable enough to provide an anchor for you in these times of change and chaos? Society is in desperate need of anchors and pillars. An anchor keeps a vessel from drifting with the winds and the waves of the ocean. A pillar provides support for a building. It must be strong, straight, and stable if the building is to withstand the negative effects of the elements. The example that your pastor sets in his personal relationships actually enables him to be an anchor and a pillar in the lives of those who exercise confidence in him. His example also adds the credibility of success to his counsel and preaching.

3. Does he know the Word of God? Is he a man of the Word, grounded in the truth and wisdom of the Scriptures? Do you sense

in him that he loves the truth and is a reverent, obedient student of the Scriptures? The one who teaches you needs to know and live by what he teaches. You should not submit your life and the lives of your loved ones to a leader who is only preaching and teaching current events. While what is occurring in the world today may be a footnote to illustrate the truth he is teaching, his messages must have as their focus the eternal truth of the Word of God (1 Timothy 4:16; 2 Timothy 4:1-2).

4. What is your sense of the genuineness of his call to pastoral ministry? Do you evidence in him the call, ordination, and anointing of God to minister through the public preaching and teaching of the Word of God? (John 15:16) This has to do with recognizing a gifting from God. God gives pastors (Ephesians 4:11). No one, no matter how charismatic or articulate, should choose for himself pastoral ministry. He must be called (Hebrews 5:4).

5. What is his vision for ministry? In what direction is he going? Do you sense, in the sharing of his heart, that he has received a vision, heard a word of revelation from God (Habakkuk 2:2-4), and is running by faith in the direction of his destiny? A good man may have the pieces of his life together in the first three areas above, but if he is not called, or even if he is called, but has not waited long enough to hear a word of God's direction and vision (Proverbs 29:18) for his life and ministry, he is not ready to lead others. Prayerfully seek God's face for His confirmation to your decision to make a pastoral leader and his church your spiritual home.

THE HOW OF PRAYER
(PART I)

Considering practical ways to put principles into practice

CHAPTER FIFTEEN

PRACTICALLY SPEAKING, HOW SHOULD YOU BEGIN?

THE YEAR WAS 1985, ABOUT 21 YEARS AFTER MY CONVERSION TO Christ. I'd grown up in church. My mother was a preacher's daughter, the sixth of nine children of saved parents. Her father was a man of God, deeply committed to the lordship of Christ, and her mother was a prayer warrior. I always believed the gospel story and the truths of Scripture, but I was lost not having committed my life to Christ. The lusts of the flesh and the attractive sights and sounds of the world of sin lured me away from what I was taught in Sunday school. Some might say that I had dormant faith because of my upbringing, but that faith was dead in the presence of the practice of sin and in the absence of a commitment to Christ.

Everything changed for me, however, the Sunday morning I wept in repentance at an altar in church. It was April 26, 1964 that the Lord began to turn my life around. I started going to church three times a week: Sunday morning, Sunday evening service, and Wednesday evening prayer meeting and Bible study. I purchased a Bible and began reading the New Testament. Soon after, I started testifying of my conversion to my friends and inviting them to commit their lives to Christ and come to church. With another believer in the church, we planned a cottage meeting that blossomed into a Friday evening service in homes. The first was held on a Friday evening, in the fall of 1964, where four young friends were invited, fed a meal, and witnessed to about the love of God in Christ to save all who believe (Romans 1:16-17). I also gave my testimony. All four prayed to receive Christ that evening, praise the Lord, and before a year had transpired, in the winter of 1965, the Lord confirmed my call to Christian ministry. In all I was experiencing, I was learning how to pray and trust the Lord for guidance through college, marriage, seminary, and being called to pastor my first church in Boston, Massachusetts at the young age of 26.

After ten years of faithful ministry, we saw that local church grow from a core of 41 members to a congregation of close to 400, from an annual budget of $12,500 in 1972 to one of almost $120,000 in 1982. I rejoiced with my church members and praised God for the growth and the successes, but I gradually came to realize I'd taken the church as far as they wanted to go. So I resigned after Sunday morning service July 4, 1982, gave the church a 90-day notice, and removed myself as pastor October 2, 1982.

One of the benefits of doing something unsuccessfully for years and gradually seeing success begin to peek its head over the horizon is you gradually grow to know by experience what works and what doesn't. Struggling for ten years (1972-1982) to pastor a small, democratically governed church in New England taught me the absolute necessity of fasting and prayer. Though the church is my business and I understand it's a spiritual business, yet in some respects, the church is like other businesses—there are relational issues (customers, church members, and visitors), physical issues (building space, church meeting space, children's space, and administration space), and financial issues where growth and progress exist; though the church is spiritual business, we also seek to achieve success that can be measured. It was in the midst of my starting all over again that I came to understand the power of prayer more fully.

Make an Appointment

In 1985, I was invited to preach a revival in a church pastored by Rev. James Anderson in Gary, IN. Alone in my hotel room, I spent my mornings praying for two requests: the success of the revival, and the deepening of my walk of faith as I was a little more than two years in the new church. My struggle with the faith walk drove me to cry out to God for *how* I could be more consistent in my prayer life. Somehow I sensed my answers to numerous questions and needs laid there. It certainly wasn't that I didn't pray, but I sensed my faith would be strengthened if I were more consistent in my prayer life. I remember that in the midst of crying out for God's help in being more consistent and faithful in prayer, I heard the Lord say, "Why not make an appointment?"

Those of you who have heard the Lord speak a word of wisdom and direction know that His words carry massive meaning. I also heard phrases echoing in the corridors of my mind: I've made appointments to do other important things—I've scheduled dentist appointments, an appointment to meet with the mayor of my city, an out-of-town preaching engagement where I'd made an appointment to catch a plane, and all of those appointments were kept, even though all of them, without fail, were appointments with people. God was saying, "Make an appointment with Me." It was so simple yet so profound. Following that spiritual encounter, I did four important things.

1. Set a Time

After examining my regular daily schedule in search of a time to pray, I found the best time for me to keep a daily appointment with God was before my day began. Therefore 5:00 AM became my prayer time, my appointment with the Father.

Before the revelation of "making an appointment," I would say in prayer every day, "I'm going to set aside some time today to spend in prayer," but most of the time the day would end with me saying, "Tomorrow Lord, I'm going to do better."

2. Select a Partner

Two are better than one (Ecclesiastes 4:9), and where agreement exists, strength for victory is certain (Genesis 11:6; Leviticus

26:8; Judges 7:17-25). The Lord taught this truth of agreement saying, "If two of you on earth agree about anything they ask for, it will be done for them by my Father in heaven" (Matthew 18:19). Of course, the "anything" in the above text means anything "according to His will" (1 John 5:14-15). Obviously, Jesus is not teaching you that the Father can be forced to do something unjust because two misguided people pray in agreement.

Whom Are You Looking For?

First, you should look for someone who wants to pray. It should not be that in your pursuit of God's presence in prayer, you are burdened with the responsibility of chasing down your prayer partner and convincing them of their need to pray. For example, if you were considering inviting a friend to enroll in a class to become a SCUBA diver with you, that friend would have to be someone who can swim and is interested in exploring underwater ocean life. Understand what I'm saying?

Second, you should look for someone faithful in their church attendance. Someone whose commitment to the church that does not lead them to attend Sunday service faithfully will probably be someone that will be unfaithful in meeting you in Early Morning Prayer meetings (EMP). Included in this matter of faithful church attendance should be the member's love of the church, enough to serve in some ministry capacity.

Third, unless you are seeking to pray with your spouse or fiancé(e), you should be looking for a brother if you are a brother or a sister if you are a sister. This does not mean that you should never pray with someone of the opposite sex, but generally speaking, you should be looking for someone of your gender to partner with in prayer. The procedure we named *tandem-praying* or *agreement praying* works very well with two believers sitting together side-by-side.

Agreement Praying

Agreement praying is praying in agreement side-by-side with another believer for various needs. A main reason this method is an extremely effective way of praying with a partner is it eliminates the need for lengthy discussions or testimonies about prayer requests. Your prayer-benefit with someone is maximized in a convenient and timely manner. Remember, two are better than one. Two can carry the prayer burden easier than one can carry it alone. Even Jesus asked His disciples to watch with Him for one hour (Matthew 26:40). Also, two praying together in agreement multiplies the strength of their praying. It has been said that if one horse can pull 700 pounds and another horse can pull 800 pounds, the two-horse team will pull their own weight plus the weight of their interaction. Therefore, yoked together, the horses can pull about 3000 pounds! This "two-horse rule" illustrates the power or strength released through the unity of teamwork, and so it is with agreement praying. The three-stage procedure of praying in agreement with a partner is simple:

Stage One

As two believers sit side-by-side to pray, one prays aloud for a need he or she knows (a few minutes). During the praying of the first, the second verbally, but quietly, agrees in prayer. It is not necessary that the second be familiar with the need for which the first is praying. The Spirit will help him as he listens and agrees with the prayer of the first (Romans 8:26-27).

Stage Two

After the first person has prayed their specific request, the second person briefly prays aloud for that same request, agreeing with the prayer of the first person (Matthew 18:19). This should take about one minute or so. Afterwards, the second person should then continue in prayer for a need he knows about. This additional prayer should take about two minutes or so. While the second person is praying for their request, the first person is verbally, but quietly, agreeing in prayer (just as had been done for him or her in stage one).

Stage Three

After the second person has concluded their prayer, the first person then prays aloud in agreement for the new request. This also should not take more than a minute or so. Afterwards, the first should then continue in prayer for a new request that they know about. And on it goes, back and forth, until their time runs out or their requests are all prayed for. This is an effective and practical way of bearing one another's burdens in order to fulfill the law of Christ (Galatians 6:2).

Prayer partnership is a productive way of providing a prayer covering[55] for a prayer partner as they provide a prayer covering for you. You also provide a prayer covering for those for whom you pray daily, including the prayer-circle[56] of persons for whom your partner prays regularly. Partners should faithfully covenant to do three things: (1) Schedule to pray together once a week in EMP. If this is not possible, praying over the phone is permissible. (2) Pray daily for each other in their private prayer and devotional time. (3) Fellowship around a meal in a home, apartment, or restaurant once or twice a month with your partner and some other prayer laborers (Ephesians 3:14-21).

3. Sanctify a Place

As a pastor, this was an easy task—I made my church my main place of prayer. The year was 1986 and our church of 300 or so believers met on Sundays at the Strand Theatre in Uphams Corner in Dorchester, a neighborhood in Boston. Since we didn't have a church building, we held our Wednesday evening prayer meetings and Bible study at a Baptist Church building in Codman Square in Dorchester. So when I sanctified a place, I announced to my church that we were starting EMP meetings. Thus, my place was with my church, the local body of Christ I pastored. In those first EMP meetings, approximately one third (almost 100 believers) of the church showed up to meet the Lord at 5:00 in the morning. We met from 5–6 AM, Mondays–Fridays, and from 7–9 AM on Saturdays. Those EMP meetings have continued since those beginning days, and in 2016 we celebrate 30 years of EMP meetings in our church. Praise the Lord!

4. Secure a Pattern

Prayer patterns are numerous. A prayer pattern is an outline you memorize that leads you step by step through worship and into prayer and intercession. The one I use most often is praying the Lord's Prayer as an outline. It has been said that the *Lord's Prayer* (Matthew 6:9-13 KJV) is the most memorized passage of Scripture in the world. Until you learn and memorize other patterns, use this one that you probably already know. The outline known as the Lord's Prayer Pattern has three sections.

Worship

> *"Our Father who art in heaven, hallowed by Thy name ..."*

This first section is where you praise the Father using His nine compound covenant names.[57] Remember, you enter the LORD's gates with thanksgiving and His courts with praise (Psalm 100:4) by exalting His names (Psalm 103:1-5) with words of praise and adoration. You address God as "Father," because you recognize the covenant relationship you have with Him as a son or daughter through your faith in Christ (Romans 8:14-17, 10:9-10; Ephesians 2:8-9). The words of praise and thanksgiving are based on the benefits He has promised in the meanings of His names. In worship, you run into the refuge of His names (Proverbs 18:10). For example, when God provided the ram in the thicket for Abraham (Genesis 22:13-14), he understood that God was saying to him, "I am *Jehovah-Jireh,* your Provider." Now, when I thank God for being my Jehovah-Jireh, the LORD my Provider, I think of the provisions God has enabled in my life through Christ and verbalize thanksgiving and praise.

Ask yourself, what has the Lord provided as a benefit of eternal salvation? Search the Scriptures and talk with other believers. The benefits are numerous, and if you began with all of the implications of just, "In him we live and move and have our being" (Acts 17:28), your worship would take several minutes, and that's just one of the nine names.

Also, during this first section of worship and praise, you get a chance to pray about specific needs you may have. Repentance and confessions of faith can be spoken during this section. In fact, in the midst of worshiping the Lord around His names, the Holy Spirit, for example, may remind you of a failure to maintain a commitment you made, or of an offense you need to correct, and in this first section, you will get your own matters straight and out of the way before you go further to intercede for others.

Intercession

> *"Thy kingdom come, Thy will be done on earth as it is in heaven. Give us this day our daily bread, and forgive us our debts as we forgive our debtors. And lead us not into temptation, but deliver us from evil..."*

In this second section of the Lord's Prayer Pattern, you have an opportunity to pray in faith to establish the will of the kingdom in the lives of those for whom you pray in three areas: (1) Their needs; (2) The security of their relationships; and (3) The achievement of their destiny. In faith, you are praying that God's kingdom will come as His will is being done on earth as it is in heaven in the lives of those you know.

The initial statement of *"Thy kingdom come, Thy will be done on earth as it is in heaven"* is the ultimate universal cry of all mature believers; it is a corporate prayer to cover the entire planet with the truth, righteousness, and justice of the kingdom of God. But the following statements break down the universal corporate decree into three bite-size pieces that are distinctly individual and local. The obvious wisdom of the text is that we pray for God's kingdom to be established everywhere, and we prayerfully work within our local spheres of influence for God's kingdom to become a reality in the lives of those we know and influence. Robert E. Coleman in his book <u>The Master Plan of Evangelism</u>[58] teaches that the plan of our Lord to take the gospel into all the world was not mass evangelism but the discipleship of an intimate core of faithful believers who determined to multiply within their individual spheres of influence. The ultimate goal is for everyone everywhere to be discipled and come under the dominion of the Church, the "last days"[59] expression of God's kingdom.

Spiritual intercession is praying for the needs of someone. You take the intercessory position of standing before God on behalf of another person. That person may be saved and in need of spiritual guidance, sick or bound and in need of healing or deliverance, or lost and in need of salvation. What they need is for you to pray in faith.

Before I go into detail about the three areas outlined in the second section of the Lord's Prayer, you must hear me say that prayer, as important as it is, is not the only thing you may be called to do. It may be that you are part of the answer to someone's need or dilemma. You may be able to feed them, help them find shelter, or clothe them to provide warmth against the elements. In many instances, your prayer to the Father for someone will be heard and answered according to the will of God in ways far beyond what you could ask or imagine, but in some instances, your prayer will be more your prayerful assistance in serving and ministering to the need at hand that you are able to meet. This could very easily come under the covering of Matthew 6:33 where Jesus, in the Sermon on the Mount, exhorts us to seek first the kingdom of God and His righteousness, and everything that we need will be added. Could it be that God's expectation is that you pray for that which only God can provide, and supply that which you can provide knowing His promise that everything you need will be added? In that regard, let me encourage your generosity; you cannot beat God in giving!

Here's the explanation of the three areas of emphasis in section two of the Lord's Prayer Pattern:

(i) *Give us this day our daily bread*

This first area of intercession deals with you praying for the needs of others to be met. The plural pronouns throughout the prayer speak to the corporate, inclusive nature of our worship and prayer experiences. Of course, it does not mean you are out of order when you pray alone. It just means that no mature believer can really be satisfied and fully complete by simply praying provisions for self. Yes I know you have need of daily provisions, but love requires your concern and care for your covenant brother or sister and even the stranger within your community. Your emphasis in this first area of intercession is praying for the needs of those you know: a job, healing, sustenance, etc. Don't be afraid to be specific!

Again, let me remind you that your prayer for yourself should be handled under the first section of worship around God's compound covenant names; during that season of worship and praise is where your personal petitions find their hearing in your worship-filled confessions of faith around the promises in God's names. But in this first part of intercession for others, by name and by need, you stand before God to pray specifically the promises in faith.

(ii) *Forgive us our debts as we forgive our debtors*

This second area of intercession deals with you praying that the relationships of others will be secure. Most broken relationships contain some form of failure to forgive. Instances of deception, betrayal, or unfaithfulness, just to name a few, are responsible for the brokenness of most relationships, and, according to rationality, some may consider the circumstances unforgiveable. But while the road to reconciliation may need to include the counsel and/or advice of a third party, an unwillingness to forgive should never be part of the mature Christian's posture. This is because the commandment to forgive is connected to your being forgiven (Matthew 6:14-15). And the meaning of the word "debt" states unequivocally that forgiveness is something you OWE.[60] This truth is poignantly portrayed by Jesus in the Parable of the Unmerciful Servant:

> [21] *Then Peter came to Him and said, "Lord, how often shall my brother sin against me, and I forgive him? Up to seven times?"* [22] *Jesus said to him, "I do not say to you, up to seven times, but up to seventy times seven.*
>
> [23] *Therefore the kingdom of heaven is like a certain king who wanted to settle accounts with his servants.* [24] *And when he had begun to settle accounts, one was brought to him who owed him ten thousand talents.* [25] *But as he was not able to pay, his master commanded that he be sold, with his wife and children and all that he had, and that payment be made.* [26] *The servant therefore fell down before him, saying, 'Master, have patience with me, and I will pay you all.'* [27] *Then the master of that servant was moved with compassion, released him, and forgave him the debt.*
>
> [28] *But that servant went out and found one of his fellow servants who owed him a hundred denarii; and he laid hands on him and took him by the throat, saying, 'Pay me what you owe!'* [29] *So his fellow servant fell down at his feet and begged him, saying, 'Have patience with me, and I will pay you all.'* [30] *And he would not, but went and threw him into prison till he should pay the debt.*
>
> [31] *So when his fellow servants saw what had been done, they were very grieved, and came and told their master all that had been done.*
>
> [32] *Then his master, after he had called him, said to him, 'You wicked servant! I forgave you all that*

debt because you begged me. *³³ Should you not also have had compassion on your fellow servant, just as I had pity on you?' ³⁴ And his master was angry, and delivered him to the torturers until he should pay all that was due to him.*

³⁵ So My heavenly Father also will do to you if each of you, from his heart, does not forgive his brother his trespasses." (Matthew 18:21-35 NKJV)

Those who refuse to pay the *debt* of forgiveness are those who do not appreciate the grace of being forgiven.

(iii) Lead us not into temptation but deliver us from the evil one

This final area of intercession deals with you praying for someone's destiny to be achieved. Your motivation should be that somebody prayed for you, had you on their mind, and took the time to pray for you. Jesus would say, "Go and do likewise" (Luke 10:37). Therefore, you are petitioning God in prayer to lead someone away from a temptation where the enemy is endeavoring to entice a brother or sister to follow a false direction away from the will of God. Your prayer would include "binding" the enemy and canceling his deceptive plan in the name of Jesus (Matthew 12:29 KJV; John 16:24; 2 Corinthians 2:11). Your consistent prayer for them should be, "Father, direct their steps, guide them by Your Spirit (Romans 8:14) into the center of Your will for them, in Jesus's name" (Romans 12:1-2). In this way, with your consistent prayer covering, by the grace of God, they will achieve their destiny in Christ.

Remember the words of the LORD to Jeremiah, "'For I know the plans I have for you,' declares the LORD, 'plans to prosper you and not to harm you, plans to give you hope and a future'" (29:11). May you never forget that the ones for whom you labor with prayer and fasting, do not belong to you, they belong to the Lord. Your responsibility is to do the prayer work necessary for the paths of righteousness to become plain to them. Pray with the confidence that the seeds of faith you sow in prayer will provide the covering your brother or sister will reap as they persevere to the achievement of their destiny.

Thanksgiving

> *"For Thine is the kingdom, and the power, and the glory, forever. Amen."*

This final section is where you bring your prayer-time to a close with the strong realization that all you are able to accomplish through prayer is due to the kingdom, power, and glory of God. In essence, you could conclude your season of prayer with the words, "Thank you Father that I know it is Your kingdom I am praying to establish; it is by Your power that Your kingdom will be established in the hearts of Your people; and, it is by Your grace that I determine to give You all of the glory for whatever is accomplished, in Jesus's name. Amen." Let us pray...

Father, increase the hunger and thirst of these readers to walk in the righteous path of being prayer warriors. Deliver them from spiritual mediocrity where prayerlessness is the norm. Bring them to prayer proficiency as they: (1) set a time, (2) select a partner, (3) sanctify a place (perhaps a war room[61] in their home or apartment), and, (4) secure a pattern. I pray they will use these admonitions and learn to approach the throne of grace with confidence. I pray that their consistent worship and their faithful intercession for others become an example others will emulate. Thank you, Father, that needs are being met, relationships are being strengthened, and destinies are being achieved by grace through faith. My desire is for Your love to fill our lives as our hearts are open to obey Your Word and do Your will. Thank you for empowering us to do the work of the kingdom. Be glorified in all we do, in the name of Jesus we pray. Amen.

CHAPTER SIXTEEN

PRACTICALLY SPEAKING, HOW DOES FAITH WORK?
(PART I)

UNDERSTANDING HOW FAITH WORKS IS FUNDAMENTAL FOR PRAYER proficiency. The necessity of faith cannot be overemphasized if you expect to have an effective prayer life. Many pray only general, non-specific prayers that could never be identified as answered because their faithless expectation handcuffs them to trying to do God's work without Him. One may even believe intellectually that God exists, but because of an absence of experiential contact with Him they only view Him as transcendent, the One way out there who watches over us, a Being with which they've had no legitimate contact or access. It's a sad state of affairs if you understand the need for light to find your way through the darkness of life's difficult circumstances but you have no faith to pray for the light of God's help. The key passage for the necessity of faith is Hebrews 11:6: "And without <u>faith</u> it is impossible to please God, because anyone who comes to him must <u>believe</u> that he exists and that he rewards those who earnestly seek him" (emphasis mine).

Though the word "prayer" does not appear in the text, yet the obvious meaning of "anyone who comes to him must believe" is a reference to prayer. Faith is the foundation upon which an effective prayer life is built. The words "faith" and "believe" are connected in the verse. You cannot please God without *faith* and anyone who prays to God *must believe*. Though the two important (underlined) words in the text are different in English, they are the same words in the original Greek. The noun *pistis* means "faith" and the verb *pisteuo* means "to believe." Both have the same root—*pist*. Therefore, to have <u>faith</u> is to <u>believe</u> and to <u>believe</u> is to have <u>faith</u>. This phrase is important enough for you to remember it so expect to see it repeated in this "how" section on faith.

<u>Hear this illustration</u>: Praying without faith is like living in a house where you are hungry and praying for food, but you never go into the kitchen to look in the pantry or open the refrigerator to get the food that's inside.

<u>Here's another important illustration</u>: Praying without examining yourself, repenting, and making the adjustments in your life to qualify in faith for your prayer to be answered is like living in a house during freezing winter weather with all the windows and doors wide open. Both illustrations highlight the place of corresponding actions in the success of your faith. (James 2:17)

The Criteria for Praying in Faith

Many believers do not have an effective prayer life because they lack an expectation that God actually moves in response to our prayers. They do not actually believe God rewards those who earnestly seek Him. Prayer for them is more ceremonial than supernatural; it may be good for opening and closing a worship service, dedicating a baby, or praying wise and appropriate words over someone being appreciated or someone being elevated to a position of leadership and trust, but the idea that prayer actually touches the heart of God and moves Him to respond is not an experience with which they are familiar or that they expect.

If this is your dilemma, the first criterion for you to be used in prayer is: *change your perspective*. Start by repenting of your doubt of the trustworthiness of God's Word and your lack of expectation of the reality of God's presence bringing change that at times could be termed supernatural. Stop expecting business as usual. This does not necessarily mean you will see dramatic miracles occur immediately, but along with the dramatic that happens every now and then there are those miracles that are not dramatic but nonetheless miraculous. People who pray in faith see those occurrences take place and rejoice to see the hand of God save someone, change a countenance, or open a cold heart to become warmed as they turn toward God. These miracles happen all the time before our very eyes but many fail to recognize them due to a non-expectant perspective. As your perspective opens so that you expect God to show up, your praying will create within you and those around you an expectation of God's gracious movement in and among His people to save, deliver, heal, encourage, strengthen, and bless. With your perspective changed and your eyes opened, you will literally live your life with a renewed appreciation for God's love and care for His people, and you will know, without any fear of contradiction, God actually answers prayer.

The second criterion for being used in prayer is: *change your company*. The Word teaches, "Do not be misled: 'Bad company corrupts good character'" (1 Corinthians 15:33). Sometimes the answer to "bad company" is leave. You heard me—LEAVE! Joseph had to run from Potiphar's wife; Lot had to leave the city of Sodom; and you may have to do as Paul exhorted the Corinthians in another passage,

> *17 ..."Come out from them and be separate, says the Lord. Touch no unclean thing, and I will receive you." 18 And, "I will be a Father to you, and you will be my sons and daughters, says the Lord Almighty."* (2 Corinthians 6:17-18).

Many times, leaving, separating yourself, getting yourself away from negative people is the best decision you can make.

The third criterion for being used in prayer is: *change what you do*. Now that you are free from negative people who can potentially contaminate you, determine no longer to become entangled in their web of gossip, low moral outlook, negative faithless talk, corrupt practices, and worldly entrapments; but instead, seek to align yourself with those who are clearly upwardly mobile in the faith-filled spiritual sense. Get a prayer partner who is hungry for more of God, like you, and when you pray with them about needs, be specific. And when God answers your specific prayer based upon a promise in His Word, your faith will soar to a new level of confidence and expectation. Stop missing services and look to sit closer to the front where the serious believers sit. Do the necessary work in your church to be included in a ministry where you can serve and be useful. When the Word is being preached, bring your Bible and notebook to review the message on your own. Write down the points and Scripture references in order to read and study them more closely. Recognize the need to know better what God requires of you, the steps you need to take to be a stronger believer, one prospering personally and relationally in church and in your community. With these changes in perspective, company, and practice, you will begin to see the will of God clearer and recognize the gifts of God better and how they work to make you someone God will use to touch your generation and the next.

Understanding How Faith Works

A prayer of faith is a prayer based upon the "will" of God. God's will is known and understood by His Word, just as others know your will by your words. Let us not equivocate about this matter. Having *faith* about something means you *believe* what was written or said about that something. You must come to terms with this matter of faith. Many in Christian circles are confused about faith because they don't understand that to have faith is to believe with all your heart; if you really believe, you have faith. Remember, the two words are the same truth. It's just that simple.

But here's the problem—there are different kinds of believing. There's intellectual believing where the mental assent to a particular truth is acknowledged without any expectation of change in what you do or don't do. Then there's the believing with all of your heart. This phrase, "with all of your heart," means you've totally committed yourself to what you believe and will not be dissuaded from performing the actions or having the attitude commensurate with that belief.

For example, Charles Blondin (born Jean François Gravelet, February 28, 1824) the famous French tightrope walker and acrobat, owed his celebrity status and fortune to crossing the Niagara Gorge (located on the American-Canadian border) on a tightrope. This he did on June 30, 1859, and a number of times thereafter, always with different theatrical variations: blindfolded, trundling a sack-laden wheelbarrow, on stilts, sitting down midway while he cooked and ate an omelet, and standing on a chair with only one chair leg on the rope.[62] Legend has it that one day after pushing a huge sack in a wheelbarrow across the falls, he asked the crowd, "Do you believe I can push a man in this wheelbarrow across the falls?" The crowd, having witnessed his tightrope-walking expertise, responded in unison with a sonorous roar, "Yes!" He then asked for a volunteer from the crowd, "Who will get into the wheelbarrow?" But there was silence. No one came forward; a poignant illustration of the difference between believing with your head and believing with your whole heart. After the silent non-commitment of the crowd, Blondin's manager stepped forward saying, "I believe you," and climbed into the wheelbarrow.

Faith is more than lip service; it requires you saying, "Yes," with what you do. God is calling for you to be more than just a hearer but a doer of His Word. That's where living faith comes alive in your reality—in your acting out what you believe as the man who got into the wheelbarrow.

An Action of Faith

Evangelist Madelyn Joell, a dear sister in the Lord, was home sick with the flu that had her bedfast with fever and body aches. On one occasion, when her sister brought her some soup, her sister's son, a toddler of about three or four years old, was with her, and when he saw his aunt in bed, he asked, "What's wrong, Auntie?"

Not willing to ignore the little boy's question, she turned to him and with a raspy quiet voice responded, "Auntie is sick, honey."

Immediately the little boy, who had attended many church meetings where he'd witnessed his aunt praying for the sick at the altar, spoke up boldly in broken English, "I pray for you."

Being a woman of God and a prayer warrior, there was no way she would refuse prayer, and so she said to him while her headache made it even difficult to keep her eyes opened, "Yes, honey. Pray for Auntie."

Though she did not expect him to pray at that moment, he pushed past his mother, laid his hand on her forehead, as he had seen her do on several occasions in church, and said, "Bud of Jesus; bud of Jesus!" and stepped back. (Of course he meant "Blood of Jesus," but no one corrected him.) Then he pointed to her as he had seen her command others she'd prayed for at the altar and said, "Get up!"

She said to me as she shared this testimony, "I felt no different; I was just as sick, feverish, and headachy as before, but I did not want to discourage that little boy. So I mustered all of my strength to force myself to get out of bed for him, and miraculously, as I got up, I was healed."

This demonstrates the truth of James 2:17b, "Faith by itself, if it is not accompanied by action, is dead." When it comes to the important matter of the will of God in prayer (1 John 5:14-15), and you believe with your whole heart that the promise is true for you, your actions will follow what you really believe. It's just that simple. Expect your miracle.

Believe with Your Whole Heart

Believing with all of your heart is like the command to love the LORD with all your heart:

> *⁴ Hear, O Israel: the LORD our God, the LORD is one. ⁵ Love the LORD your God with all your heart and with all your soul and with all your strength.* (Deuteronomy 6:4-5)

No one questions the fact there are various levels of love. For some, their love is no more than lust, meaning, they are determined to benefit themselves at the expense of others. That's certainly not the love God intends for His people to have for Him or for one another. In terms of the love we are to have for one another, Jesus gave us a new commandment stating that the love we have for one another must follow the pattern of the love He demonstrated for us (John 13:35-35). And of course, the love demonstrated for us is the kerygma of the gospel—the sacrificial death of Christ on the cross, His burial, and His resurrection (1 Corinthians 15:1-4). On the cross, the definition of love was portrayed before the whole world: love determines to benefit others at your own expense (John 3:16; Romans 5:8), and God did it.

So then, whole heart *believing* is real *faith*, like loving with all your heart, soul, and strength. You believe with all your heart, with every part of your inner spirit; with all your soul, with every fiber of your mental faculties; and with all your strength, with all the power of your physical ability to act, as best you can without reservation or doubt. Is this difficult? Yes, but possible because Jesus said, "Truly I tell you, if you have faith as small as a mustard seed, you can say to this mountain, 'Move from here to there,' and it will move. Nothing will be impossible for you" (Matthew 17:20).

What then should your posture be? Good question. Realize faith deals with unseen things you are believing will appear in your future, be it next minute, day, week, month, year, etc. The time it takes should not be a faith issue since timing is God's job. Your job is to keep your faith-switch turned on. Paul encouraged the Galatians, "And let us not be weary in well doing: for in **due season** we shall reap, if we faint not" (Galatians 6:9 KJV, emphasis mine). Keeping the faith-switch turned on means not becoming weary in doing good, and being aware that your "due season" is in God's hands. You believe to reap a harvest of blessings from the faith-filled prayers you've prayed based upon the truth of God's promise(s), so DO NOT FAINT, DO NOT GIVE UP! Your due season is coming, so keep faith with a hope-filled expectation (Hebrews 11:1).

In the interim—between your praying and your "due season" of receiving—say "AMEN" with worship and thanksgiving to the promise(s) you are holding onto, remembering what Paul wrote in his second epistle to the Corinthians, "For no matter how many promises God has made, they are 'Yes' in Christ. And so through him the '**Amen**' is spoken by us to the glory of God" (2 Corinthians 1:20, emphasis mine). Since you are "in Christ," the promises of God are "Yes" for you! You must believe the truth of His promises with all your heart and boldly confess "Amen" to the glory of God. The "Amen" you speak means, "So let it be!" It is a faith confession you are making. Ostensibly, you are saying, "I'm saying, 'Amen' to the truth and trustworthiness of God's holy Word, and I believe to receive what God has promised!"

This is the truth of making a "*good* confession." Unfortunately, the word *confession* in many church circles is only used in connection to verbally admitting sin or some other type of wrongdoing. But there's another side to confession you need to know in the faith fight. Paul spoke of it in his first epistle to Timothy (1 Timothy 6:12; cf. also Hebrews 10:23). Timothy's "good confession in the presence of many witnesses" was probably at a church gathering during a time of testimony, perhaps the confession of Jesus Christ as the Lord of his life was included (Romans 10:9-10); maybe it was Timothy giving witness of his faith commitment before being baptized. But when you fully understand what God has done in you through your act of faith in the blood of Christ, and the truth of it finds its way into your prayers or in a testimony service in church or in a time of sharing your faith with a friend, you are making a *good confession.*

Also, a good confession progresses into saying verbally in prayer what the Word says about you: who you are *in Christ,* what you have *in Christ,* and what you can do *in Christ.* It can be something you say aloud like a declaration when you're alone or maybe as a part of your early-morning-prayer time. In whatever way at whenever time your good confession is spoken your goal is for its truth to brand itself to the bone marrow of your spirit. When that happens, the power of that truth will set you free from all bondages, especially the ones connected to doubt and unbelief (John 8:31-32).

You enter into the warfare aspect of prayer with a good confession. You put on the full armor of God (Ephesians 6:10-18) and fight against demonic principalities with spiritual weapons[63] (2 Corinthians 10:4) in the process of making a good confession. As Paul wrote to Timothy, you "take hold of the eternal life to which you were called" when you maintain a good confession (1 Timothy 6:12).

This battle is called the "good fight of faith" because you cannot lose. With a good confession, you take territory for the kingdom of God within your spheres of influence because you are not praying in a defensive way where your prayers lacking faith are characterized by begging and pleading, but with confidence you stand in faith upon the bedrock of God's eternal Word that's forever settled in heaven (Psalm 119:89 KJV). This is because you've gone further in praying the prayers of faith, speaking the sword of the Spirit, the Word of God, to demolish demonic strongholds in the name of Jesus. Prayer becomes the battleground where this combative activity takes place. You are not just making your requests known (Philippians 4:6-7), as good as that is, but with the *anointing* of the Spirit and the *authority* of the Word, you wield a decisive blow against the enemy, where in the power of the Spirit you speak with authority the Word of God and in faith gain *access* to grace in the name of Jesus (Romans 5:2). That grace is the power of God bestowing His strength on His heirs (2 Corinthians 12:9).

A good confession is saying about you what God's Word says about you. The word *"confess"* is translated from the Greek word *homologeo* (the verb form "to confess") and *homologia* (the noun form "confession"). It's used in the Greek New Testament about 29 times: confess and/or confession (19 times); profess and or profession (eight times); promised (one time); and giving thanks (one time). It's a compound word from two Greek words *homo* meaning *"same"* and *logeo* meaning *"to say or speak."* Therefore, to make a good confession literally means to *say the same thing* God says about you. A good confession should find its way into your prayer life as thanksgiving and praise. That's warfare praising and praying!

A significant prayer warrior, Dr. David D. Ireland, recognizes this truth in his book, *The Weapon of Prayer: Maximize Your Greatest Strategy Against the Enemy*. He characterizes prayer as an offensive weapon. It speaks volumes of his experiential understanding of the faith fight. He aptly defines offensive praying as seeking "to advance your life, your ministry, and the penetration of the gospel message into the world around you." He expands his definition, saying offensive praying is "not reactionary…not backward looking"—it is not praying "in a counteractive way"—but with faith and vision you seek to "initiate action" in the sense of moving forward, "driven by tactical steps that preclude any problem, cut off or reduce future distractions, and annihilate satanic schemes designed to trip you up."[64]

E.M. Bounds, in his book *The Weapon of Prayer*, mentions the words of the apostles concerning the first administrative difficulty of the early church: the neglect of the Hellenistic widows in the daily distribution of food. Bounds rehearses the words of the apostles who turned the problem over to seven men to solve as the apostles shared a telling statement, "But we will devote ourselves to prayer and to the ministry of the Word" (Acts 6:4 ESV). Bounds follows this backdrop of the story in Acts with these words,

> It is better to let the work go by default than to let the praying go by neglect. Whatever affects the intensity of our praying affects the value of our work. "Too busy to pray" is not only the keynote to backsliding, but it mars even the work done. Nothing is well done without prayer for the simple reason that it leaves God out of the account.[65]

I recall the seniors in my home church making a similar statement that rhymed, "If you don't pray, you won't stay; if you don't fast, you won't last." Therefore, by all means, add a *good confession* of what God promises in His Word to your praying and fasting, laboring and loving, and you will see the dawn of your answers to prayer rise over your spiritual eastern sky.

The Faith-fight Sometimes Requires Rebuke

Sometimes your answer to prayer is not a matter of waiting for your due season to arrive as you keep the faith-switch turned on. It may be that the hindrance to the blessing is the work of the enemy and you need to exercise authority over him. Take, for example,

Jesus ministering to the man whose son had a condition like epilepsy that was caused by an evil spirit.

> [21] *Jesus asked the boy's father, "How long has he been like this?" "From childhood," he answered.* [22] *"It has often thrown him into fire or water to kill him. But if you can do anything, take pity on us and help us." * [23] *"'If you can'?" said Jesus. "Everything is possible for one who believes." * [24] *Immediately the boy's father exclaimed, "I do believe; help me overcome my unbelief!" * [25] *When Jesus saw that a crowd was running to the scene, **he rebuked the evil spirit**. "You deaf and mute spirit," he said, "I command you, come out of him and never enter him again." * [26] *The spirit shrieked, convulsed him violently and came out. The boy looked so much like a corpse that many said, "He's dead." * [27] *But Jesus took him by the hand and lifted him to his feet, and he stood up.* (Mark 9:14-27, emphasis mine)

Notice in the text we see Jesus raising the need for the father to have faith. The immediate response is the father exclaiming, "I do believe; help me overcome my unbelief!" (v. 24), and the result is Jesus casting out the evil spirit and the boy being delivered and healed. This is an example of when the faith of the one ministering overrode the unbelief of the one needing ministry. The expectation is that the weak one will grow in faith enough to hold on to their healing or deliverance.[66]

Deliverance from a Distance: An Illustration

My cousin, Jerry, was unsaved and deeply embroiled in a sinful lifestyle. We'd grown up together since our mothers were sisters and best friends. We attended Sunday school and church together as young people. Once I grew to a place in my prayer life where I determined that no one I felt close to would be lost, I started praying for my cousin every day. Whenever I'd see him at a family gathering, I tried to share truth with him with the view of encouraging him to take inventory of his life and change, but those few sessions never reaped any immediate results. Actually, I don't remember why I changed the way I'd been praying for him, but I thought on one occasion, "He's so trapped by the sins of his lifestyle, maybe I should pray against those individual sins first." So the next time I prayed for him, I took on the sin of smoking. Now of course, I know there are believers who smoke and don't see smoking as a sin, but my cousin grew up in the same church with me where we were taught that saints don't smoke. So I knew that smoking was a sin to him.

My prayer against his smoking habit was simple and specific: I prayed, "Father, I rebuke the smoking habit in my cousin, and the next time he lights up a cigarette, I'm asking that You make him so sick, he'll have to go to the hospital. Thank you Father in Jesus's name." We lived in different cities, I in Boston and he in Philadelphia. Well, after several weeks, I drove to Philly to visit my parents, and whenever I was in my hometown, my pastor would ask me to preach his Wednesday evening service. My cousin was not in the service, but his younger sister, who's a believer, was present, and after the service she shared with me, "Cuz, guess what; Jerry stopped smoking!"

My joyous response was, "Praise the Lord!"

"Yes," she continued, "He lit up a cigarette and became so sick that he went to the Emergency Room. They didn't find anything wrong with him, but he threw away his pack of cigarettes, quit smoking, and hasn't had another cigarette since." I continued to rejoice with her at the news, knowing her love for her brother and her many prayers for his salvation, but I privately took note that God had answered my prayer specifically. Getting answers from specific prayer requests strengthens your faith.

I then continued my prayers for his salvation by attacking his living arrangement. He was divorced and living with his girlfriend. My prayer was that she would come to Christ, kick him out, or he would leave on his own. And the next thing I heard from my family was that Jerry had moved and was living with his oldest daughter who is a believer; praise the Lord, another prayer was answered specifically. And it had been answered even better than I'd imagined, because his daughter would watch Christian television, and Jerry fell in love with Bishop T.D. Jakes while he was living with her. Sometime after that, I don't know how long, Jerry committed his life to the lordship of Christ, married his girlfriend, answered the call to preach the gospel, and eventually preached his trial sermon in our home church.

Difficult scheduling precluded my being present at his trial sermon, but before he went to be with the Lord, one of my sons and I drove to Philly because I'd heard he was sick and in need of a heart transplant. We sat together—Jerry, his wife, my son, and me—in their bedroom. He was in bed as we shared together for almost two hours, during which time he wept about a half dozen times rejoicing over the glory of being saved. He never got the transplant, but I know I'll see him on the other side.

Bathe yourself, your family, your business, and your work in the kingdom in prayer daily. This will prepare you to care prayerfully and strategically for your community and city without the personal distractions many in ministry feel. Prayer will help you stay focused on the goals you strategically set and enable you to guard against the self-exalting pride of effective accomplishments. When there is travailing prayer that's effectual and fervent (James 5:16b KJV) you can stay balanced knowing that whatever is accomplished—whether spiritual, relational, physical, or financial—this is about God's kingdom and not about you. It is all about Jesus, for without Him, no significant impact will happen today and no generational influence will arise tomorrow. Jesus did not give *you* the job to build His Church. Building the Church is *His* job; your job includes being a prayer warrior, being one who hears His voice, knows His Word, and follows the leading of the Spirit in Jesus's name. This is true not only for pastors or church ministry leaders or workers, but it is also true for the business owner or worker who labors in a secular occupation. Prayer proficiency will pull you into supernatural increase and benefit, especially when you are a mature believer who understands God favors you to support in every way the work of your church.

CHAPTER SEVENTEEN

PRACTICALLY SPEAKING, HOW DOES FAITH WORK?
(PART II)

Multigenerational Faith in Action

WARRIOR PRAYER ADVANCES THE WORK OF THE KINGDOM, BECAUSE a prayer-energized gospel will penetrate the hearts and lives of multiple generations in your area and especially in your local church. The local church Jesus is building is all about touching the next generations. This is what He meant when He said to Peter and the disciples, "On this rock, I will build *my* church, and the gates of Hades [death] will not overcome it" (Matthew 16:18, emphasis mine). Basic to the fact that Jesus is building His Church and that death cannot stop what He is building, is the truth— we are commissioned to make disciples of all nations (Matthew 28:19-20). The phrase "all nations" most assuredly includes all generations within those cultural contexts. The Great Commission in the Matthew 28 text ends with the statement, "And surely I am with you always, to the very end of the age." (Vs. 20) The immediate contextual sense of that text is that Jesus promised to add the powerful approval of His presence to those who partner with Him in multinational and especially multigenerational evangelism and discipleship. Those agreeing to prioritize this salvation kingdom work demonstrate *faith in action*.

Christian Character is Faith in Action

When you strive to see a multigenerational expression of the church, it will force you to discipline yourself to be the kind of example others will follow. Irrespective of their ages, others will remember much more of who you are than of what you said. It's part of the truth that we remember more of what you see than what you hear. It's probably why Jesus said, "Let your light shine before men, that they may *see* your good deeds and praise your Father in heaven." (Matthew 5:16, emphasis mine)

You cannot *make* your light shine; you can only *let* your light shine. So, the light others will see is that which shines through *who* you really are. And being strong in faith is part of that light they need to see. Literally, it is a light of *faith in action* that the world is in desperate need of seeing in your action and your words. You have an opportunity to make an impact upon the next generation by being REAL. Real in your commitment to Christ; real in your walk of faith; real in your genuine balanced Christian lifestyle!

The next generation is hungry to see and hear the simple, balanced, spiritual truth that is evidenced by your experienced sharing. Amen? Now let me remind you of the difference between faith, foolishness, and presumption and how the qualifying of your faith-stand positions you to experience what God has promised. This is *faith in action* that can effectively minister to others.

Faith, Foolishness, and Presumption

Do you remember the discussion about *Faith, Foolishness, and Presumption* in chapter fourteen? The same principles apply here. You are acting in *faith* when your prayer has its foundation in the Word of God, written or spoken; you are acting in *foolishness* when your prayer has no foundation in the Word of God, written or spoken; and you are acting in *presumption* when you pray without first examining the Scriptures and considering whether or not you qualify for the promise you want fulfilled in your life. Some years ago, while teaching on faith, I heard myself say, "You cannot demand by promise what you deny by principle."

There is a part you must play in this challenge of praying and believing by faith. An old word of wisdom I've heard spoken several times in the church I grew up in is, "Pray like it's all God and work like it's all you." You should not exempt yourself from any responsibility in solving your problem or finding a way out of your dilemma. Do you need money because you have a family and bills to pay? By all means, pray for God to open the door for employment, get up early every day, wash your face, brush your teeth, comb your hair, put on business clothing, and go out with your resumé in hand and/or an understanding of your skillset and apply.

Are you sick, do you have a toothache, or are you in pain? Going to a doctor, making a dentist appointment, or receive the services of a chiropractor. This does not mean you have no faith. Your challenge is to pray, believe, and walk in faith knowing that God can move to solve your situation on His own or use someone with His knowledge to help you. In the final analysis, it all depends on God anyway, and if you will attack the challenges of life with faith-filled praying, you will be strengthened to deal with those difficulties or circumstances that no physical professional person, procedure, or medicine can solve.

Faith from the Text

You are called to operate in faith—to live by faith and not by sight (2 Corinthians 5:7). As a mature believer who prays, you are not to be ruled by your senses. Though what you see or feel is part of your physical reality, your spiritual reality that speaks through the word of faith you believe (Romans 10:8) is what you must hear and pay attention to. You must determine to believe what God says though it may contradict what you see or feel.

The British Evangelist, Smith Wigglesworth, an apostle of faith, is credited with having said, "I'm not moved by what I see; I'm not moved by what I feel; I'm moved only by what I believe!" Learning to give more credence to the promises you believe and less credence to what you see or feel is the process of becoming a person strong in faith (2 Corinthians 4:18).

Connected to that process is growing in your knowledge of God's Word. The strength of your faith, in large measure, is commensurate to how well you know God's Word. In fact, the reason the devil fights so hard to discredit the Bible is because those who honor God, who have a superior knowledge of His Word, and who know how to pray in faith the promises of the Word literally become the devil's worst nightmare. In spiritual warfare, they are believers to be reckoned with because they draw spiritual water from the wells of salvation found in Scripture. Therefore, love, study, and honor the truth and trustworthiness of the Scriptures, the holy Word of God.

Given the powerful authority you have in the Word, and the miraculous healings and deliverances that have been experienced by mature believers throughout salvation history, your primary responsibility is to get the Word into the minds and hearts of the people you influence. Then, let the Word do its work![67]

The Inspired Scriptures: God-breathed

A key reason for believing the truth of God's Word above empirical evidence is the fact the Scriptures are inspired—*God-breathed* (2 Timothy 3:16-17). Charles T. Studd, the founding pioneer of the Worldwide Evangelization Crusade (WEC), a faith missionary[68] to China, India, and central Africa (the Belgian Congo), is credited with saying, **"God said it, that settles it!"** If you truly believe what God said is true and you exercise your faith by acting upon the promise you believe, as you receive the benefit, blessing, or provision because of your faith, you will be able to proclaim with faith walkers like Charles T. Studd, George Mueller, Hudson Taylor, C. H. Mason, Dr. Lillian B. Yoemans, MD, John G. Lake, William J. Seymour, and Dr. Helen Roseveare, MD—God said it, that settles it!

The Word of Faith

Along with the faith you receive to see miracles performed because the simple truth of the Scriptures is believed as it is preached and taught, there is an even greater measure of faith you can receive that rises from your intimate walk with Christ. Let me explain.

There are two main Greek words translated into English as "word" in the New Testament. They are *logos* and *rhema*. While there are other Greek words translated "word," these two are used by the writers of the New Testament far more frequently. A careful examination of their usage in the Synoptic Gospels indicates the Greek word *logos* is used to refer to a word spoken or message delivered (e.g. Matthew 2:13; 12:32), and while there are exceptions where Jesus was speaking a word that brought healing and deliverance (cf. *logos* used in Matthew 8:16), the Greek word *rhema* is always used of a spoken "word"[69] heard or recalled by an authority, usually Jesus.

While the two words in the epistles are seemingly used interchangeably, yet in the key passage where believing faith is explained, the Greek word used is *rhema*. The distinction in the text is a word that is near you, a word you hear, a word that's revealed out of your intimate relationship with Christ. While all of us pray over spoken requests for needs in various areas, there are those prayers you pray out of a revelation word you hear in your spirit. That "heard word" is a "word of faith." The key passage teaching this truth is Romans 10:8-17 NASB,

> [8] *But what does it say? "The word is near you, in your mouth and in your heart"-that is, the* **word of faith** *which we are preaching,* [9] *that if you confess with your mouth Jesus as Lord, and believe in your heart that God raised Him from the dead, you will be saved;* [10] *for with the heart a person believes, resulting in righteousness, and with the mouth he confesses, resulting in salvation.* [11] *For the Scripture says, "Whoever believes in Him will not be disappointed."* [12] *For there is no distinction*

between Jew and Greek; for the same Lord is Lord of all, abounding in riches for all who call on Him; [13] for "Whoever will call on the name of the Lord will be saved." [14] How then will they call on Him in whom they have not believed? How will they believe in Him whom they have not heard? And how will they hear without a preacher? [15] How will they preach unless they are sent? Just as it is written, "How beautiful are the feet of those who bring good news of good things!" [16] However, they did not all heed the good news; for Isaiah says, "Lord, who has believed our report?" [17] So faith comes from hearing, and hearing by the word of Christ.
(Emphases mine)

The truth about the word of faith is that God's spoken word contains the powerful authority of heaven in the earth realm. It is a word of God's intention or will in a particular event at a specific time. We see this operation in the ministry of Jesus healing the man at the Pool of Bethesda (John 5:1-9). According to the commentary in the text, many sick people were gathered at the pool waiting for the troubling of the waters, but Jesus only healed one person, a man who had been infirm for about 38 years. Doubtless, Jesus only heard the Father speak about healing that one man and not the others (cf. John 6:38; 8:28-29; 10:38; 12:49-50; 14:31). There's a lesson to be learned in this: if Jesus could walk through a place where the sick and infirmed were gathered in large numbers to be healed, and He only healed one person, it says that though healing generally is the will of God, at times, there are specific circumstances in terms of the Spirit's leading that should be respected. Hearing the Lord speak to you with specific instruction about what to do in those times takes faith to another level and instills a strength of confidence that makes ministry success inevitable. Hearing God's spoken word is power.

God created the world by His spoken word; He said, "Let there be...," and it was (Genesis 1; cf. Hebrews 11:3). His word is the highest authority in all of creation history: "Your word, LORD, is eternal; it stands firm in the heavens" (Psalm 119:89). When deliverance or healing was needed in the life of believers, the Psalmist wrote, "He [God] sent out his word and healed them; he rescued them from the grave" (Psalm 107:20).

Hearing a Word of Faith: An Illustration

We were in the last service of a revival. The evangelist, Madeline Joell, one whom God used on several occasions to inspire faith for healing, at the close of the sermon called for those who wanted hands laid on them in prayer for healing to come forward. First to come was the 12-year-old son of a couple in the church. His parents were long-time members and their only child suffered from chronic nosebleeds. He had one as they arrived for service and had been in the basement of the church trying to get the bleeding to stop. On past episodes, his parents had to resort to going to the Emergency Room at the local hospital where a doctor would cauterize his nose tissue to stop the bleeding. But on this occasion, they were in church and decided to wait until the service was over before they made the trek to the Emergency Room.

However, when they saw there would be prayer for healing, they had an usher retrieve their son from the basement so he could be prayed for. The evangelist and I prayed for him first, given his obvious need for healing. I'd never seen a nosebleed quite like that: a steady stream of blood flowed from both nostrils. The usher who'd brought him to the front held a small trash basket full of blood soaked tissues. It was both scary and intimidating. We laid hands on him and prayed, but to no avail. We prayed again and again for his nose to stop bleeding, but without the slightest bit of success. Finally, the evangelist left him and went on to pray for others who had come to the altar for healing, and the young man went and sat on the front pew. I went with him and stood in front of him continuing to pray. Here was a young boy, 12 years old, who had given his life to Christ under my ministry, and we could not get him healed from a simple nosebleed.

I remember praying, "Father, I've been preaching to these, Your people, that it is Your will to heal them, and the first chance we get to demonstrate that truth, we fail. This is embarrassing! If you weren't going to heal anybody tonight, why didn't you send someone who has a hidden condition? That way, no one would know we failed, but this nosebleed shouts loud and clear, NO HEALING HERE! Why have we failed?"

When I asked the question in all sincerity, I realized for the first time that *we* had failed. Since there's no failure in God, the failure is always with us. So I prayed, "Lord, how did we miss it? Where did we fail?"

It was then I heard Him say distinctly, "Ask him, is he saved."

I looked at him sitting in front of me, "Junior, are you saved son?" I asked.

"No pastor, I'm backslidden." By then, his parents were on their way to the front to retrieve their son and take him to the Emergency Room. I gently ushered Junior and his parents into a prayer-room next to the altar. When there, I said to his parents, "Junior is not saved."

His mother responded, "Pastor, I thought you knew Junior had backslidden."

"No, I didn't know," I said. Then I looked at their son and said, "Junior, in order to be healed, you must be on healing ground. Healing is the children's bread. Now get on your knees and repent of your backsliding and God will heal you without anyone having to pray for you. I'll know you got through to God because your nose will stop bleeding." When I said that, I was tempted to fear, given how long we'd prayed for him without success, but I was emboldened by having heard the Lord say, "Ask him, is he saved." Somehow, I knew this was a healing moment. He knelt down, closed his eyes and prayed while I watched his nose. The Bible says to watch as well as pray. I saw the miracle with my own eyes and his parents saw it also. In just a matter of a few seconds, the bleeding went from streams to drips to a gentle spray. He opened his eyes. I asked, "Did you get through?"

He answered, "Yes, Pastor."

Dabbing his nose with the tissue in my hand, I asked, "Where is your nosebleed?" Some would say he was healed by the power of God, but I would say, "It surely was God's power, but it did not happen until he got on healing ground." And the faith that brought it came from hearing the word of Christ.

Multigenerational Agreement

We examined agreement praying with a partner in chapter 15 Praying with a partner in faith is further strengthened when practiced multi-generationally, meaning an older person praying with someone from the next generation. This enables the cross pollination of ideas and strengths: the younger will grow in their knowledge of the Word and in fervency from the older prayer warrior, and the older will grow in the language usage and request interests of the younger prayer warrior. Very important!

Summary Conclusion

The place of prayer in faith cannot be over-emphasized. Though faith in the promises of Scripture is powerful, you must recognize that the ones who moved in faith in Scripture did so because they heard God speak to them and not because they read about the miraculous movings of God in the Bible. Let me repeat—they HEARD God speak to them and faith came alive within them.

Faith is, by all means, gained as the Word is preached and taught, read and understood. Understanding the truth of *hearing a rhema word* does not in any way negate the truth of the impartation of faith through the written Word. In fact, the two work together to support the veracity you need to act in faith. Because God does not contradict Himself, what He says to you as a *rhema word* will never contradict the truth principles taught in the Scriptures. Therefore, you need a thorough understanding of the truths of the Bible, the intimacy gained in prayer, faithful living, and kingdom ministry to hear His voice (John 10:27). Let us pray...

> Father, open the eyes of my heart to know Your ways. Teach me to listen to Your still small voice and to walk in faith productively and circumspectly. I want to please You. Lead me into pastures green; give me a heart to share with others and to nourish them with what I learn. Use me to establish truth that will set others free, in Jesus's name I pray. Amen.

CHAPTER EIGHTEEN

PRACTICALLY SPEAKING, HOW DOES AGREEMENT WORK?

IN ORDER TO EXAMINE HOW THE TRUTH OF AGREEMENT IMPACTS YOUR prayer life you will need to understand what agreement is, why agreement is important, and how agreement is achieved. Knowing agreement's definition, importance, and how to maximize its strength will not only benefit your pursuit of prayer proficiency, but it will also help you push past those unseen barriers that prohibit your growth. Unfortunately, the truth of agreement is rare in the church, but it's not rare in businesses where the owners' vision permeates the culture of the company, or in the military where in "boot camp" recruits are trained to submit to the authority of their superiors. Though the truth of agreement is taught and exemplified in Scripture, the average believer and the average local church are unaware of its teaching and ignorant of its benefits. What you learn here about agreement will impact your life. As you incorporate its truth in your prayer life, in your personal life, and in your professional life, others will witness the strength of its benefits. Walking in and modeling agreement can potentially catapult you into new levels of achievement and even prosperity. Let's begin.

What is Agreement?

The Greek word *sumphoneo* is translated by the English word "agree" in the context of agreeing with someone in prayer (Matthew 18:19). It means,

> "...agreeing in sound; metaphorically accordant, harmonious, agreeing...to sound together, to be in unison, be in accord; tropically to agree with, accord with in purport, Acts 15:15; to harmonize with, be congruous, suit with, Luke 5:36; to agree with, make an agreement, Matt. 18:19; 20:2, 13; Acts 5:9."[70]

Without having the benefit of studying Koine Greek, the language of the New Testament, you can understand the meaning of the Greek word *sumphoneo* in addition to the Greek Lexicon definition given above because our English word *symphony* comes from that Greek word. A symphony is a harmonious musical composition or arrangement that is usually performed by an orchestra with a conductor. Though the orchestra is made up of many different musical instruments, and though the musicians are playing different notes at the same time, yet the symphony is always harmonious because the conductor overseeing the performance knows exactly how he wants the symphony interpreted and all the musicians are submitted to the volume, intensity, and pace of the conductor. Thus, a symphony, despite all of its moving parts with various sections playing different roles in the composition, yet when the musicians play their musical instruments under the conductor's direction, the symphony pictures the beauty and harmony of *agreement*.

Why is Agreement Important?

Dr. Edwin Louis Cole, the founder of the Christian Men's Network, a precursor to the great ministry to men, Promise Keepers, said, "The place of agreement is the place of power." Agreement is important because it releases power into the lives of those who venture to *agree*. It is emphasized by the teaching of Jesus on prayer to His disciples as a guarantee that the Father will move in response to two believers praying in agreement: "Again, I tell you that if two of you on earth agree about anything you ask for, it will be done for you by My Father in heaven" (Matthew 18:19). Though the text does not reference the will of God, remember, the full meaning of a passage needs to take into account what the Bible teaches elsewhere on that subject. Notice the truth concerning prayer according to the will of God in 1 John 5:14-15. Clearly, two believers agreeing in prayer in line with the will of God get the job done.

Another corroborative example of the power of agreement is found in the Old Testament account of God's words about the builders of the Tower of Babel. This is perhaps one of the most telling historical examples of the importance behind why we should strive to agree: "The LORD said, 'If as one people speaking the same language they have begun to do this, then nothing they plan to do will be impossible for them'" (Genesis 11:6; cf. 11:1-8). The agreement of Genesis 11 is a phenomenal example of what can happen when people are united ("as one people"), are all understanding one another ("speaking the same language"), and agree to work together ("they have begun to do this"); with these agreement pieces of the puzzle solidly in place, the LORD says, "…then nothing they plan to do will be impossible for them." That's the important power of agreement you and I need in our everyday lives, and especially within the work of the kingdom.

God confused their languages (vv. 7-8) so they could not understand each other. Evidently, the LORD did not want them to build a city for themselves with a tower that reached to the heavens, so that they might make a name for themselves and not be scattered over the face of the whole earth (v. 4). So I say again, agreeing in prayer in line with the will of God gets the job done.

How is Agreement Achieved?

Basically, the building of agreement is achieved when four necessary pillars are in place: (1) Leadership; (2) Integrity; (3) Vision; and (4) Submission. Let's briefly consider each to gain a basic understanding of this truth.

Leadership

The question of how agreement is achieved is answered in the example of a symphony being played by numerous musicians in the harmony of agreement because everyone is following the leadership of the conductor. Local church ministry leaders are called gifts from God (Ephesians 4:8-11), and the pastor could be considered the conductor. He's the one, along with the other elders, responsible for the oversight of the believers in that church (Hebrews 13:7, 17). Secular leaders understand the leadership model of authority flowing down from the top. Unity of function that brings financial success is achieved by agreement with those who have been given authority. The necessity of leaders is obvious.

The work that gifted leaders provide by their wise direction in the church, in the community, or in business, is invaluable. Their lifestyle examples to those they influence speak volumes to the necessity of their position. This is true of spiritual and secular leaders. And if they work together in agreement in the local church, they are a formidable force for truth and change.

One person alone will accomplish little, but together, great things are achievable. God gives various gifts that solve various problems, and the leader is the one God gifts to supply the vision and chart the course where direction and action are coordinated. It is not a matter of competition or of who will receive credit. It's the matter of seeking the harmony unity brings as everyone recognizes their gifts are from God (Romans 11:29; 12:6). Mature believers rejoice to focus on achieving the vision the leader has received from God. It's a harmonious orchestration of unity that is selfless, and the song of unity's achievement is music in the Lord's ears. This is leadership worth following.

Integrity

Synonyms for integrity are: honesty, truthfulness, honor, veracity, reliability, uprightness, completeness, and wholeness. Because the enemy knows how important leadership is, he exalts false leaders who end up doing more harm than good, often leading their followers down a negative path of failure and destruction. The enemy's goal is to instill hesitation and fear in the hearts of people following God-commissioned leaders because of the publicized failures of leaders with little or no character. The result of this is the leader's ability to catch the vision and proclaim the direction to submitted followers becomes crippled by a lack of trust. And out of fear, the people produce regulations and perimeters that limit the ability of a leader to do what God gifted him to do. This dilemma is commonplace in churches everywhere, and it needs to be solved.

The answer is to resist fear and hesitation by seeking to follow a person with integrity who you sense is called and gifted by God to do what he is envisioning doing. Then, allow him to prayerfully lead you and the church into green pastures. Is he following in faith the vision he has? Is he open to instruction? Is he one under authority? Is he praying? Does he know the Word? Does his personal and family life exemplify what he says? In other words, do his talk and his walk agree? If yes, follow him and the vision he teaches (Proverbs 29:18).

Vision

Within the realm of faith, there are two sources of vision: (1) The Baptism with the Holy Spirit; and (2) Prayer. On the Day of Pentecost, in his message, the apostle Peter quoted the Old Testament prophet Joel (Acts 2:16-17; cf. Joel 2:28-29) that the gift of the Holy Spirit would bring dreams and visions to Spirit-filled believers. This sought-after encounter with the Holy Spirit, resulting in an outpouring that believers receive, results in power to perform effective ministry (Acts 1:8). Vision is part of the by-product of seeking to be used by God to touch others for Christ.

The second source of vision is *prayer*, and the classic key passage teaching this is Habakkuk 2:1-4. The prophet climbs the steps of a tower to seek God in prayer for an answer to a serious dilemma in his nation, and the Lord speaks to him a vision (v. 2 KJV, "revelation" NIV), and he's instructed to write it down and share it with those he influences. He is told further about the timeframe for the vision so that his faith might be strengthened as he waits for the vision's fulfillment. It is interesting to note that just because you hear a word of revelation or receive a vision directly from the Lord does not mean the fulfillment of the vision will occur without difficulty; faith will be necessary throughout the process, beginning with receiving the vision to concluding with walking into the glorious fullness of the accomplished goal.

Submission

Very little will ever be accomplished without the confident strength of character to submit your part of the plan to the overall vision of the Leader. When submission to the authority of visionary leadership is in place, the progress toward making the collective faith become sight is achievable as the leaders and their teams work together. Though there may be questions about timing and organizational priorities, success inevitably follows the faith filled trust that exists in the God given vision of the Leader.

Submission occurs at various levels in the process of organizing multiple pieces of the vision where different leaders chosen to guide teams to work on different aspects of the vision humbly press forward aware that their part is connected to other parts contributing to the success of the vision as a whole. Key to this is a summitted attitude of cooperation with the contributions of other teams while at the same time submitted to the focus of the vision of the Leader; this attitude of focus for the success of the vision is crucial. Each piece of the puzzle will find its place in the overall fulfillment of the vision as the Leader fulfills his responsibility to hear and see the vision, share what he hears and sees with the leaders under him as they are submitted to doing their part in agreement to submit to the vision of the Leader and work with their respective teams, who are submitted to them, in order to achieve seeing the vision become a reality. Thus, the success is realized as those working on different parts of the vision are mature believers whose prayer life keeps them balanced in their perspective that they are working to achieve God's vision, do God's work, and in the process feel grateful and privileged to be God's fellow workers in His vineyard (2 Corinthians 6:2) to see this vision become a reality.

Understanding what you have learned about the truth of agreement, let us consider three (3) progressive steps to follow to achieve agreement in prayer.

1. <u>Find a believer whose faith is strong enough to agree in prayer with you for the specific request(s) you have</u>. Bear in mind that just because someone is a believer does not mean his or her faith is strong enough to sustain agreement over the time it may take for faith to become sight. Therefore, choose wisely; the miracle you need may hang in the balance of the faith agreement of your partner.

2. <u>Take the time to pray fully over every aspect of the request upon which you are set to agree with your partner so that no misunderstanding surfaces later to unsettle your faith in the request being the will of God</u>. Not only should you take time to choose your prayer partner well, but even after you are confident of the faith of your partner, taking the time to pray with them about every aspect of the request's fulfillment should secure the confidence you both need that God's will is in line with this specific request.

3. <u>Remember that prayer is warfare and you are called to put on the whole armor of God and fight the good fight of faith</u>. This is a matter of you fighting and wrestling against demonic principalities and powers who threaten to hinder you from gaining access by faith into the grace-power in which you are called to stand. Add to your faith-stand these few practices:

- In your faith fight, whether you're alone or praying with your partner, in the name of Jesus, bind and rebuke any doubts or fears the enemy might bring.
- In your faith fight, remember worship is a weapon (2 Chronicles 20:21-23), so with praise and thanksgiving

rejoice in the Lord always that you are confident in your faith stand (Philippians 4:4).

- In your faith fight, remember that in addition to you having a partner standing in agreeing faith with you (Deuteronomy 32:30; Ecclesiastes 4:9-12; Matthew 18:19), you also have the greater One living in you (1 John 4:4) and there are more with you than with the enemy (2 Kings 6:16-17). Fear not!
- In your faith fight, remember that the Word of God is the sword of the Spirit (Ephesians 6:17), so say and pray a confession full of the promises in the Word of who you are, what you have, and what you can do as a believer who is *in Christ* (Hebrews 10:23). Encourage yourself in the Word in between when you first pray and you finally receive (Psalm 42:5). And remember, effective ministry is not about the promotion of *self* but the elevation of *Christ* as you respond to the call to *serve*.

Let us pray…

> Thank you Father for the spiritual strength to stand in faith and the wisdom to walk in agreement. Help me to stand unswervingly upon the truth of Your Word and faithfully to confess who I am, what I have, and what I am able to do because I am in Christ; in Jesus's name I pray. Amen.

EPILOGUE

6 Then they gathered around him and asked him, "Lord, are you at this time going to restore the kingdom to Israel?"

7 He said to them: "It is not for you to know the times or dates the Father has set by his own authority. 8 But you will receive power when the Holy Spirit comes on you; and you will be my witnesses in Jerusalem, and in all Judea and Samaria, and to the ends of the earth."

9 After he said this, he was taken up before their very eyes, and a cloud hid him from their sight.

10 They were looking intently up into the sky as he was going, when suddenly two men dressed in white stood beside them. 11 "Men of Galilee," they said, "why do you stand here looking into the sky? This same Jesus, who has been taken from you into heaven, will come back in the same way you have seen him go into heaven."

—Acts 1:6-11

STORY HAS IT THAT A MAN DREAMED HE WAS PRESENT WHEN JESUS ascended in Acts chapter one. He saw himself standing on the mount of ascension with Christ and His disciples when Christ was taken up before their very eyes. To his amazement, in the dream, the man ascended with Christ and heard a conversation between the Lord and the two angels, called "two men dressed in white," as they passed each other.

One angel asked, "Lord, how did the mission of the redemption of mankind go on the earth?"

Jesus responded, "Mission accomplished: My blood was shed as I gave My life as a ransom for many (Matthew 20:28). Then I commanded My disciples whom I trained for over three years to wait for the promise of the Father, the Baptism with the Holy Spirit (Luke 24:49; Acts 1:4-5); and I commissioned them to go preaching the gospel of My love shown through My death on the cross (Romans 5:8) and make disciples of all nations, baptizing them in the name of the Father and of the Son and of the Holy Spirit, and to teach the new disciples to obey everything I have commanded them." (Matthew 28:19-20)

Upon hearing the Lord's answer, the other angel then asked a serious follow-up question, "But Lord, what if Your disciples fail to take the gospel, the good news of Your love for the world (John 3:16-17) and Your desire to save all who believe; what if they fail to make disciples by teaching the truth of Your offer of eternal salvation? What backup plan have You put in place? What is Your plan B?"

The man having the dream said he saw a somewhat strange expression come over the Lord's face as he responded to the second angel, saying, "I have no other plan."

The truth, dear friend, is that in a sin-cursed world where rebellion and disobedience reign, the only remedy for the lost is faith in Christ—believed, prayerfully mirrored, and shared by mature believers who love the Lord and care enough to share the truth they know and experience with those they can touch.

God's Will for Your Life

God created you unique; no one else has your DNA, your fingerprints, or your smell. A bloodhound could track the path you walked through the forest because every place you stepped, you left behind your unique smell, a little bit of your scent with each step you took. If this is true, and it is, can you also wrap your mind around the truth—if God created you unique, could it be that He has a plan for you that is also unique, tailor-made just for you? The words of the Old Testament prophet Jeremiah agree.

> [11] *"For I know the plans I have for you," declares the LORD, "plans to prosper you and not to harm you, plans to give you hope and a future.* [12] *Then you will call upon me and come and pray to me, and I will listen to you.* [13] *You will seek me and find me when you seek me with all your heart."* (Jeremiah 29:11-13)

While many simply find these verses interesting, let me urge you to consider seriously that God's purpose for creating you unique is that you will seek Him for His specific plan for your life. Further, you should know that the will or plan God ordained for your life is divided into two steps: *general* and *specific*.

God's *general* will for you, and everyone else, is *righteousness*. He wants the world to be imbued with righteousness and He wants to use you as an exponent. (How you should be used as an exponent draws upon the personality gifts you were born with and the spiritual gifts you were given when you were born again (John 3:3). It gets over into the *specific* area which we'll cover below. But let's just deal with this *general* area first). Righteousness is key! It's why the Old Testament prophet Amos cried out, "Let justice roll on like a river, **righteousness** like a never-failing stream" (Amos 5:24, emphasis mine). And it's why Jesus encouraged believers to "seek first his (God's) kingdom and his **righteousness**, and all these things will be given to you as well" (Matthew 6:33, emphasis and parenthesis mine).

God created you on purpose for purpose. You are no accident! Even if your parents did not plan for your birth, you are supposed to be who God created you to be, regardless of your background, difficult upbringing, or parentage. And God did not save you just because He loves you. More importantly, He saved you because He also loves the people in your life He intends to use you to touch. He expects you to grow in the grace and knowledge of your Lord and

Savior Jesus Christ (2 Peter 3:18) to become a mature believer He can use to reach the lost within your spheres of influence.

Generally and specifically speaking, God saves you by grace through faith and gives you right standing with Him (righteousness) (Romans 5:1), and He intends that you become the righteousness of God in Christ (2 Corinthians 5:21) so that by the power of the Holy Spirit you can affect spiritual transformation in the lives of those you influence.

Righteousness is twofold: in Romans 5:17, we see Paul teaching that righteousness is a gift, "…those who receive God's abundant provision of grace and of the *gift of righteousness* reign in life through the one man, Jesus Christ" (emphasis mine). You became *right* with God and at *peace* with God when you were *justified by faith* (Romans 5:1). It is the path of salvation outlined again and again in vivid detail in Holy Scripture. This is the *vertical* side of your salvation experience where you sing, "Blessed assurance Jesus is mine; O what a foretaste of glory divine."[71] But wait! Don't make the mistake of sitting on your *justification* by grace through faith, or resting on your receiving *righteousness* as a gift from God. The gift part of righteousness is not the end of the story. It's like the words I heard from the lips of the late Danniebelle Hall, "God loves you just the way you are, but He also loves you too much to leave you the way you are."

Righteousness has another side; notice Romans 5:19, "For just as through the disobedience of the one man the many were made sinners, so also through the obedience of the one man the many will be *made righteous*" (emphasis mine). Receiving righteousness as a gift is the first step (the vertical step) of your personal salvation by grace through faith, but being "made righteous" is the second step (the horizontal step) that includes you fulfilling your God-given destiny to allow the power of righteousness that includes love, truth, fairness, justice, and equity to impact the lives of those within your various spheres of influence. This is where having a strong prayer life and building intimacy with the Father is important and necessary. You will not experience ultimate success without the guidance you must receive through prayer intimacy.

When you get to this second step, your search for the *specifics* of God's will and purpose for your life begins with you becoming a mature believer "in Christ." It is where you are no longer just a saved believer who is ignorant to the truth; it is where your understanding of truth matures you to hunger and thirst for righteousness to be filled in you and flow through you (Matthew 5:6). You begin to understand the authority you have "in Christ" to gain access by faith into this grace in which you now stand (Romans 5:2) for the *specific* purpose of reaching others. You even grow to love and care enough to reach beyond your comfort zones for the purpose of ministry. This is effective horizontal righteousness in action.

Beloved, this is the theological thinking of the apostle Paul writing to the carnal Corinthian church members in an attempt to bring them to the maturity where the specifics of ministry purpose could be fulfilled.

> *[17] Therefore, if anyone is in Christ, the new creation has come: The old has gone, the new is here! [18] All this is from God, who reconciled us to himself through Christ and gave us the ministry of reconciliation: [19] that God was reconciling the world to himself in Christ, not counting people's sins against them. And he has committed to us the message of reconciliation. [20] We are therefore Christ's ambassadors, as though God were making his appeal through us. We implore you on Christ's behalf: Be reconciled to God. [21] God made him who had no sin to be sin for us, so that in him we might become the righteousness of God. As God's co-workers we urge you not to receive God's grace in vain.*
> (2 Corinthians 5:17-6:1)

When this passage is interpreted within the immediate context of chapter five and the extended context of both Corinthian epistles, you readily see the apostle is dealing with carnal believers (1 Corinthians 3:1-4), some of whom, though members of the church, may not really have become members of the Body of

Christ: the sexually immoral brother (ch. 5), the lawsuits between members (ch. 6), or the discrimination associated with the Lord's Supper (ch. 11); these are just a few in the first epistle that give us pause about the depth of their commitment or at least raise questions as to whether some of them ever made a genuine commitment. And in the second epistle, let's remember the beginning context of chapter five:

> *[10] For we must all appear before the judgment seat of Christ; that everyone may receive the things done in his body, according to that he hath done, whether it be good or bad. [11] Knowing therefore the <u>terror</u> of the Lord, we persuade men…"* (2 Corinthians 5:10-11a KJV)

Do you recognize the warning there? Do you hear what I hear? Paul is trying to push those on the fence toward being saved and those who are hesitant about a deeper commitment into saying yes to living for Christ seriously and not just for themselves:

> *[14] For Christ's love compels us, because we are convinced that one died for all, and therefore all died. [15] And he died for all that **those who live should no longer live for themselves** but for him who died for them and was raised again.* (2 Corinthians 5:14-15, emphasis mine)

Clearly, Paul emphasizes that Christ is the One who "…died for all, and therefore all died," and he endeavors to raise the consciousness of the *few* out of the *all* for whom Christ died. Though Christ died for all, only a few had faith to believe. They are the ones included in the statement, "those who live [i.e. those who by faith are born again] should no longer live for themselves [should stop being the ones who "receive God's grace in vain" (6:1) because they never achieved the purpose of righteousness] but to live for him who died for them and was raised again." The summary that makes sense is to view this chapter from the perspective of Paul seeking to prompt believers into deepening their commitment to seek God's face in prayer for His specific will or plan for their lives in terms of righteousness.

And now we come to it: "Therefore, if anyone is in Christ, he is a new creation; the old has gone, the new has come!" (5:17) The conditional statement preceded by the word "if" immediately says that it is possible for someone not to be in Christ. It also says that, if the old has *not* gone and the new has *not* come, chances are you've met someone who is *not* in Christ. Do you hear the subtle pressure Paul is putting on the carnal church members hearing this read? Then add the words of *reconciliation* in verses 18 and 19: "God...reconciled *us* to himself through Christ and gave *us* the *ministry of reconciliation*" (v. 18, emphasis mine). Do you hear Paul's subtle emphasis with his words where he includes himself in the *"us"* of the text? The push of the text from Paul is that all of us, not just me (Paul), but all of us by virtue of God reconciling *us* to Himself through Christ, have been given the "ministry of reconciliation." He then adds the truth that "God was reconciling the world to himself in Christ, not counting people's sins against them. And he has committed to us the message of reconciliation" (v. 19). In other words, Paul is saying the "ministry of reconciliation" is not just *mine* but *yours*.

This verse has gotten the theological vehicle of some stuck in the mud of contextual confusion where they interpret a verse in contradiction to its context and to what the Bible teaches in other clear passages on the subject of salvation. I will not mince words: no one should ever think that anyone can feed a profligate, sinful lifestyle with the cravings of the flesh, the lust of the eyes and the boasting of what he has and does and legitimately believe that God is not counting his sins against him (cf. 1 John 2:15-17). The only interpretation of this verse that makes sense is that God did not allow the sinful history of humankind to preclude His sending Christ to reconcile the world to Himself. And the fact that, in verses 18 and 19, Paul is pushing for believers in Corinth (this includes you too, wherever you live) to perceive they have been given the *ministry and the message of reconciliation* militates against anyone thinking all are saved by some inclusion of the cross.

Everyone Has Two Choices

There are two basic choices you can make with your life (Joshua 24:15): the *first* is you can choose to believe and live a life based upon saving faith (Ephesians 2:8-10), and the *second* is you can choose NOT to believe and not to live a life based upon saving faith (Psalm 14:1). Remember, to believe is to have faith, and to have faith is to believe. This believing is what I call "true-believing," not some sort of intellectual assent where no commitment to the truth is made and no real transformation of behavior takes place. The true believer is one who exercises his or her faith and experiences change. The pseudo-believer has no real faith and though he or she may go through the motions of a Christian commitment, he experiences no real change.[72] This difference is taught by Paul in 2 Corinthians 7:10, "Godly sorrow brings repentance that leads to salvation and leaves no regret, but worldly sorrow brings death." When you truly believe the gospel, you experience godly sorrow for your sin (unbelief) that brings repentance (change, transformation) that leads to salvation (deliverance). Worldly sorrow brings death, spiritual separation from God, because it doesn't lead to repentance.

The two choices have two possible outcomes: if you choose to believe and live your life as a believer with the accompanying changes and the promises of the Bible are either false or true, here are the outcomes. If they are false and there is no eternal salvation with God in an afterlife called heaven, you really have not made a non-productive choice. As a believer, you lived an honest, honorable life where you loved and served others in an attempt to improve their lives and make the world a better place. Since you reap what you sow, you sowed love, kindness, mercy, and forgiveness (just to name a few), and you reaped those qualities from the people you touched, including your children. BUT, if the promises are true, you will go to the place the Bible calls *heaven* and spend eternity in the presence of your Lord and with all those who believed and had genuine faith like you.

Now let's consider if you choose not to believe what the Bible teaches and you live a life of unbelief where faith is absent (Hebrews 11:6). This may or may not be an immoral life of pursuing pleasure and selfish gain, but let's consider that the promises of the Scriptures are either false or true. If they are false and there is no life after death, no rewards or punishments, you still will have made a non-productive choice. As a non-believer, you most likely lived a selfish lifestyle where you served yourself at the expense of others. Because you sowed a selfish lifestyle devoid of real love, kindness, mercy, and forgiveness (just to name a few), you failed to reap those qualities from the people you touched, including your children. The world did not become a better place within your spheres of influence. Before God, your existence, however long or short, would be judged spiritually unprofitable. But fortunately for you, if the promises are false and there is no life after death, no judgment or punishment, you simply cease to exist. BUT, if the promises are true, and after you die physically you are called to stand before an almighty God who judges you to be punished for eternity away from Him and your family— that will be the saddest day of your life.

The Righteousness of God in Christ

The passage in 2 Corinthians 5:17-21 culminates with Paul including the Corinthian church with himself: "We are therefore Christ's ambassadors, as though God were making his appeal through us. We implore you on Christ's behalf: Be reconciled to God (vs. 20)—let us. The insistent tone you hear in the apostle's words is probably due to the immaturity of church members refusing to shoulder their spiritual responsibility to propagate righteousness. Paul is saying that, with the *ministry and message of Reconciliation (vss. 18-19)* call upon us (he includes himself), we are *therefore* Christ's ambassadors (representatives of the kingdom of light to the kingdom of darkness). Our corporate response as a church should be: to understand that God Himself is making His appeal through us to speak on Christ's behalf to our world of family, friends, and neighbors—*be reconciled to God*—let us therefore seize the day to be reconciled ourselves, and to proclaim to others, "Be reconciled to God!"

The inspired foundation in verse 21 announces loud and clear the truth that Christ who had no sin was <u>made to be</u> sin for us, so that in Him we might <u>become</u> the righteousness of God. Let me emphasize further—Christ was **made** to **be** sin for us, so that **in Him** we **might become** the righteousness of God. You become saved by grace through faith in an instantaneous moment of believing and receiving, but you becoming the righteousness of God in Christ is a matter of prayer and consecration to seeking the Lord's face. Understand? At issue is your maturity in Christ, evidenced by your strength in prayer, in the ministry of the Word (cf. Acts 6:4), and in the grounded state of knowing your place in His plan for your life.

The church of God should, by all means push past the nonsensical drama that dominates our many agendas and go all out to becoming as much as we can, as soon as we can, *the righteousness of God in Christ*. Not doing so is tantamount to you receiving the grace of God in vain because you fail to achieve your grace-gift, new-birth purpose and potential of operating in God's specific will for your life (Romans 12:2). Experiencing the powerful joy of finding your place in His plan, discerning the gifts and callings the Lord placed in you (some placed in you when you were born and some when you surrendered your life to Christ and were born again) is part of the responsibility of seeking His face in prayer for the specific meaning of your part in His plan. Don't let your surrender to the call of eternal salvation be in vain because you failed to discover the *why* of your life "in Christ" (2 Corinthians 6:1) in prayer. My prayer is that God the Father will bless and keep you in His love as you determine through prayer and consecration to grow in grace and in the knowledge of Christ.

ENDNOTES

1. For an explanation of what it means to "pray through," see Mother Elizabeth Juanita Dabney's *What it Means to Pray Through.* Bloomington, IN: iUniverse, Inc., 1945. Reprint 2012.

2. "Honor your father and your mother, so that you may live long in the land the LORD your God is giving you" (Exodus 20:12).

Section One: Prayerlessness: The Problem Considered
Chapter Two: An Interesting Comparison

3 Barna.org. "Only Half Of Protestant Pastors Have A Biblical Worldview." January 12, 2004. Accessed April 2, 2016. https://www.barna.org/component/content/article/5-barna-update/45-barna-update-sp-657/133-only-half-of-protestant-pastors-have-a-biblical-worldview#.VwALBaQrKM8. Emphasis mine.

4 Barna. "Protestant Pastors."

Section Two: The WHAT of Prayer (Part I)
Chapter Three: The Questions Answered

5 Frank Capra, et al. "It's a Wonderful Life" [United States]: Liberty Films, 1947.

6 See chapter 14 below.

7 Mrs. C. H. Morris. "The fight Is On." *Hymnary.org.* Accessed April 2, 2016. http://www.hymnary.org/text/the _fight_is_on_the_trumpet_sound_is_rin.

8   Lit., "seize upon... to struggle to obtain eternal life." Joseph H. Thayer, D.D. *Thayer's Greek–English Lexicon of the New Testament*. Grand Rapids, MI: Associated Publishers &Authors, Inc., 1895. s.v. *epilambano*.

9   See Arthur Wallis. *Pray in the Spirit: The Work of the Holy Spirit in the Ministry of Prayer*. Fort Washington, PA: CLC Publications, 2009.

10 The truth of praying in the Spirit deserves this level of explanation and balanced clarification in order to help lift it past the prejudice of some doctrinal disputations and non-biblical practices. Praying in the Spirit is a basic, practical truth that will strengthen your prayer life. Someone with a strong prayer life can endure and even make sense of the predictable changes, the unexpected difficulties, and the tragic circumstances that occur in the normal Christian life. A strong prayer life is part of the foundation of obedience Jesus taught in the concluding parable of the Sermon on the Mount (Matthew 7:24-27).

Chapter Four: What Prayer Basics Do You Need To Know?

11 Around 1975, three significant leaders in Christendom received revelation knowledge about how to effectively impact our modern society: the founder of Campus Crusade for Christ, Bill Bright, the founder of Youth with a Mission, Loren Cunningham, and Francis Schaeffer. The revelation they received was that in order to impact any nation for Jesus Christ we must affect the seven spheres, or mountains of society that are the pillars of any society.

12 L.L. Morris. *New Bible Dictionary*. Edited by I. Howard Marshall, A. R. Millard, J. I. Packer, and D. J. Wiseman. 3rd edition. Downers Grove, IL: InterVarsity Press 1996. s.v. redeemer, redemption.

13 Clearly, the price for the redemption of the Church was the blood of Christ. Since Jesus Christ was sinless, "knew no sin" (2 Corinthians 5:21 KJV), "did no sin, neither was guile found in His mouth" (1 Peter 2:22 KJV; see also vv. 23-24,

cf. Hebrews 4:15), as God the Son, His was eternal blood of eternal value (1 Peter 1:18-19; cf. also Acts 20:28).

14 "Progressive revelation—the view that the divine disclosure of doctrine did not come in a single deposit, but that at divers times in its historical development later revelation added to former disclosures." N.L. Geisler and W.E. Nix. *A General Introduction to the Bible*. Revised edition. Chicago: Moody Press, 1986. p. 604.

15 W.E. Vine. *Vine's Concise Dictionary of Old and New Testament Words*. Nashville, TN: Thomas Nelson, Inc., 1999. p. 113.

16 Smith Wigglesworth. "The Power of the Name." Www.smith-wigglesworth.com. Accessed April 11, 2016. http://www.smith-wigglesworth.com/sermons/eif3.htm.

17 The serious Bible Study student needs to have in his or her library at least the following two reference tools: *Strong's or Strongest Exhaustive Concordance of the Bible* (available in KJV, NIV, and NASB), and *Vine's Expository Dictionary of Old and New Testament Words*.

18 Confucius. *Confucius Quotes*. Goodreads.com. Accessed April 11, 2016. https://www.goodreads.com/author/ quotes/ 15321. Confucius. Emphasis mine.

19 Obviously, the absence of faith and the presence of ungodliness resulted in God not being **pleased**. Paul in the New Testament rehearses the failure of many in Israel in 1 Corinthians 10:5-11. *"God was not **pleased** with most of them."* Some deluded inter-preters mitigate *"God was not pleased"* with God's goodness, but the writer to the Hebrews, speaking of the same people wrote, *"…but the message they heard was of no value to them, because those who heard did <u>not combine it with faith</u>…God has said, 'So I declared on oath in my anger, "They shall never enter my rest"'"* (Hebrews 4:2b-3b). Cf. also Proverbs 16:7, *"When a man's ways are <u>pleasing</u> to the LORD…"* indicating the "ways" of a man's life is the result of spiritual change. The word *"please,"* Heb. râtsâh meaning "pardon, please, reconcile self." James Strong, *Strong's Exhaustive Concordance of the*

Bible. Peabody, MA: Hendrickson Publishers. #7521 p. 110. Cf. also Hebrews 11:5.

20 Hal Lindsey. Beliefnet's Inspirational Quotes. Accessed April 14, 2016. http://www.beliefnet.com/Quotes/ Inspiration/H/Hal-Lindsey/Man-Can-Live-For-About-Forty-Days-Without-Food-An.aspx#k6WZq5f0Fs82HY 23.99.

21 Biblical criticism is defined as the origins, the history, contents, and purposes of the canonical books of Scripture. Higher Criticism and Textual Criticism are the two parts of the science of Biblical criticism. Textual Criticism deals with the study of the text of Scripture. It examines the manuscripts, different versions and codices seeking to determine the original words written by the authors of the text. Higher Criticism examines the authorship, the historical background, dates of the books of the Bible (especially the Old Testament), and, in summary, is the study of the literary structure of the books of the Bible.

22 Unfortunately, the Theory of Evolution has been substituted for creation; Adam and Eve are a myth; Moses didn't write the Pentateuch, but the first five books of the Old Testament are the combination of at least four sources according to the Wellhausen Documentary hypothesis and are the result of some redactors (probably during the time of Ezra) who brought the various sources (JEDP theory) together; Noah's ark and the universal flood is a myth; Jonah was not swallowed by a big fish; Jesus did not walk on water nor did He feed more than 5,000 people from a little boy's lunch. These are some of the anti-supernatural biases taught as "fact" on many college, university, and seminary campuses, and they serve to discredit the authority and veracity of the Scriptures.

Chapter Five: What Does Prayer Empower You to Do?

23 The compound Greek word "hupoakouo" is translated by the English verb "to obey." It literally means, "to hear under." Obedience is to submit your life under the authority of the truth you hear and know.

24 There are three key New Testament passages dealing with gifts of the Holy Spirit: Romans 12:6-8 (The Motive Gifts); 1 Corinthians 12:7-11 (The Manifestation Gifts); and Ephesians 4:11 (The Ministry Gifts).

25 See The Rev. Dr. Martin Luther King, Jr.'s "I Have a Dream" speech at the 1963 Civil Rights March on Washington DC. Accessed May 11, 2016. http://www.americanrhetoric.com/speeches/mlkihaveadream.htm.

26 "Talk: Tim Duncan." Wikiquote. August 26, 2015. Accessed April 29, 2016. https://en.wikiquote.org/wiki/Talk:TimDuncan

27 Prayer warriors are powerfully connected to the prayer assistance aspect of the Ministry of the Holy Spirit (Romans 8:26), and you cannot have that level of intimacy without experiencing in reality the fruit of the Spirit that includes *joy* (Galatians 5:22-23).

Section Three: The WHAT of Prayer (Part II)
Chapter Six: What About Prayer and the Will of God?

28 Johnson Oatman, Jr. "Higher Ground." Public Domain, 1889

Chapter Seven: What About Prayer and Christian Unity?

29 M. Coogan, ed. *The New Oxford Annotated Bible.* New York, NY: Oxford University Press, 2001. p. 309.

Chapter Eight: What About Prayer and Kingdom Ministry?

30 Though it is sad and unfortunate that Judas Iscariot was lost, it says that if Jesus, the Son of the living God, the greatest teacher in all of human history and the picture of the love and grace of God, could not save Judas, you need to recognize two truths: (1) Even the superior ministry of Jesus of Nazareth could not save everyone (Matthew 26:24; Mark 14:21); and (2) You should not beat yourself up over the inability of your love and witness to turn some from darkness to light.

Section Four: The WHY of Prayer
Chapter Nine: Why Should You Pray?

31 If you have not yet confessed Christ as Lord and Savior, do it now by praying this simple prayer: "Father, thank You for loving me and for sending Your Son, the Lord Jesus Christ, to die on the cross to save me. I repent today; as an act of my will, I turn from the practice of sin and wrongdoing, and I surrender my life to You; boldly confessing—Jesus Christ is my Lord, I believe He is raised from the dead. Therefore, by faith, I thank You for the gift of salvation in the name of Jesus. Amen." (Cf. Romans 5:1, 6:23; 10:9-10).

32 Frank C. Huston. "Keep On Believing." ©1945 Word Music, LLC.

33 "In the short-term, Operation Ceasefire was very successful: in the four years (1996-2000) after the program was started the number of youth homicides (13-24) in Boston was cut in half. <u>In fact, in the two-year period (1996-1997) there were no teenage homicides</u>. **This was the Boston Miracle**. Many sides have taken credit for this amazing achievement—depending on whether you are talking to police and probation officers, politicians, street-workers and youth organizations, or valiant black pastors who had taken to the streets and Organized TenPoint Coalition." UrbanMinistry.org, "The So-Called *Boston Miracle*." (July 2010) Accessed May 5, 2016. http://www.urbanministry.org/wiki/boston-miracle.

34 From 1986-1991, our local church's EMP meetings were held at 340 Blue Hill Avenue. After Palm Sunday, 1991, the meetings were moved to the church's new facility: 1500 Blue Hill Ave., Mattapan, MA.

35 E. E. Hewitt. "Wonderful Power in Prayer." Hymnary.org. ©1909 by Char. H. Gabriel. Accessed June 20, 2016. http://www.hymnary.org/text/no_matter_how_hard_goes_the_battle_of_li.

Chapter Ten: Why is Praying with Power so Difficult?

36 William Earnest Henley. "Invictus." Public Domain, 1875.

37 Remember from Chapter Seven: In essentials, unity; in non-essentials, liberty; and in all things, charity. Stay within this biblically balanced path; don't fall into the ditch on the left that is liberalism, or the ditch on the right that is legalism.

38 Earlier in this chapter I gave a brief outline of another passage, Psalm 24:3-4, that outlines four criteria you should know to qualify as a prayer warrior. For a full explanation of this passage, see chapter 12.

Chapter Eleven: Why Do I Pray in the Early Morning?

39 You should not assume the departed are finished running their race. While it is true the apostle Paul stated, "I have finished the race..." (2 Timothy 4:7 NIV), yet the word *race* literally means *course* and is translated *course* in several other translations (NASB, Young's Literal Translation, ASV, The Complete Word Study Bible, and The Interlinear Literal Translation of the Greek New Testament: KJV). Paul finished the earthly *course* of his race, but there is a sense in which we will never stop running. This helps us understand how those Old Testament saints who did not receive what was promised during their lifetime are *made perfect* by their promises being fulfilled in us (Hebrews 11:39-40). This may also be applicable to New Testament saints, who have died, being *made perfect* by you receiving what they were promised. You may be connected to the prayers of, let's say, a godly grandmother who prayed for you before you were born and never saw the believer you've become. She is part of that great cloud of witnesses surrounding your life.

40 This phrase and its teaching is from the book by Stephen R. Covey, *First Things First: Coping With the Ever Increasing Demands of the Workplace*. New York: Simon & Schuster Publishers, 1994.

41 C. Austin Miles. "In the Garden." Public Domain, 1912.

Section Five: The WHO of Prayer
Chapter Twelve: Who Qualifies to Pray Effectively?

42 The text of Matthew 6:33 does not say, "Seek *only* the kingdom of God..." There are other important pursuits of life and God is fully aware that they demand your attention. God is simply saying in the text, do not prioritize any person, thing, or practice above His kingdom and His righteousness.

43 Dr. Edwin Louis Cole. *Coleism.* "Ed Cole Library." Accessed May 21, 2016. http://www.edcole.org/index.php?fuseaction=coleisms.showColeism&id=96&keywords=viewall&page=10.

44 Navigators is a discipleship ministry you can find online at navigators.org. Order their Topical Memory System (TMS) to assist you in Scripture memory.

Chapter Thirteen: Those Committed to Knowing the Word

45 Cf. Gideon A. Thompson, *Systematic Theology: A Summary of the Seven Major Doctrines in Scripture.* Contact Sanctuary Books, the bookstore of Jubilee Christian Church in Boston, for this comprehensive study: 617-296-4651, www.jubilee-boston.org.

46 The Greek word *ekklesia,* translated by the English word "church," literally means "a calling out." James Strong. *Strong's Exhaustive Concordance of the Bible.* Peabody, MA: Hendrickson Publishers. *Greek Dictionary of the New Testament,* p. 26. Thus, the Church consists of those who, through faith experience, have been delivered from (called out of) the dominion of darkness into the kingdom of light (cf. Colossians 1:12-13).

47 James Hill. "What a Day That Will Be." ccli.com. Accessed June 1, 2016. https://us.songselect.com/ songs/32046/what-a-day-that-will-be/viewlyrics.

48 The necessity of understanding the power of being "in Christ" was adequately dealt with in the section entitled "Your Position

in Christ" in Chapter Four: What Prayer Basics Do You Need to Know?

Chapter Fourteen: Those Committed to Knowing God's Ways

49 James Strong. *Strong's Exhaustive Concordance of the Bible.* Peabody, MA: Hendrickson Publishers. p. 24.

50 Mark Galli and Ted Olsen, eds. *131 Christians Everyone Should Know.* Nashville, TN: Broadman & Holman Publishers, 2000. p. 378.

51 "Jim Jones." Wikipedia. Accessed June 2, 2016. https://en.wikipedia.org/wiki/Jim_Jones.

52 "David Koresh." Wikipedia. Accessed June 2, 2016. https://en.wikipedia.org/wiki/David_Koresh.

53 Jaroslav Pelikan. *The Vindication of Tradition: The 1983 Jefferson Lecture in the Humanities.* New Haven, CT: Yale University Press, 1984. Accessed June 2, 2016. http://www.goodreads.com/work/quotes/713639-the-vindication-of-tradition.

54 James M. Kouzes and Barry Z. Posner. *The Truth About Leadership.* San Francisco, CA: Jossey-Bass Publishers, 2010. p. 105.

Section Six: The HOW of Prayer
Chapter Fifteen: Practically Speaking, How Should You Begin?

55 A prayer covering is the spiritual oversight you provide through prayer and through teaching. The mature prayer-warrior sees himself as a "teaching priest." As a prayer-warrior, you are a priest: one who represents others before God; as a teacher, you represent God before them in the sharing of truth that can potentially set them free (cf. 2 Chronicles 15:3 NASB; Ezekiel 22:30; John 8:31-32).

56 A prayer-circle consists of those persons closest to you for whom you pray daily.

57 There are nine (9) compound covenant names for Jehovah: Jehovah-Jireh (Provider); Jehovah-Tsidkenu (Righteousness); Jehovah-M'Kaddesh (Sanctifier); Jehovah-Shalom (Peace); Jehovah-Nissi (Banner); Jehovah-Shammah (Present); Jehovah-Rohi (Shepherd); Jehovah-Rapha (Healer); Jehovah-Sabbaoth (Captain). There are more than these nine names for God, but these nine are the ones I use most often.

58 Robert E. Coleman. *The Master Plan of Evangelism*. Grand Rapids, MI: Revell Publishers, 1993.

59 The phrase "last days" is prophetic for the final move of God to save lost humanity through the Church, the *ekklesia*, "the called out ones," the literal meaning of the Greek word translated "church" in the Bible. See Isaiah 2:2; Joel 2:28 comp. with Acts 2:17; Micah 4:1; 2 Timothy 3:1; 2 Peter 3:3.

60 The word used in the text, "debts," is the Greek word *opheile*, meaning "that which is owed." It is translated "debt" in Matthew 18:32. Where it appears in Romans 13:7 it is translated "dues." W.E. Vine. *Concise Dictionary of Old and New Testament Words*. Nashville, TN: Thomas Nelson Inc., 1999. p. 84.

61 By all means watch the full-length feature film, *War Room*, directed by Alex Kendrick (FaithStep Films, Affirm Films, Red Sky Studios, TriStar Pictures, 2015) about the powerful weapon of prayer in the hand of a mature Christian.

Chapter Sixteen: Practically Speaking, How Does Faith Work?: Part I

62 "Charles Blondin." Wikipedia. Accessed May 26, 2016. https:// en.wikipedia.org/wiki/ Charles_Blondin; "Blondin Broadsheet [image]." *Niagara Falls Public Library*. February 27, 2006. Accessed May 26, 2016. http://www.nflibrary.ca/nfplindex/ show.asp?id=89311&b=1; Karen Abbott, "The Daredevil of Niagara Falls." *Smithsonian.com*. October 18, 2011. Accessed May 26, 2016. http://www.smithsonianmag.com /history/ the-daredevil-of-niagara-falls-110492884/?no-ist.

63 The spiritual weapons are: (1) Faith in the truth of the Word of God that you know; remember, Jesus quoted from memory three

times, "It is written" (Matthew 4:4, 7, 10) in His battle against Satan. (2) The weapon of godly character that frees you from hypocrisy (Matthew 7:3-5) and enables you to be an example others can follow to peace and discipleship (Philippians 4:9; Hebrews 12:1-3). (3) The weapon of full surrender to God's will for your life (Romans 12:1-2; Hebrews 10:7). Knowing who you are in Christ and working out of your gifting in the center of God's will for you instills a confidence that seriously threatens the foothold of the enemy in your area of ministry. (E.g. God sustained and used Daniel again and again as he was in his place in God's plan. Daniel 1, 2, 5, 6, 8, 9, 12.)

64 David D. Ireland, PhD. *The Weapon of Prayer: Maximize Your Greatest Strategy Against the Enemy.* Lake Mary, FL: Charisma House, 2015. p. 128.

65 E.M. Bounds. *The Weapon of Prayer.* Grand Rapids, MI: Baker, 1975. p. 13.

66 Unfortunately sometimes they don't hold on to their deliverance. See *Deliverance: a personal example* in Chapter Four above.

Chapter Seventeen: Practically Speaking, How Does Faith Work?: Part II

67 Let me balance this strong faith teaching with the fact we are not against doctors and medical science. That's why I say, "We pray like it's all on God, and we work like it's all on us." There may be some physical circumstances where the care of a doctor is necessary for life. Taking medication and following a doctor's instructions do not have to negate your faith. Keep on believing as you take the medication by speaking prayer-focused words to your organs pronouncing healing and health. Remember, faith is the victory that overcomes the world (1 John 5:4).

68 A "faith missionary" is one who is called of God to minister in a specific part of the world, foreign or domestic, and is not delayed by the need to raise financial support. Their faith says, "If God guides, He'll provide." They go to the field in faith believing that since God called them, He will provide for them.

69 See also Matthew 4:4; 12:36; 18:16; 26:75; 27:14; Mark 14:72; Luke 1:38; 2:29; 3:2; 4:4; 5:5.

Chapter Eighteen: Practically Speaking, How Does Agreement Work?

70 William D. Mounce. *The Analytical Greek Lexicon.* New York: Harper & Brothers Publishers. p. 384

Epilogue

71 Fanny Crosby. "Blessed Assurance." Public domain, 1873.

72 Dietrich Bonhoeffer wrote against the kind of Christianity where Christians profess to believe but their faith does not translate into change in *The Cost of Discipleship* (New York, NY: Touchstone, 1995).

INDEX OF SCRIPTURE REFERENCES

Colossians

1:11-14	103, 156, 237#48
1:13	16
1:16-17	145
1:27	70
2:15	102, 120, 147
3:1-3	37
4:2-5	104

1 Thessalonians

1:10	82
3:5	19
4:15-5:11	148
5:16-18	125
5:17	104, 111, 123

1 Timothy

3:2, 7	170
3:4-5	170
4:16	85, 111, 145, 166, 171
5:6	39
6:12	25, 120, 195, 196

2 Timothy

2:15	82
3:1	238#61
3:16-17	55, 204
4:1-2	171
4:2-5	20-21, 171
4:7	235#41

Titus

2:11	146, 154
2:12	148, 156

2:13	145
2:14	103
3:10	86

Hebrews

1:1-2	145
1:6	145
2:14-16	147
4:2b-3b	232#21
4:14-16	62, 102, 231#15
4:16	29, 62
5:4	171
6:17-19	88, 153, 156
8:8-13	91
9:14	146
9:28	148
10:7	239#65
10:19, 22	40
10:23	48, 195, 217
10:36	151, 152
11:1	150, 153, 194
11:3	55, 206
11:5	232#21
11:6	53, 145, 150, 188, 226
11:8-10	27, 154
11:8-16	154
11:39-40	123, 236#41
12:1	35, 77, 79, 123, 124, 165, 167, 239#65
12:1-3	239#65
12:14	35, 156
13:5	20
13:7	214
13:17	169

CPSIA information can be obtained
at www.ICGtesting.com
Printed in the USA
FFHW012039080119

9 781545 642801